Study Guide

# BUSINESS LAW:
# PRINCIPLES AND PRACTICES

**Study Guide**

# BUSINESS LAW: PRINCIPLES AND PRACTICES

*Fourth Edition*

**Arnold J. Goldman**
Law Firm of Goldman & Goldman

**William D. Sigismond**
Monroe Community College

HOUGHTON MIFFLIN COMPANY   BOSTON   TORONTO
Geneva, Illinois   Palo Alto   Princeton, New Jersey

Editor-in-Chief: Bonnie Binkert
Senior Project Editor: Paula Kmetz
Editorial Assistant: Adrienne Vincent
Senior Manufacturing Coordinator: Marie Barnes
Marketing Manager: Michael Mercier

Copyright © 1996 by Houghton Mifflin Company. All rights reserved.

No part of this work may be reproduced or transmitted in any form or by any means, electronic or mechanical, including photocopying and recording, or by any information storage or retrieval system without the prior written permission of Houghton Mifflin Company unless such copying is expressly permitted by federal copyright law. Address inquiries to College Permissions, Houghton Mifflin Company, 222 Berkeley Street, Boston, MA 02116-3764.

Printed in the U.S.A.

ISBN: 0-395-74661-2

12345678-CS-99 98 97 96 95

# Contents

*To the Student*  ix

## PART I  UNDERSTANDING THE LAW  1

Chapter 1  Foundations of Law  2
Chapter 2  The U.S. Court System and Its Constitutional Foundation  5
Chapter 3  Public Wrongs/Crimes  11
Chapter 4  Private Wrongs/Torts  17
Chapter 5  Litigation and Alternatives for Settling Civil Disputes  23

Review  Part I  28

## PART II  CONTRACTS  35

Chapter 6  The Basics of Contract Law  36
Chapter 7  Agreement: Offer and Acceptance  41
Chapter 8  Consideration  46
Chapter 9  Competent Parties  50
Chapter 10  Legal Purpose  53
Chapter 11  Contracts That Must Be in Writing  58
Chapter 12  Transfer of Contract Rights and Obligations  63
Chapter 13  The Termination of Contracts: Discharge  69
Chapter 14  The Termination of Contracts: Breach of Contract  75

Review  Part II  80

## PART III  PURCHASE AND SALE OF GOODS UNDER THE UCC  87

Chapter 15  The Sales Contract: Key Concepts  88
Chapter 16  The Sales Contract: Transfer of Title and Risk of Loss  93

v

Chapter 17    The Sales Contract: Performance, Breach, and Remedies for Breach   97
Chapter 18    Product Liability: Negligence, Warranties, and Strict Liability   101
Review   Part III   106

## PART IV   COMMERCIAL PAPER   111

Chapter 19    Nature and Types of Commercial Paper   112
Chapter 20    Issue, Transfer, and Discharge of Commercial Paper   115
Chapter 21    Rights and Duties of Parties to a Negotiable Instrument; Holder in Due Course Status   118
Chapter 22    Checks, Electronic Fund Transfers, and the Banking System   122
Review   Part IV   128

## PART V   AGENCY, EMPLOYMENT, AND LABOR LAW   133

Chapter 23    Employer-Employee Relationship   134
Chapter 24    Principal-Agent Relationship   138
Chapter 25    Principal-Agent, Employer-Employee, and Third-Party Relationship   143
Review   Part V   147

## PART VI   BUSINESS ORGANIZATION AND REGULATION   151

Chapter 26    Sole Proprietorships and Partnerships   152
Chapter 27    Corporations and Franchising   157
Chapter 28    Government Regulation of Business   162
Review   Part VI   165

## PART VII   REAL AND PERSONAL PROPERTY   169

Chapter 29    Basic Legal Concepts of Property   170
Chapter 30    Renting Real Property   174
Chapter 31    Buying and Selling Real Property   178
Review   Part VII   181

## PART VIII   BAILMENTS   185

Chapter 32    Nature and Creation of Bailments   186
Chapter 33    Bailments: Types, Rights, and Responsibilities   189
Chapter 34    Special Bailments   192
Review   Part VIII   196

## PART IX   INSURANCE   199

Chapter 35    Property and Casualty Insurance   200
Chapter 36    Automobile Insurance   204
Chapter 37    Personal Insurance   207
Review   Part IX   210

**PART X   WILLS AND ESTATE PLANNING   213**

    Chapter 38    Wills and Intestacy   214
    Chapter 39    Estate Planning   217

    Review   Part X   220

**PART XI   CONSUMER AND CREDITOR PROTECTION   223**

    Chapter 40    Protecting the Consumer and the Taxpayer   224
    Chapter 41    Protecting the Borrower   228
    Chapter 42    Protecting the Creditor   231

    Review   Part XI   235

**ANSWER KEY   241**

# To the Student

We have designed this *Study Guide* for use with *Business Law: Principles and Practices*, Fourth Edition. Each chapter of the *Study Guide* corresponds to a chapter in the textbook and contains several types of activities: *True-False Questions, Multiple-Choice Questions, Matching Questions, Completion Questions, Short-Answer Questions, Case Problems, Case Analysis, Analysis of Legal Documents, Opinion Questions,* and an *Ethical Dilemma Question*. These questions are all based on material in the textbook chapter under study. If you follow the suggestions below, the *Study Guide* will help you review and master the important legal principles discussed in the text:

1. Read the assigned chapter in the textbook and review your classroom lecture notes. If you need to make additional notes on key concepts and principles brought out in the chapter, do so. You may even wish to re-read the "Summary of Important Legal Concepts" at the end of the chapter.
2. Turn to the *Study Guide* chapter that corresponds to the textbook chapter you have just read and complete the exercises.
3. Check your answers with the Answer Key at the back of the *Study Guide*.
4. If the exercises you completed showed any weaknesses in your knowledge of the principles of law presented in the assigned chapter, then review the chapter material and your lecture notes for that chapter again.

If you use the *Study Guide* as suggested above you should be able to improve your results on quizzes and examinations. This *Study Guide* will prove to be an invaluable learning tool only if used in conjunction with textual readings and classroom instruction. It is not a substitute for attending class. Your instructor's lectures as well as class discussions are a significant part of the course. Remember, your grades can be positively affected by worthwhile class contributions and regular class attendance. We wish you much success in your business law course.

AJG
WDS

# PART I

# UNDERSTANDING THE LAW

# Chapter 1

# Foundations of Law

## CHAPTER OUTLINE

Why Laws Are Needed
The Nature of Law
The Relationship Between Law and Ethics
Functions of Law
    Protection of the Individual
    Protection of Society
    Protection of Property
    Promotion of Worthwhile Social
      Objectives
Development of Law
    Roman Law
    Common Law

Sources of Law
    Constitutions
    Statutes
    Court Decisions
    Administrative Regulations
Civil Law Versus Criminal Law
The Role of Business Law
The Changing Nature of Law

## TRUE-FALSE QUESTIONS

On the line at the right of each statement, write the word *true* if the statement is true. If the statement is false, write the word or expression that should be substituted for the underlined word or expression to make the statement correct.

1. Law is a set of rules for controlling both individual and group conduct.     *TRUE*

2. The Uniform Commercial Code makes the laws of commercial transactions uniform from one state to another.     *TRUE*

3. Administrative regulations are court rulings that are used as a basis for deciding later cases.    *PRECEDENTS*     *FALSE*

4. The case title *State of Ohio* v. *Moran* indicates a criminal action.     *TRUE*

5. The system that grants relief for a wrongdoing based on what is fair and just rather than on legal principles is called criminal law.     *FALSE*
                      *EQUITY*

6. As society changes, laws change to reflect the changes in society.   TRUE

common (case) 7. Statute law refers to decisions made by English courts that were based on local customs.   FALSE

8. The federal and state governments generally initiate actions against an accused individual.   TRUE

9. An important concept in our legal system is that the law protects people and at the same time imposes legal duties on them.   TRUE

10. A person harmed because of a violation of civil law by another person may sue that person and ask for money damages.   TRUE

## MULTIPLE-CHOICE QUESTIONS

On the line next to each statement, write the letter of the best answer.

B  1. Unwritten law based on previous court decisions is known as (a) statute law, (b) common law, (c) moral law, (d) constitutional law.

A  2. In a conflict among laws, the law that takes precedence over all others is (a) constitutional law, (b) common law, (c) statute law, (d) criminal law.

B  3. Laws passed by cities, towns, and villages are called (a) decrees, (b) ordinances, (c) acts, (d) moral laws.

C  4. The fundamental written law of a state or nation that defines the rights and duties of individuals and describes the powers and limitations of government is called (a) business law, (b) common law, (c) constitutional law, (d) an ordinance.

D  5. Laws enacted by legislative bodies that protect society from the harmful acts of individuals and that impose fines or imprisonment for violations are called (a) moral laws, (b) civil laws, (c) natural laws, (d) criminal laws.

A  6. Laws that protect the rights and property of individuals from harm by other individuals and that provide remedies for any harm caused are called (a) civil laws, (b) criminal laws, (c) constitutional laws, (d) administrative laws.

D  7. The main reason rules or laws were established was to (a) provide jobs for people, (b) restrict people's movement in society, (c) make majority rule possible, (d) protect individual rights against the acts of others.

A  8. Tate maliciously broke into her neighbor's house. Tate's action is governed by (a) criminal law, (b) natural law, (c) equity law, (d) administrative law.

D  9. After common law is revised and adopted by a state legislature, it is known as (a) administrative law, (b) commercial law, (c) federal law, (d) statute law.

C  10. The Social Security Act is an example of a (a) local ordinance, (b) state statute, (c) federal act, (d) constitutional amendment.

A  11. A Federal Communications Commission restriction on cigarette advertising on television is an example of (a) administrative law, (b) constitutional law, (c) criminal law, (d) statute law.

D  12. The first kind of law, other than Roman law, to come into existence was (a) constitutional law, (b) administrative law, (c) statute law, (d) common law.

**4** | CHAPTER 1

A  13. The type of action indicated by the case title *William Beebe* v. *Katherine Coyle* is (a) civil, (b) criminal, (c) punitive, (d) bankruptcy.

A  14. A person who violates criminal law is subject to (a) punishment, (b) a ruling in equity, (c) *stare decisis*, (d) a moral action in a court of law.

A  15. In law, *equity* means (a) fair and just, (b) to stand by a decision, (c) a violation of the law, (d) precedent.

## SHORT-ANSWER QUESTIONS

Answer each of the following questions in the space provided.

1. List and describe the four sources of law in the United States.

   CONSTITUTIONS - FUNDAMENTAL WRITTEN LAW OF A STATE / NATION
   STATUTES - LAWS FORMALLY PASSED BY LEGISLATIVE BODIES NOT COURT
   COURT DECISION - (CASE LAW) MODERN VERSION OF COMMON LAW
   ADMINISTRATIVE REGULATIONS - AGENCIES CREATED TO MAKE RULES

2. Discuss the significance of the *stare decisis* concept.

   CONCEPT OF FOLLOWING DECISIONS IN PRIOR CASES
   WHEN A SIMILAR CASE OCCURS. EASY WAY OF CONCLUDING
   A TRIAL OF SIMILAR ACTIONS AS PAST TRIALS

3. Under what circumstances is a remedy in equity available to an injured party seeking relief in court?

   WHEN NO PHYSICAL DAMAGES HAVE BEEN COMMITTED
   AND THE THREAT OF COMPETITOR RECIEVING
   INFORMATION CONCERNING SOMETHING THAT MAKES YOU MORE
   PROFITABLE

4. Discuss the differences between law and ethics.

   LAW - A SET OF INFORCEABLE RULES MADE TO REGULATE
   THE CONDUCT OF INDIVIDUALS & GROUPS IN SOCIETY. ETHICS -
   STUDY OF WHAT IS RIGHT OR GOOD FOR HUMAN BEINGS AS THEY LIVE
   EACH DAY

5. Discuss the significance of the case of *Robinson* v. *California* (370 U.S. 660).

   IT MADE ADDICTION DEFINED AS A DISEASE &
   NOT A CRIMINAL ACT

# Chapter 2

# The U.S. Court System and Its Constitutional Foundation

## CHAPTER OUTLINE

**The Court System in the United States**
**The State Court System**
   Trial Courts of Limited Jurisdiction
   Trial Courts of General
     Jurisdiction
   Intermediate Appellate Courts
     and the Court of Final Resort
**The Federal Court System**
   Federal Trial Courts
   Intermediate Courts of Appeal
   The U.S. Supreme Court

**Participants in the Legal System**
   The Role of the Attorney
   The Role of the Paralegal
   The Role of the Judge and the Jury
**The Constitutional Framework of the United**
     **States Legal System**
   Separation of Powers
   Judicial Review
   Accommodation of Interests
   Litigation
   The Bill of Rights

## MATCHING QUESTIONS

Use the following terms to identify the phrases below. On the line next to each phrase, write the letter of the term that most closely relates to it. Do not use a term more than once.

a. Judicial review
b. Court of original jurisdiction
c. Executive branch
d. *Marbury* v. *Madison*
e. Congress
f. Litigation
g. Diversity of citizenship
h. Fourth Amendment
i. Commercial claims court

j. Separation of powers
k. U.S. Bankruptcy Court
l. $50,000
m. Small claims court
n. Appellate court
o. Fifth and Sixth Amendments
p. Fourteenth Amendment
q. *U.S.* v. *Wade*
r. $10,000

# CHAPTER 2

B  1. Where a case is first tried

~~I~~  2. Where a small business person can sue a debtor up to a certain limit without the help of an attorney

F  3. A lawsuit or legal action

N & ~~Q~~  4. Has the authority to affirm or reverse the decision of a trial court

O  5. Guarantee the right to due process

K  6. Where financially troubled debtors are relieved from paying some of their debts

A  7. Gives higher courts the power to re-examine the decisions of lower courts

D  8. The Supreme Court case that established the basis for the concept of judicial review

E  9. The branch of the federal government that has the power to make law

G  10. Grounds for jurisdiction in the federal courts when the person suing and the person being sued live in different states

L  11. The minimum claim in a diversity-of-citizenship case

K  12. Protects the individual's right to privacy by prohibiting unreasonable search and seizure by the government

## MULTIPLE-CHOICE QUESTIONS

On the line next to each statement, write the letter of the best answer.

C  1. The power of a court to hear a case is known as (a) certiorari, (b) venue, (c) jurisdiction, (d) none of these.

D A  2. A court that has the power to hear almost any case brought before it has (a) appellate jurisdiction, (b) constitutional jurisdiction, (c) limited jurisdiction, (d) general jurisdiction.

C D  3. The U.S. Supreme Court's jurisdiction is (a) appellate only, (b) original only, (c) appellate and original, (d) unlimited.

D  4. The most common means of bringing an appeal before the U.S. Supreme Court is called (a) case, (b) certification, (c) centaurus, (d) certiorari.

B  5. The major trial courts of the federal court system are called (a) circuit courts, (b) district courts, (c) claims courts, (d) courts of appeal.

A  6. A court of original jurisdiction is called a (a) trial court, (b) higher court, (c) review court, (d) criminal court only.

C  7. The United States has two separate and distinct court systems. They are (a) federal and county systems, (b) federal and local systems, (c) federal, state, and local systems, (d) state, county, and local systems.

C  8. The U.S. Supreme Court derives its judicial power from (a) Congress, (b) the president, (c) the Constitution, (d) the state courts.

D  9. Howell, a landlord, is involved in a dispute with a tenant over unpaid rent. Howell should bring suit against the tenant in (a) district court, (b) U.S. Tax Court, (c) probate court, (d) small claims court.

D 10. All of the following are part of the federal court system *except* (a) the circuit courts of appeal, (b) U.S. Tax Court, (c) district courts, (d) juvenile courts.

C 11. A typical state court system includes all but which of the following? (a) lower-level trial courts, (b) intermediate-level appeals courts, (c) bankruptcy courts, (d) small claims courts.

A B 12. Most state court systems include small claims courts to settle minor disputes. In small claims courts (a) technical rules of evidence and procedure normally followed in a court trial are not strictly followed, (b) attorneys are not permitted, (c) the maximum amount for which a person may sue is not established, (d) a judge and jury consider the evidence and render a decision.

## SHORT-ANSWER QUESTIONS

Answer each of the following questions in the space provided.

1. Briefly explain the meaning of the following statement: Our legal system is known as an adversary system.

   TWO PARTIES EXPRESS THEIR SIDES OF THE STORY TO BRING OUT EVIDENCE THAT WILL RESULT IN TRUTH

2. The U.S. system of government and law is determined by the doctrine of separation of powers. Explain the meaning of this doctrine.

   NO GOVERNMENT LAW CAN BE PASSED WITHOUT THE ABSOLUTE AGREEMENT OF ALL FACILITIES CHECKS & BALANCES

3. Explain why the concept of judicial review is important in our judicial system.

   BECAUSE SOME TRIALS ARE DECIDED WRONGLY & ARE UNFAIR SO TO MAKE IT MORE JUST APPEALS ARE

4. What is the main difference between a court with general jurisdiction and a court with limited jurisdiction?

GENERAL - THE POWER TO HEAR ALMOSS ANY CASE BROUGHT BEFORE IT
LIMITED - POWER TO HEAR CERTAIN CASES LIMITED BY TYPE OF CASE, AMOUNT OF MONEY INVOLVED, GEOGRAPHIC AREA

5. Give reasons why the opportunities for the successful appeal of a case are limited.

HAS TO SHOW IF AN ERROR OF LAW HAD NOT BEEN MADE THEY WOULD WIN CASE - COST OF CASE

6. How does a court gain jurisdiction over a person in a civil case? In a criminal case?

SUMMONS IN A CIVIL CASE BRINGS DEFENDENT PARTY UNDER THE JURISDICTION OF COURT (CRIMINAL CASE) ARREST MADE BY WARRANT ISSUED BY JUDGE BRINGS PERSON ACCUSED OF CRIME INTO COURT

7. Name four specialized federal courts.

U.S. BANKRUPTCY COURT
U.S. COURT OF INTERNATIONAL TRADE
U.S. TAX COURT
U.S. CLAIMS COURT

8. At both the federal and state levels there are civil and criminal courts. What types of cases are handled in civil courts? In criminal courts?

CIVIL COURTS - DISPUTES BETWEEN INDIVIDUALS, PERSON & BUSINESS / BUSINESSES BETWEEN ONE ANOTHER ... CRIMINAL - CASES BETWEEN GOV. MENTAL UNITS STATE / FEDERAL GOV. (ACTING FOR SOCIETY) PERSON/BUSINESS ACCUSED OF CRIME

(AWARDED MONEY 2 WINNING PARTY)

9. List three advantages to taking a case to small claims court.

TECHNICAL RULES OF EVIDENCE & PROCEDURE ARE NOT STRICTLY APPLICABLE - NO ATTORNEYS - ECONOMICALLY FEASABLE

10. What is the significance of the Supreme Court decision in *Roe v. Wade* (410 U.S. 113; 93 S. Ct. 705; 35 L. Ed. 2d 147)?

    *GAVE EXAMPLE OF COURTS POWER TO EXERCISE Judicial REVIEW*

11. The Fourteenth Amendment guarantees the equal protection of the law to all persons. What is the meaning of the phrase *equal protection*?

    *STATE & FEDERAL GOV. CANNOT TREAT ONE PERSON DIFF. FROM ANOTHER UNLESS THERE IS A LEG. REASON FOR DOING SO*

## CASE PROBLEMS

Read the case problems below and then answer the questions that follow.

1. Johnson refused to file a federal income tax return, claiming that it was a violation of his right to privacy. He was arrested and charged with a violation of the Internal Revenue Code of the United States.
    a. Is this a state or a federal case?  *FEDERAL*
    b. Which court has jurisdiction to hear this case?  *DISTRICT COURT*
    c. If Johnson is convicted, to which court may he appeal?  *COURT OF APPEALS*

2. Alden had her car radiator repaired by Smokey Garage for $125. She was not happy with the results and decided to sue the garage owner to get her money back.
    a. In what court would her case most likely be heard?  *SMALL CLAIMS*
    b. Does she need a lawyer to represent her in this court?  *NO*
    c. Would this kind of case normally be heard by a judge or by a jury?  *JUDGE*

3. Boulder got into a fight with Smyth and fractured Smyth's jaw. Smyth sued Boulder for his injuries.
    a. Would this case be tried in a civil or a criminal court?  *CIVIL*
    b. Is this a state or a federal case?  *STATE*
    c. Would this case be heard in a trial or an appellate court?  *TRIAL*

4. Metz, a citizen of Georgia, is injured in an auto accident in Atlanta. The driver of the other vehicle is a citizen of Maine. Metz wishes to recover the $5,000 she incurred for medical expenses and repairs to her car. Can Metz bring an action in federal court based on diversity of citizenship?  *NO*

## ACTIVITY: EXPRESSING YOUR LEGAL OPINION

Is the appeals process, which is both time consuming and costly, really necessary? Or should a verdict reached in a trial court presided over by a judge who has knowledge of law and trial procedures be final? Explain your answer in the space below.

*If the appealing party cannot prove that the decision could be reversed do to what ever than it should be final*

# Chapter 3

# Public Wrongs/Crimes

## CHAPTER OUTLINE

**Nature of Public Wrongs**
**State and Federal Criminal Laws**
**Common Crimes**
    Assault
    Robbery
    Arson
    Burglary
    Theft
    Driving While Intoxicated
    Drug Law Violations
    Computer Crimes
**Defenses to Crimes**
    Infancy
    Insanity

    Involuntary Intoxication
    Duress
    Justification
    Entrapment
**The Criminal Justice System**
    Police
    Courts
    Corrections
**The Juvenile Justice System**
    The Role of the Police
    Juvenile Court
    Corrections

## COMPLETION QUESTIONS

In the statements below, important words have been omitted. Fill in the blanks to complete each statement.

1. The U.S. criminal justice system is composed of three elements: police, courts, and _Corrections_.

2. The punishment for committing a felony could be imprisonment for more than _1 year_, usually in a state or federal prison.

3. Shoplifting is a form of _LARCENY_.

4. The criminal defense of _ENTRAPMENT_ applies when a person is persuaded to commit a crime by a law enforcement officer.

5. A(n) _INDICTMENT_ is a charge by a grand jury that a certain person has committed a felony.

6. A misdemeanor is an act punishable by imprisonment for _NO MORE THAN_ one year.

7. A young person who commits an unlawful act but who has not yet reached the age at which he or she can be treated as an adult criminal offender is called a(n) _JUVENILE DELINQUENT_.

8. Intentionally stealing money or the personal property of another without the use of force is called _EMBEZZLEMENT_.

9. The rights read to a suspect who has been arrested and is about to be questioned are called the _MIRANDA WARNING_.

10. Another name for blackmail is _EXTORTION_.

## SHORT-ANSWER QUESTIONS

Answer each of the following questions in the space provided.

1. A person suspected of committing a crime is dealt with through the criminal justice system. Describe the process this person must go through.

   _Crime - arrest - initial - Preliminary hearing - grand jury proceeding - arraignment - Guilty - sentence / Not Guilty - pretrial proceedings - Trial_

2. List three rights and three defenses a person has after being arrested on suspicion of having committed a crime.

   Rights:
   - right 2 remain silent
   - right against self incrimination
   - right 2 know reason for arrest

   Defenses:
   - INSANITY
   - JUSTIFICATION
   - ENTRAPMENT

PUBLIC WRONGS/CRIMES | 13

3. List four similarities and four differences between the adult and the juvenile criminal justice systems.

   Similarities:                                    Differences:

   _____                      _____

   _____                      _____

   _____                      _____

   _____                      _____

4. For each situation described below, identify the crime or crimes committed by the person underlined.

   a. A <u>fuel truck driver</u> was charged with skimming more than 100,000 gallons from gasoline deliveries to government agencies and then selling the fuel at cut-rate prices.
      
      *FRAUD*

   b. A <u>rock band member</u>, tired of having obscenities yelled at him by another band member, struck the other band member over the head with the base of his microphone stand, causing permanent brain damage.
      
      *ASSAULT & BATTERY*

   c. <u>Higgins</u> was charged with entering the Larder residence and taking a handgun, jewelry, coins, and bonds valued at over $1,500.
      
      *BURGLARY*

   d. An <u>escaped prisoner</u> entered a Conway Ice Cream store, pointed a gun at the clerk, and demanded all the money in the cash register.
      
      *THEFT*

   e. <u>Driscoll</u>, a store manager, filled out and signed time cards for nonexistent employees and then cashed the paychecks himself.
      
      *EMBEZZLEMENT*

## MULTIPLE-CHOICE QUESTIONS

On the line next to each statement, write the letter of the best answer.

_B_ 1. McCurdy's Department Store delivered merchandise to Willis by mistake. Although she knew the merchandise was not hers, she kept it. Willis is guilty of (a) nothing, (b) larceny, (c) burglary, (d) robbery.

_B_ 2. Weinberg was walking into the South Town Mall when he was attacked. Morrow, the attacker, knocked him down and took his wallet, which contained $50. Weinberg was seriously injured. Morrow was apprehended by the police and charged with (a) assault and burglary, (b) assault and robbery, (c) burglary and robbery, (d) robbery and criminal mischief.

_D_ 3. Barnum, the bookkeeper for Time Wise Food Wholesalers, made false entries in the company books so that she could take the company's money for her own use. Barnum was guilty of (a) fraud, (b) larceny, (c) robbery, (d) embezzlement.

**14 | CHAPTER 3**

_D_ 4. One defense against crime is (a) privilege, (b) the assumption of risk, (c) consent, (d) involuntary intoxication.

_D_ 5. Which of the following crimes cannot be easily committed through the assistance or use of a computer? (a) larceny, (b) criminal fraud, (c) embezzlement, (d) arson.

## ACTIVITY: CASE ANALYSIS

1. Read the case problem below and then answer the questions that follow.

   **FACTS:** Three police officers went to the home of Chimel in Santa Ana, California, with a warrant for his arrest for a coin store burglary. When they arrived, the officers identified themselves and asked to enter the house. Chimel's wife let them in. When Chimel arrived, the officers arrested him and searched him and the immediate area. Although they did not have a search warrant and although Chimel objected, the police then searched the entire house. In the course of this search, they seized a number of coins suspected of being from the coin shop burglary. In a lower court, Chimel was convicted of burglary based on the introduction of the coins as evidence. He appealed his case to the U.S. Supreme Court on the grounds that the officers' search of the entire house without a warrant was unlawful.

   **SUPREME COURT DECISION:** The Fourth Amendment prohibits "unreasonable searches and seizures" by government agents. Here, because the arrest was lawful, the Supreme Court found that a search of the arrested person and the "area of immediate control" was justified. However, the Court could find no justification for the warrantless search of the entire house. In the Court's interpretation of the Fourth Amendment, police officers are required to obtain a search warrant from a court before conducting a search unless some special circumstance justifies a warrantless search. In this case, the Court found no special circumstances concerning the search of the entire house. Therefore, the Court held that such a search should have been limited to the area where the arrest occurred (_Chimel_ v. _California_, 395 U.S. 752).

   a. Identify and define the crime involved in this case.

   _Burglary - entering private property & taking what doesn't belong to you_

   b. Briefly summarize the facts of the case.

   _Arrest warrant - can arrest accused look around without moving anything_

   c. What was the lower court's decision?

   _Conviction of Burglary_

d. What was the Supreme Court's decision regarding the officers' search of Chimel and of the entire house?

*Wasn't Search of Chimel fine — search of house was not*

e. Do you agree with the Supreme Court's findings? Why or why not?

*Yes — the officers could only arrest on probability there was no evident reason for them to search the premises*

## CASE PROBLEMS

Read the case problems below. For each problem, answer yes or no, and then explain your answer in the space provided.

1. At 3:00 a.m., Benton entered a store through an unlocked window. He gathered several valuable items, intending to steal them. When he heard the police coming, he left everything there but was caught by the police as he climbed out the window. Can Benton be charged with burglary even though he took nothing?

*Yes — the intent was there*

2. Reese bought a set of high-quality stereo speakers for $50 from someone selling them from the back of a van. The police stopped Reese several blocks away and arrested him for possession of stolen property. Can Reese claim in defense that he is not guilty because he did not know the speakers were stolen?

*No — he should be weary of the van and the low price of speakers — ignorance isn't claimable*

3. Customs and immigration officials suspected Marx of smuggling drugs into the United States. An undercover agent from the Bureau of Immigration suggested that Marx contact a certain drug kingpin in order to buy illegal drugs to sell in this country. Marx at first refused, but at the insistence of the undercover agent he later agreed. As he entered the country with the drugs, Marx was arrested and charged with smuggling. Marx claimed that he was "set up" and does not have criminal responsibility for what he did. Is Marx correct?

*Yes — the undercover entrapped Marx by pursuading him to cross the boarder*

## ACTIVITY: WHAT'S YOUR OPINION?

1. List reasons that prompt people to commit crimes.
   *Quick & easy money, lazy, want to be caught*

2. How can a police officer avoid lawsuits for false arrest?
   *Be certain of the person committing crime, obtain warrant before arrest*

# Chapter 4

# Private Wrongs/Torts

## CHAPTER OUTLINE

**An Overview of Tort Law**
**Intentional Torts**
    Assault and Battery
    False Imprisonment
    Infliction of Mental Distress
    Defamation
    Invasion of Privacy
    Wrongful Death
    Malicious Prosecution
    Fraud
    Interference with Contractual Relations
    Trespass
    Conversion
    Nuisance
**Defenses to Intentional Torts**
**Torts Resulting from Negligence**
**Defenses to Negligence**
**Strict Liability in Tort**
**Remedies for Torts**
**Tort Reform**

## MATCHING QUESTIONS

Use the following terms to identify the torts below. On the line next to each description, write the letter of the term that most closely relates to it.

a. Assault
b. Negligence
c. Trespass
d. Public nuisance
e. Conversion
f. Wrongful death
g. Private nuisance
h. Malpractice
i. Infliction of mental distress
j. Invasion of privacy
k. Malicious prosecution

_B_ 1. At Elmwood General Hospital, an 81-year-old patient died after a nurse accidentally gave him a toxic liquid instead of his medication.

_F_ 2. A 21-year-old student was paralyzed from the neck down when a poorly maintained platform collapsed at Wonder Amusement Park.

H 3. A surgeon performing eye surgery failed to follow standard postoperative procedure in measuring and minimizing pressure on the eye. As a result, the 7-year-old patient lost the sight in one eye.

D 4. Neighbors complained that Huber's property was "a junkyard and a breeding ground for rodents." County health investigators confirmed that the property was "a source of filth and a health hazard that affected the entire neighborhood."

J 5. Because of poor management practices in his department, a high-level hospital staff member was being investigated. Hospital officials searched his desk, including his personal papers and belongings, while he was at lunch. They discovered that he had once been under psychiatric care.

## COMPLETION QUESTIONS

In the statements below, important words have been omitted. Fill in the blanks to complete each statement.

1. Using a person's name or picture for an advertisement or other commercial purpose without consent is a(n) ~~CONVERSION~~ INVASION OF PRIVACY.

2. A(n) INTENTIONAL tort occurs when one person deliberately does some act that interferes with another and thereby causes injury or property damage.

3. A person who commits the tort of conversion also may be guilty of the crime of THEFT.

4. A(n) INJUNCTION is a court order that restrains a person from performing or continuing to perform some act.

5. Truth is a defense to a lawsuit for DEFAMATION.

6. The Supreme Court decision in N.Y. TIMES Vs. SULLIVAN made it more difficult for a public figure to sue for defamation.

7. The concept of liability without fault sometimes is called Strict liability.

8. Negligence occurs when a person gets CARELESS.

9. The tort of MALPRACTICE occurs when a professional's improper, immoral, or illegal conduct in rendering services causes the recipient of those services to suffer an injury or loss.

10. A victim of negligence must prove that the defendant's carelessness was the PROXIMATE cause of the victim's loss.

## MULTIPLE-CHOICE QUESTIONS

On the line next to each statement, write the letter of the best answer.

_D_ 1. The main difference between libel and slander is that (a) libel concerns adults only; slander, minors only, (b) libel concerns minors only; slander, adults only, (c) libel concerns those things spoken; slander, those things in print, (d) libel concerns those things in print; slander, those things spoken.

_C_ 2. Tort law is primarily (a) criminal law, (b) statutory, (c) case law, (d) Roman law.

_D_ 3. All of the following are intentional torts *except* (a) trespass, (b) fraud, (c) defamation, (d) malpractice.

_B_ 4. Comparative negligence can be used as a defense for (a) battery, (b) negligence, (c) conversion, (d) fraud.

_D_ 5. Martino, a bill collector, was kicked and punched by Beaden while trying to collect an overdue account from Beaden. Beaden could be held for the tort of (a) libel, (b) embezzlement, (c) extortion, (d) assault and battery.

_C_ 6. Breaking a car window and destroying a car phone is an example of (a) fraud, (b) invasion of privacy, (c) trespass, (d) defamation.

_D_ 7. By orally repeating a rumor she knew to be false, Marny damaged Jewell's reputation. Marny was guilty of (a) nothing (b) libel, (c) assault, (d) slander.

_A_ 8. Public officials cannot collect damages for false and defamatory statements made about them unless they can prove (a) actual malice, (b) strict liability, (c) invasion of privacy, (d) malicious prosecution.

_D_ 9. Benzer bought a television that, unknown to him, was stolen. Benzer refused to surrender the television until he was reimbursed the money he paid the seller. Benzer is liable for the tort of (a) fraud, (b) trespass, (c) negligence, (d) conversion.

___ 10. Curtis built a fence on what she thought was the border between her property and her neighbor's. A month later, she found that the fence was on her neighbor's property. The neighbor could hold Curtis liable for (a) nuisance, (b) trespass, (c) a criminal wrong, (d) nothing because the act was unintentional.

___ 11. To determine negligence, the court compares the conduct of the defendant with the conduct of (a) the attorneys involved in the case, (b) the judge, (c) a reasonable person, (d) a witness in the case.

___ 12. Lovell threatened to hit Farrin. If Lovell did hit Farrin and Farrin suffered injury or damages she could sue Lovell for (a) nuisance, (b) assault only, (c) battery only, (d) assault and battery.

___ 13. All of the following are a defense in a negligence suit *except* (a) assumption of risk, (b) contributory negligence, (c) comparative negligence, (d) strict liability.

___ 14. A person accused of shoplifting was detained in a store for an unreasonable length of time, but a search revealed no evidence of shoplifting. The detained person can sue for (a) robbery, (b) larceny, (c) false arrest, (d) trespass.

___ 15. A surgeon performed an appendectomy on Frank. One month later, Frank discovered that the surgeon had left some gauze in his incision, causing infection, considerable pain, and additional hospital expenses. Frank sued the surgeon to recover money damages. The basis for Frank's lawsuit was (a) nuisance, (b) invasion of privacy, (c) conversion, (d) malpractice.

___ 16. DiBella, a dentist, received a very derogatory letter from a former patient who was not satisfied with DiBella's work. If no one ever saw the letter, DiBella can sue this patient for (a) libel, (b) slander, (c) conversion, (d) none of these.

___ 17. Strict liability in tort has been applied to (a) the sale of defective products to the public, (b) cases involving assault and battery, (c) cases involving free speech under the First Amendment, (d) libel and slander cases.

___ 18. Martin leaves her garbage in open containers, causing foul odors in her neighborhood. This is an example of (a) fraud, (b) trespass, (c) nuisance, (d) defamation.

___ 19. A tort is (a) a breach of contract, (b) an offense against the state, (c) a private wrong, (d) a crime.

___ 20. Actual malice must be shown by (a) a private citizen attempting to recover damages for defamation, (b) a public figure in order to recover damages for defamation, (c) both public figures and private individuals, (d) a person suing for negligence.

## CASE PROBLEMS

Read the case problems below. For each problem, answer yes or no, and then explain your answer in the space provided.

1. Reed, a store loss prevention officer, thought she saw Jones leaving the store with merchandise he had not paid for concealed under his coat. Reed stopped Jones and asked if he would please come to the store manager's office. Jones agreed and followed Reed to the office. At the office, Reed explained to Jones why he was being detained and then asked if he would mind emptying his coat pockets. Jones agreed. Satisfied that Jones had stolen nothing, Reed released him with an apology. Later Jones claimed that he was the victim of false arrest. Was he correct?

_____
_____
_____

2. Langley, a state beauty contest winner, was sunning herself by the pool at the hotel where she was staying. Without her permission, King took a photo of her and sold the photo to Dansig for use in an advertising campaign. Langley has sued Dansig for damages for the unauthorized use of her picture. Can Langley recover?

_____
_____
_____

3. Dr. Springer tried unsuccessfully for over a year to collect a $1,000 debt from Byrd, a prominent citizen of the community, for services rendered. One evening at a dinner party, Springer casually mentioned to several of his business friends, including the president of the local bank, that he had not been able to collect the overdue debt from Byrd. As a result, Byrd was denied a personal loan he had applied for at the bank. Byrd claims that Springer's remark was slanderous and that Springer owes him damages. Is Byrd correct?

___

4. Marvelle had just mopped and waxed an area of the floor of his restaurant. He placed signs around the waxed area warning customers of the danger. Despite the warnings, Davis walked onto the waxed area. He slipped, fell, and broke an arm and a leg. Davis now claims that Marvelle is liable for the injuries he sustained. Is Davis correct?

___

## SHORT-ANSWER QUESTIONS

Answer each of the following questions in the space provided.

1. The torts of false arrest and false imprisonment often are confused. They are similar in some ways and different in others. Explain the difference between false arrest and false imprisonment, and give a brief example of each.

___

2. A person bringing a lawsuit for negligence must generally show the presence of four elements. List and describe these elements.

___

3. Two common defenses in a lawsuit based on negligence are contributory negligence and comparative negligence. What are the differences between them?
___
___
___
___

4. The law of defamation has been significantly affected by the Supreme Court's decision in *New York Times Co.* v. *Sullivan*. Discuss.
___
___
___
___

# Chapter 5

# Litigation and Alternatives for Settling Civil Disputes

## CHAPTER OUTLINE

Prologue
Scenario
How a Lawsuit Begins
Pretrial Proceedings
The Trial
Posttrial Proceedings
Alternatives for Settling Disputes
    Arbitration
    Mediation
    Minitrials
    The Summary Jury Trial
    Private Trial
    Informal Settlement Between Parties

## TRUE-FALSE QUESTIONS

On the line at the right of each statement, write the word *true* if the statement is true. If the statement is false, write the word or expression that should be substituted for the underlined word or expression to make the statement correct.

1. At the conclusion of a civil trial, jurors render a <u>motion</u>.
2. The examination of potential jurors to determine their qualifications to serve as jurors is called a <u>voir dire</u> examination.
3. <u>Grand</u> jurors render a verdict.
4. The official decision of the jury, which is entered into the court record, is called the <u>award</u>.
5. The term <u>litigation</u> refers to a lawsuit.

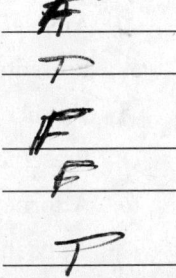

## 24 | CHAPTER 5

6. A major reason for not bringing a lawsuit is that the person you are thinking about suing may be <u>judgment proof</u>.   T

7. In order to fully understand your options, the first step in deciding whether or not to sue is to discuss your legal problem with a <u>friend</u>.   F

8. The failure of the defendant in a civil lawsuit to acknowledge receipt of a summons gives the plaintiff the right to a <u>judgment by default</u>.   T

9. The pretrial steps taken by the plaintiff and the defendant to learn in detail the nature of the other's claim in a civil lawsuit is called <u>direct examination</u>.   F

10. If the plaintiff and defendant do not demand a jury trial in a civil lawsuit, the evidence in the case is presented only to a <u>judge</u>.   T

## MULTIPLE-CHOICE QUESTIONS

On the line next to each statement, write the letter of the best answer.

C̶B̶   1. An unwilling witness must be served with a (a) motion, (b) summons, (c) subpoena, (d) *voir dire*.

C   2. The questioning of a witness for the plaintiff by the attorney for the defendant is called (a) direct examination, (b) redirect examination, (c) cross-examination, (d) indirect examination.

A   3. When a judge advises the jurors of the rules of law that must be applied to the facts presented during a trial, the judge is (a) instructing the jury, (b) asking for a judgment on the part of the jury, (c) asking for a motion, (d) requesting a verdict.

B   4. In a civil action, the paper that contains the defendant's statement of his or her defense is called a(n) (a) summons, (b) answer, (c) complaint, (d) award.

A̶ D   5. In a civil case, in order to "win," the plaintiff must establish the truth of his or her claim by (a) proving the facts beyond a reasonable doubt, (b) cross-examination, (c) direct examination, (d) a preponderance of the evidence.

## CHRONOLOGY

Rearrange the following events in the order in which they occur.

2 Summons and complaint
1 Discovery proceedings
3 Attorneys' opening statements
7 Answer
5 Presentation of evidence for the defendant
8 Verdict
4 Presentation of evidence for the plaintiff
6̶ 8 Attorneys' closing statements
9 Appeal

1. Summons & complaint
2. Answer
3. Discovery proceedings
4. Attorneys' opening statement
5. Presentation plaintiff
6. Defendant
7. Closing statements
8. Verdict
9. Appeal

## SHORT-ANSWER QUESTIONS

Answer each of the following questions in the space provided.

1. What are the differences among litigation, arbitration, and mediation?

   _____
   _____
   _____
   _____
   _____

2. What is the purpose of discovery as a pretrial step?

   _____
   _____
   _____

3. List three discovery techniques used by attorneys.

   _____
   _____
   _____

4. What are some of the problems that the losing party in a civil lawsuit can encounter if he or she decides to appeal the decision of the lower court?

   _____
   _____
   _____

5. What are the advantages of an informal settlement versus litigation or any of the alternatives to litigation described in Chapter 5?

   _____
   _____
   _____

## ACTIVITY: DOCUMENT ANALYSIS

---

SUPREME COURT OF THE STATE OF NEW YORK
COUNTY OF MONROE

WILLIAM JORDAN, Plaintiff

— against —

MARY MARTIN, Defendant

Complaint

The plaintiff, by his attorney, Peter Leffer, complaining of the defendant, alleges:

1. That on or about the 6th day of July, 1991, the plaintiff was lawfully upon Monroe Avenue, at its intersection with Winton Road, which is a public highway in the City of Rochester, New York, and was in the act of crossing said street at the same time that an automobile, owned and operated by the defendant, was passing over and along Winton Road.

2. That said defendant so negligently and carelessly managed and operated said automobile that in sole consequence thereof and without negligence or fault on the part of the plaintiff, plaintiff was suddenly and without notice or warning thrown violently to the street by said automobile.

3. That by reason of the foregoing the plaintiff suffered great bodily injury and became and still continues to be sick, sore, and disabled, and was obliged to spend large sums in attempting to cure himself, and was prevented for a long time from attending to his business, and was otherwise injured to his damage One Hundred Thousand Dollars ($100,000).

Wherefore, plaintiff demands judgment in the sum of $100,000, together with the costs and disbursements of this action.

PETER LEFFER
Attorney for Plaintiff
Office and P.O. Address
Platt Building
No. 175 Main Street
Rochester, New York
Telephone: 716-389-1462

---

1. What is the purpose of this document?

2. What is the basis for this complaint?

3. In the legal process, a complaint often accompanies what other legal document?

4. What are the statements made in this complaint called?
_____

5. When the defendant receives this complaint, what should she do?
_____
_____
_____

## ACTIVITY: WHAT'S YOUR OPINION?

State your opinion to the following questions after reviewing the scenario in Chapter 5.

1. Do you think that the $3,000,000 for medical expenses, "pain and suffering," and court costs that Allen was asking for was too high?
_____
_____
_____

2. The attorney for the Laiden Trucking Company, the defendant, could have used legal tactics to delay the lawsuit. In turn, this would have delayed a possible verdict in Allen's favor. What do you think can be done to eliminate legal delays in courtrooms?
_____
_____
_____

# Review

# Part I
# Understanding the Law

## TRUE-FALSE QUESTIONS

Indicate whether each statement below is true or false by circling T or F in the column on the right.

1. Law is strongly affected by ethical concepts.     T   F
2. In a criminal case, the state or the federal government represents society against the individual accused of the crime.     T   F
3. Laws passed by Congress and by state legislatures are called common laws.     T   F
4. Any law enacted by a state legislature or municipality that conflicts with that state's constitution may be declared invalid by a court of law.     T   F
5. A federal court decision always can be appealed to the U.S. Supreme Court.     T   F
6. The primary difference between a felony and a misdemeanor is the seriousness of the act committed.     T   F
7. Most serious crimes are punishable by a sentence of a year or more in a state or federal prison.     T   F
8. The prior criminal record of a defendant may affect the punishment given for a crime.     T   F
9. Small claims courts usually hear cases involving minor crimes.     T   F
10. *Stare decisis* means to "stand by a decision" and refers to cases that were decided previously.     T   F
11. Compensatory damages are imposed on a wrongdoer by the court as punishment for an intentional tort.     T   F
12. Tort law is concerned with "private" wrongs.     T   F
13. Strict liability is based on the concept of liability without fault.     T   F
14. All persons taken into police custody have the right of due process.     T   F
15. Jurors are selected for jury duty through a process called *voir dire*.     T   F

## MULTIPLE-CHOICE QUESTIONS

On the line next to each statement, write the letter of the best answer.

_____ 1. The function of the grand jury is to (a) prosecute the defendant, (b) judge the defendant guilty or not guilty of the charges, (c) decide whether there is sufficient evidence to bring a case to trial, (d) prove to the court that the defendant is guilty as charged.

_____ 2. Once a case has been brought to trial, the first court procedure in a lawsuit is (a) jury selection, (b) the jury's verdict, (c) the attorneys' opening statements to the jury, (d) the judge's charge to the jury.

_____ 3. While playing football in an empty lot, Matthews hit a passerby in the eye with the ball. This is an example of a(n) (a) felony, (b) tort, (c) misdemeanor, (d) infraction.

_____ 4. Libel and slander are forms of (a) negligence, (b) conspiracy, (c) fraud, (d) defamation.

_____ 5. The refusal to return to its rightful owner stolen property that you purchased is a tort called (a) attachment, (b) trespass, (c) conversion, (d) injunction.

_____ 6. Blain's neighbor charged him with assault and battery. Blain was handed a legal notice directing him to appear in court to answer the charges. This notice is known as (a) an answer, (b) a subpoena, (c) a summons, (d) none of these.

_____ 7. Potter won her negligence lawsuit against Mann. The $100,000 awarded to Potter is called a(n) (a) judgment, (b) sentence, (c) indictment, (d) injunction.

_____ 8. Fleming leaves her garbage outside in an uncovered barrel. The resulting bad smell bothers her neighbors. This is an example of (a) fraud, (b) trespass, (c) nuisance, (d) conversion.

_____ 9. The person who initiates a civil action is called the (a) defendant, (b) plaintiff, (c) state, (d) district attorney.

_____ 10. A grand jury has the authority to issue a(n) (a) judgment, (b) indictment, (c) verdict, (d) award.

_____ 11. An example of an act classified as a crime is (a) arson, (b) nuisance, (c) slander, (d) invasion of privacy.

_____ 12. A valid defense that a defendant's attorney could introduce during a criminal trial is (a) the defendant did not know the act was wrong, (b) entrapment, (c) the defendant was instructed to perform the illegal act as a joke, (d) the defendant committed the act out of necessity.

_____ 13. The case title *United States* v. *Powers* indicates a (a) state civil case, (b) state criminal case, (c) federal civil case, (d) federal criminal case.

_____ 14. Common law often is referred to as (a) written law, (b) administrative law, (c) equity law, (d) unwritten law.

_____ 15. Judges' practice of following the precedents established by past decisions is called (a) equity, (b) indictment, (c) *stare decisis*, (d) an act of Congress.

_____ 16. If Bartel dumped trash on Frank's land, Bartel could be held liable for (a) fraud, (b) negligence, (c) conversion, (d) trespass.

_____ 17. Taking money that belongs to someone else and that has been given to you for safekeeping is the crime of (a) embezzlement, (b) robbery, (c) forgery, (d) arson.

18. The questioning of a plaintiff's witness by the defendant's attorney is known as (a) direct examination, (b) indictment, (c) cross-examination, (d) objection.

19. An effort to make laws similar among states has been attempted through (a) the Uniform Commercial Code, (b) amendments to the state constitutions, (c) an amendment to the U.S. Constitution, (d) local ordinances within each state.

20. Common law is a system of law that developed (a) after the eighteenth century, (b) after the United States was founded, (c) in the early American colonies, (d) in England, with precedents established from prior disputes.

21. Punitive damages are awarded to someone injured by another person's intentional tort (a) so the injured party can make a profit, (b) so the injured party is compensated for hospital and doctor bills, (c) to punish the party who committed the tort, (d) so the person who committed the tort can make a profit.

22. When Bond's lease ended, her landlord inspected the apartment and found no damage beyond ordinary wear and tear. The landlord promised to return her $300 security deposit within a week, but several months later, Bond still was trying to get her money. For an inexpensive, quick, fair settlement, Bond should (a) ask the public defender to represent her at state expense in a local court, (b) take her case to small claims court, (c) take her case to the highest state court, (d) obtain a writ of execution to seize and sell the landlord's property.

23. Carmel struck a legally parked car while backing carelessly out of his driveway. Carmel could be found guilty of the tort of (a) nuisance, (b) negligence, (c) assault and battery, (d) conversion.

24. A body of law that states the rights and limitations of both the federal government and of state governments is classified (a) administrative, (b) constitutional, (c) common, (d) statutory.

25. A convicted criminal claimed that his constitutional rights had been violated. The highest court that can pass judgment on his claim is (a) the highest state court, (b) the U.S. Court of Claims, (c) a federal district court, (d) the U.S. Supreme Court.

26. Laws enacted by legislative bodies that forbid conduct harmful to society and that impose fines or imprisonment for violations are called (a) moral laws, (b) civil laws, (c) natural laws, (d) criminal laws.

27. In the United States, law is derived from (a) written laws, such as constitutions, statutes, and ordinances, (b) case law, which is based on judicial decisions, (c) administrative agencies' rules and regulations, (d) all of these.

28. If Larson breaks into Pick's house while Pick is away and steals a painting, Larson may be found guilty of (a) burglary and robbery, (b) arson and misrepresentation, (c) burglary and larceny, (d) arson and robbery.

29. A person who suffers mentally as a result of another person's extreme conduct can sue for (a) battery, (b) conversion, (c) emotional distress, (d) trespass.

30. Detaining a person in a restaurant to see whether the bill has been paid would be considered (a) battery, (b) a nuisance, (c) trespass, (d) false imprisonment.

31. The relief granted in a civil action is (a) punishment, (b) confinement in a state prison, (c) confinement in a county jail, (d) money damages.

32. A court of original jurisdiction is called a (a) trial court, (b) higher court, (c) review court, (d) criminal court.

33. Some states have passed a law that allows a cause of action against a bar or tavern owner in favor of third parties injured by an intoxicated patron. This law is called the (a) dram shop act, (b) alcoholic beverage control act, (c) intoxicated patrons act, (d) Federal Controlled Substance Act.

34. A court that has the power to hear any case brought before it is said to have (a) original jurisdiction, (b) appellate jurisdiction, (c) venue jurisdiction, (d) general jurisdiction.

35. In addition to having jurisdiction over the subject matter, before a court can hear a case it must have (a) jurisdiction over the state, (b) jurisdiction over the person, (c) jurisdiction in general, (d) appellate jurisdiction.

## COMPLETION QUESTIONS

In the statements below, important words have been omitted. Fill in the blanks to complete each statement.

1. A court decision that has the force of law is a(n) _____.

2. A person who violates a criminal law is subject to _____.

3. The usual remedy available to the injured party in a civil lawsuit involving a tort is _____.

4. A pretrial device used by the plaintiff and defendant to learn in detail about the nature of the other's claim or defense is called _____.

5. The defendant in a slander case is not liable if he or she can prove that the statement made about the plaintiff was _____.

6. In law, the average individual is referred to as a(n) _____ person.

7. Another name for negligence is _____.

8. The tort of _____ is based on injury resulting from false statements that are made deliberately to deceive.

9. Trespass is a wrong against the property of another; false imprisonment is a wrong against another's _____.

10. _____ damages are imposed on a wrongdoer by the court as punishment for an intentional tort.

## CASE PROBLEM

Read the case problem below and then answer the questions that follow.

Ring, age 35, was convicted of driving while intoxicated (DWI). Six months later, he was arrested and again charged with DWI.

1. What do you call the formal charge the grand jury issued against Ring?

2. How would you classify DWI? What kind of "wrong" is it?

3. Who presents the charges against Ring in court?

4. By what means can an unwilling witness to the accident be ordered to appear to give testimony in court?

5. Suppose it can be shown that Ring, while intoxicated, had been served alcoholic beverages in a restaurant and as a result injured another person. Is the restaurant owner liable? Explain your answer.

## SHORT-ANSWER QUESTIONS

Answer each of the following questions in the space provided.

1. List and describe four primary sources of law in the United States.

2. Under the law, torts are classified in three ways. Briefly identify and describe them.

3. List the primary steps in the adult criminal justice system.

   _____
   _____
   _____
   _____
   _____
   _____

4. List and describe three alternatives to litigation as a way to settle legal disputes.

   _____
   _____
   _____

5. Why is it important for you to understand the law and how it works?

   _____
   _____
   _____
   _____
   _____

# PART II
# CONTRACTS

# Chapter 6

# The Basics of Contract Law

## CHAPTER OUTLINE

What a Contract Is
The Elements of a Valid Contract
Contract Terminology
    Bilateral and Unilateral Contracts
    Valid, Void, Voidable, and Unenforceable Contracts
    Formal and Informal Contracts
    Express and Implied Contracts
    Executory and Executed Contracts

## MULTIPLE-CHOICE QUESTIONS

On the line next to each statement, write the letter of the best answer.

\_\_\_\_ 1. Oral contracts (a) are not legal, (b) cannot be enforced in court, (c) lack agreement, (d) are harder to prove than written contracts.

\_\_\_\_ 2. An illegal contract generally would be considered (a) valid, (b) voidable, (c) implied, (d) void.

\_\_\_\_ 3. Carlson fully performed her part of a contract to the complete satisfaction of Briggs, who has not yet paid Carlson. This is an example of a(n) (a) executory contract, (b) executed contract, (c) formal contract, (d) void contract.

\_\_\_\_ 4. Contracts that involve important or complicated matters should be (a) implied in fact, (b) written, (c) breached, (d) implied in law.

\_\_\_\_ 5. If either party fails to perform her or his duties under the terms of a contract, the contract has been (a) performed, (b) breached, (c) enforced, (d) executed.

6. Another name for a contract implied in law is a(n) (a) executed contract, (b) written contract, (c) quasi contract, (d) express contract.

7. Bart agreed to sell Sean his motorcycle for $900. Sean paid Bart $900, and Bart promised delivery the next day. This is an example of a(n) (a) implied contract, (b) executed contract, (c) executory contract, (d) void contract.

8. For a contract to be valid, four essential elements are required. All of the following are essential elements of a valid contract *except* (a) offer and acceptance, (b) competent parties, (c) consideration, (d) written form.

9. Peters promised to pay Carter $25 if he repaired a lawnmower. Carter repaired the lawnmower but has not been paid yet. At this point, this contract is (a) valid, unilateral, and executory, (b) valid, bilateral, and executory, (c) valid, bilateral, and executed, (d) valid, unilateral, and executed.

10. To create a legally binding contract, both parties to the agreement must be (a) able to read and write, (b) able to speak and understand English, (c) financially responsible, (d) competent.

11. A bilateral contract involves a(n) (a) act for an act, (b) act for a promise, (c) promise for a promise, (d) promise for an act.

12. Bentley, a minor, bought a set of golf clubs for $89.95 from Mickey's Sporting Goods Shop. This is an example of a (a) void contract, (b) voidable contract, (c) quasi contract, (d) social agreement.

13. A contract implied in fact (a) does not exist in the eyes of the law, (b) can be expressed orally or in writing, (c) arises from the actions of the parties rather than from a specific agreement, (d) generally is not enforced by the courts because competent parties are lacking.

14. An express contract is one in which (a) no specific oral or written agreement is made, (b) the agreement is stated specifically, (c) neither party can enforce the contract against the other in court, (d) no legal obligation is intended.

15. A contract that can be enforced unless a party legally entitled to avoid the contract does so is called a (a) void contract, (b) voidable contract, (c) quasi contract, (d) contract implied in law.

## CASE PROBLEMS

1. Read the case problems below. For each problem, answer yes or no, and then explain your answer in the space provided.

    a. Armond and his girlfriend went to the movies. Without saying anything, Armond handed the ticket seller $10. The ticket seller, also without speaking, handed Armond two tickets. Was any type of contract formed?

b. Berger fainted at a shopping mall. A security guard arranged with police to have her taken to a hospital for emergency treatment. When she regained consciousness and was about to be discharged, the business office asked her to sign papers arranging for her insurance company to pay the bill. Berger refused to sign, claiming she had not made an agreement with the hospital for treatment. The hospital sued Berger. Would a court require Berger to pay the bill?

_____
_____
_____
_____

c. Stevens agreed to take his friend Anderson to lunch. He said to Anderson: "Meet me at the Royal Scot Restaurant at 12:30 tomorrow afternoon." Anderson agreed. Stevens never showed up. Does Anderson have a legal claim against Stevens for breach of contract?

_____
_____
_____
_____

d. Mason, who has a degree in business administration, interviewed for two positions, one as a credit manager for a large bank and the other as a financial planner. He received a phone call offering him the credit manager's position, which he accepted. Two days later he was offered the financial planner's job, his first choice. He also accepted this position and then called the bank to say he had changed his mind about taking the credit manager's position. Has Mason breached a contract with the bank?

_____
_____
_____
_____

e. The Isaac Heating Company randomly sent out letters to residents of the town where it did business. The letter read: "Special—We offer to clean your furnace for 50% off our regular price." Martell received one of the letters. Did a contract result between Isaac Heating Company and Martell when Martell received the letter?

_____
_____
_____
_____

f. Serono agreed to sell her horse to Branston. Unknown to either of them, the horse had been hit by a car and killed. Can either party still enforce the contract in court?

_____
_____
_____
_____

2. Read the case problem below and then answer the questions that follow.

> On January 7, Harry Owens, owner of Custom Cleaners, offered to clean the carpets in Jane Harrington's law office for $350. Harrington agreed to this offer on January 9. On January 20, Owens cleaned the carpets and was paid $350.

a. Who is the offeror? _____
b. Who is the offeree? _____
c. When was the offer accepted? _____
d. What did each party give as consideration to bind the agreement? _____
_____
e. Was the contract executed? _____

3. Read the following contract and then list at least four items that are missing.

> This agreement is made between David Richardson and Edward Warren. Richardson agrees to clean and paint the outside surface of Warren's frame dwelling, using paint and materials supplied by Edward Warren and applying two coats of paint. In consideration of this, Edward Warren agrees to pay David Richardson on satisfactory completion of the work.

a. _____  c. _____
b. _____  d. _____

## SHORT-ANSWER QUESTIONS

Answer each of the following questions in the space provided.

1. "All contracts are agreements, but not all agreements are contracts." What does this statement mean?

_____
_____
_____
_____
_____

2. Why should a contract involving an important or complicated matter be in writing?

_____
_____
_____
_____

3. Other than money, what forms can consideration take?
   _____
   _____
   _____

4. How is a quasi contract related to the law of contracts?
   _____
   _____
   _____

5. What is the difference between a unilateral and a bilateral contract?
   _____
   _____
   _____

# Chapter 7

# Agreement: Offer and Acceptance

## CHAPTER OUTLINE

How Agreement Is Reached
The Offer
    Offer Must Be Seriously Intended
    Offer Must Be Definite
    Offer Must Be Communicated
    Invitations to Make Offers
    How an Offer Ends

The Acceptance
    Acceptance Only by Offeree
    Acceptance Must Agree with the Offer
    Acceptance Must Be Communicated to the Offeror
    Silence as Acceptance

## MULTIPLE-CHOICE QUESTIONS

On the line next to each statement, write the letter of the best answer.

_____ 1. The Budget Office Furniture Company advertised a 60- × 30-inch executive desk for $220.99 in its office supplies catalog. Marlow went to the store and told the salesperson that she wanted to buy one of the advertised desks. Marlow's action was a(n) (a) agreement, (b) acceptance, (c) offer, (d) bilateral contract.

_____ 2. An example of a valid offer is a(n) (a) notice of a reward for finding a lost dog, (b) advertisement to sell a car, (c) offer that is made in jest, (d) offer to sell a stolen stereo.

_____ 3. If no fixed time is stated for an offer to remain open, the offer (a) ends automatically after 30 days, (b) ends after a reasonable time, (c) ends when the offeree states that it has ended, (d) remains open indefinitely.

_____ 4. Your friend made the following statement: "I might sell my car next month if I can get a good price." This statement is (a) an offer to a formal contract, (b) an offer to a unilateral contract, (c) an offer to a bilateral contract, (d) not an offer.

5. When goods are sold at an ordinary auction, acceptance takes place when (a) the auctioneer lets the gavel fall, (b) the offeree pays for the goods, (c) the auctioneer accepts a bid from the highest bidder, (d) the auctioneer presents the goods for sale.

6. Carelli bid $125 for an antique table at a flea market auction. Legally this bid is considered a(n) (a) acceptance to an offer, (b) bilateral contract, (c) counteroffer, (d) valid offer.

7. Revocation of an offer takes place when (a) the offeror has been properly notified, (b) the offeree has been properly notified, (c) a proper counteroffer is made, (d) the offeree properly refuses the offer.

8. Unless stated otherwise, acceptance of an offer made by mail takes place as soon as the letter of acceptance is (a) written by the offeree, (b) mailed by the offeree, (c) received by the offeror, (d) received by the offeree.

9. Fowler, an antique dealer, wrote a letter to Gorcey on May 9 offering to sell Gorcey the grandfather clock that Gorcey had seen at Fowler's antique show. The letter stated that the acceptance had to be received by May 15. Gorcey mailed a letter of acceptance on May 15 that reached Fowler on May 16. A valid contract was made (a) on May 15, (b) on May 9, (c) on May 16, (d) at no time.

10. If Stornelli pays Mooney $50 to keep an offer for the sale of a personal computer open for a definite length of time, their agreement is called a(n) (a) counteroffer, (b) option, (c) breach, (d) quasi contract.

11. Preston offered to sell a camera to Bellino, but then withdrew the offer before Bellino could accept. Preston's withdrawal of the offer is known as (a) revocation, (b) an option, (c) a counteroffer, (d) acceptance.

12. Caldwell offered to sell his used car to Jones for $2,000. Jones refused. The offer has been terminated by (a) performance, (b) mutual agreement, (c) revocation, (d) rejection.

13. Thomas said to Winton: "I'll sell you my computer for $2,000." Winton replied: "I'll take it if you will include a used printer." Winton's reply legally resulted in (a) a binding contract, (b) a counteroffer, (c) revocation, (d) substitution.

14. Which of the following statements most likely would *not* be considered a counteroffer? (a) "I accept, but only if you also include a CD player," (b) "I accept, but please ship the merchandise to my home rather than my place of business," (c) I accept, but only if you give me 30 days to pay," (d) "I accept, but only if you give me a discount."

15. A person who makes a counteroffer becomes the (a) acceptor, (b) offeree, (c) offeror, (d) promisee.

## CASE PROBLEMS

Read the case problems below. For each problem, answer yes or no, and then explain your answer in the space provided.

1. Archer, in Chicago, wrote to Ganze in New York City offering to purchase her antique car. When she received the letter, Ganze mailed an acceptance. After she mailed the letter, Ganze

changed her mind and sent a telegram rejecting the offer. The telegram and the letter reached Archer at the same time. Did a contract result?

2. Jordan said to Beacher, "I'll sell you my telescope for $150." Beacher replied, "I won't give you $150, but I will give you $75." Jordan said no. Beacher then changed his mind and said, "Okay, I'll give you $150." Jordan refused to sell the telescope to Beacher, saying it was too late and he had decided to keep it. Beacher now is claiming breach of contract. Did a contract arise between Jordan and Beacher?

3. Wurzer subscribed to *Weight Lifters* magazine. About 3 months before the subscription ran out, he received a letter from the publishing company stating that his subscription would be renewed on the renewal date unless he notified the company to the contrary. Wurzer did not reply or renew his subscription. Is Wurzer bound by contract for the subscription renewal?

4. Perez offered a $25 reward for the return of an expensive calculator watch he had lost. Jarvis saw the notice in the newspaper and returned the watch, but Perez refused to give her the reward. Does Jarvis have a legal right to the reward?

5. Earle offered Grant $450 for her computer printer and told her that she had until noon the following day to accept. At 9:00 the next morning, Earle called Grant and withdrew his offer. Nevertheless, at 11:00 a.m. Grant called Earle back and accepted his offer, noting that Earle had given her until noon of that day to accept. Is Grant's acceptance legally binding?

## MATCHING QUESTIONS

Use the following terms to identify the method of terminating the offer in the descriptions below. On the line next to each description, write the letter of the term that most closely relates to it.

a. Lapse of time
b. Rejection
c. Counteroffer
d. Revocation
e. Illegality

_____ 1. Benson received a letter from a college offering her the position of director of admissions. Before she could reply, she received a telegram from the college president stating that the board of trustees had decided that because of budget restrictions, a director would not be appointed now.

_____ 2. Three months ago, Petrus offered to sell a friend several shares of a popular stock. The friend as yet has not accepted the offer.

_____ 3. Janice offered to sell her friend two tickets to a live rock concert but was told by this friend that she did not want them.

_____ 4. Hawkins offered to sell her necklace to Haines for $350. Haines replied that she would pay $300.

_____ 5. Carter, a wholesaler, offered to sell Horton, the owner of a retail drugstore, several items classified as drug paraphernalia. Before Horton accepted the offer, a local law was passed banning the sale of drug paraphernalia.

## ACTIVITY: CASE ANALYSIS

Read the case below and then answer the questions that follow.

Following the assassination of President Abraham Lincoln on April 14, 1865, by John Wilkes Booth and John H. Surratt, one of Booth's suspected accomplices, the secretary of war published the following reward offer in various newspapers:

$25,000 reward to the person who apprehends John H. Surratt and a $10,000 reward for information leading to the arrest of John H. Surratt.

Sometime afterward, a notice revoking the offer was published. Shuey, unaware that the offer had been revoked, reported information on the whereabouts of Surratt to the proper government officials. The information furnished by Shuey led to Surratt's arrest. (Based on *Shuey* v. *United States*, 92 U.S. 73, 23 L. Ed. 697, 1875)

1. Was Shuey legally entitled to the reward? Explain your answer.

_____

_____

_____

_____

2. If Shuey had provided the information on Surratt before the reward offer was revoked, would he be entitled to $25,000? Why or why not?

_____
_____
_____
_____

# Chapter 8

# Consideration

## CHAPTER OUTLINE

The Requirement of Consideration
The Nature of Consideration
Adequacy of Consideration
Moral Consideration
Past Consideration
Special Problems Relating to Consideration
    Pre-existing Contractual Agreement
    Pre-existing Duty to Pay a Debt
    Pre-existing Duty to Perform a Legal Obligation
**Agreements Enforceable Without Consideration**
    Promises to Charitable Organizations
    Promissory Estoppel

## MULTIPLE-CHOICE QUESTIONS

On the line next to each statement, write the letter of the best answer.

_____ 1. An agreement is unenforceable because of lack of consideration when (a) consideration is inadequate, (b) consideration is not in the form of money, (c) a person gives up his or her legal rights, (d) no promise is given or act completed for the offeror's promise.

_____ 2. Lee owes Chaney $450. Both Lee and Chaney agree on the amount owed. The debt will be discharged if Chaney (a) accepts $300 and a set of books worth $125 from Lee, (b) accepts $375 in full payment, (c) accepts $400 in full payment, (d) orally agrees to cancel the debt.

3. After Buckman found Conrad's wallet, Conrad orally promised to pay Buckman $15. Conrad is not legally bound to pay because the consideration for her promise was (a) present, (b) past, (c) future, (d) illegal.

4. Altier orally promised his daughter a silver bracelet as a gift. Altier is not legally bound because (a) a promise to make a gift is unenforceable, (b) he never intended to give the gift, (c) the consideration was inadequate, (d) the gift was too expensive.

5. When a debtor and a creditor disagree on the amount owed on a debt and agree to compromise, the debt is (a) not paid legally, (b) not binding legally, (c) settled legally, (d) partially settled.

6. A police officer is not entitled to a reward offered for the arrest of a criminal because (a) the officer has a legal duty to arrest criminals, (b) a reward is not legal consideration, (c) the reward is not an offer, (d) the reward is too high.

7. Your uncle gave you a TV. He could not claim lack of consideration and demand its return because (a) the promise of a gift is unenforceable, (b) the TV is future consideration, (c) consideration is unimportant once an agreement is executed, (d) the consideration was inadequate.

8. McIntyre was struck by a car driven by Gaines, who orally promised McIntyre $1,500 if she would not bring suit for injuries. McIntyre agreed. McIntyre (a) has made a void agreement, (b) is entitled only to actual expenses, (c) has no rights because she gave no consideration for Gaines's promise, (d) has a right to $1,500 because she refrained from doing what she had a legal right to do.

9. Chang owed Scott $800 but was unable to pay Scott on the due date. Scott agreed to let Chang pay him the following month. This agreement (a) is not binding legally, (b) is binding legally, (c) is enforceable by Chang, (d) contains adequate consideration by Scott.

10. Allen repaired Hansen's house while Hansen was sick. When she found out about the repairs, Hansen promised to pay Allen $50. Hansen's promise is not enforceable in a court of law because it was (a) not adequate, (b) for past consideration, (c) for future consideration, (d) too indefinite.

11. Which of the following agreements is unenforceable because of lack of valid consideration? (a) Johnson agreed to donate $1,000 to the United Hospital Building Fund. Based on this and similar promises, construction was started, (b) Davis promised to give his neighbor's son $50 if the boy would refrain from trespassing on his property. Because of Davis's promise, the boy complied, (c) Boyd agreed to sell his used motorboat to Yates for $500. Yates offered the $500, (d) Philips promised his nephew $200 if the boy would refrain from smoking until he reached age 21. Because of this promise, his nephew did not smoke.

## CASE PROBLEMS

Read the case problems below. For each problem, answer yes or no, and then explain your answer in the space provided.

1. Adler was a medical research assistant at Mills General Hospital. Before his contract with the hospital expired, he was offered a position with another hospital at a higher salary. Mills General Hospital then offered Adler an increase in salary if he would complete his

employment contract. Adler agreed to stay at Mills General Hospital. Is Adler entitled to the increase in salary offered by the hospital?

2. Gurbowski, who was heavily in debt, offered to sell her motorcycle, which was valued at $1,200, for $800. Marconi accepted the offer. After thinking it over, Gurbowski decided not to deliver the motorcycle, claiming that $800 was not enough. Is Marconi entitled to delivery of the motorcycle?

3. Visca, who was visiting a friend's house, was injured by a ceiling tile that fell and hit her on the head. The friend gave her money for one visit to a doctor and for prescriptions ordered by the doctor. In return, Visca agreed not to sue for injuries. Later Visca complained of severe headaches and had to see a doctor several times and continue on medication. Visca then decided to sue for additional money. Can Visca collect?

4. Springer promised to give his son a car on his twentieth birthday. Is Springer legally bound by this promise?

5. Jenkins claimed he owed LaFond only $500; LaFond insisted the debt was $600. After much discussion, they agreed to settle for $550. Later, evidence proved that LaFond was correct. He sued to recover the $50. Will he win?

## SHORT-ANSWER QUESTIONS

Answer each of the following questions in the space provided.

1. Name four circumstances that lead the courts to question whether the consideration received by each party is fair.

2. Why is the performance of a pre-existing contractual obligation by the offeree not consideration for an offeror's promise? Give an example.

3. What is the basis for enforcing a contract under the doctrine of promissory estoppel?

4. Discuss the different theories for enforcing promises to charitable organizations.

# Chapter 9

# Competent Parties

## CHAPTER OUTLINE

**Competent Parties**
**Minors**
  Minors' Liability on Ordinary Contracts
  Misrepresentation of Age by a Minor
  Ratification by a Minor
  Minors' Liability for Necessaries
  Parents' Liability for Minors' Contracts
  Minors' Liability for Torts
**Persons Under the Influence of Alcohol or Other Drugs**
**Mentally Ill Persons**

## MULTIPLE-CHOICE QUESTIONS

On the line next to each statement, write the letter of the best answer.

_____ 1. Kavik has been declared legally insane by a court. Her purchase of an electric corn popper for $43.95 is (a) voidable by Kavik, (b) void, (c) valid if the price of the corn popper is reasonable, (d) valid if the store declares it valid.

_____ 2. Two months before reaching the age of majority, Marcus bought a radar detector for $129.95. She paid cash. Nine months later, she sought to avoid the agreement. Marcus's delay in avoiding the agreement (a) made her liable to the merchant for fraud, (b) did not prevent her from avoiding the agreement, (c) most likely constituted a ratification of the agreement, (d) entitled her to only a partial refund of the purchase price.

_____ 3. A minor who disaffirms an executed agreement with an adult (a) is bound for life, (b) ends the agreement with no further obligation, (c) must inform the adult orally, (d) must return any consideration received from the adult.

4. An emancipated minor who purchases a prescription in a drugstore is required to pay (a) any amount the druggist wants to charge, (b) the reasonable value of the prescription, (c) an amount decided on by the minor, (d) the price set by the manufacturer.

5. Lewis, a minor, sold her indoor exerciser to Francis, an adult. Francis then resold the exerciser to Beacon, a good faith purchaser. Beacon's title is (a) voidable, (b) valid, (c) void, (d) unenforceable.

6. Agreements of people who suffer from periods of temporary insanity but who have not been declared legally insane by a court can be disaffirmed by (a) the temporarily insane person in a period of normalcy, (b) the temporarily insane person at any time, (c) the other party to the agreement, (d) either party.

7. Cigarette lighters, jewelry, and electronic games are classified legally as (a) necessaries, (b) luxury items, (c) adult items, (d) entertainment items.

8. Thompson, a minor, bought headphones for her stereo from The Stereo Store. This agreement is (a) voidable by The Stereo Store only, (b) voidable by either party, (c) voidable by Thompson only, (d) binding on both parties.

9. An emancipated minor can avoid a contract to pay for (a) having a tooth filled by a dentist, (b) jeans and shirts that are part of a school wardrobe, (c) room and board at a private roominghouse near the private school he is attending, (d) archery equipment used in sports tournaments.

10. An emancipated minor's contracts are voidable unless they are (a) for luxury items, (b) for necessaries, (c) made with other minors, (d) made with adults.

11. A person who enters into a written contract while intoxicated and does not understand the consequences of the agreement (a) still is bound by the written contract, (b) may avoid the contract under certain conditions on becoming sober, (c) can do nothing, (d) waives all rights in that agreement.

12. The best illustration of a legally competent party is (a) a person under the influence of alcohol, (b) a 14-year-old, (c) a 65-year-old, (d) a person who is legally insane.

## CASE PROBLEMS

Read the case problems below. For each problem, answer yes or no, and then explain your answer in the space provided.

1. A month before his 18th birthday, Karlson purchased a VCR for $450 from Langley. He agreed in writing to pay $50 down and the balance in monthly payments of $40. After making three payments, Karlson tried to return the VCR and have his money refunded, less depreciation. Was he within his legal rights in returning the VCR and asking for a refund?

2. Cordaro, age 17, who is self-supporting, injured herself while biking across the country. The injury was serious enough to require immediate medical attention. After being treated by a physician, Cordaro refused to pay the bill, claiming that her parents were still liable for her medical bills. Is Cordaro's refusal legal?

3. Roper, age 17½, bought a new car for her personal use. A few days after her 18th birthday, she asked the dealer to take the car back. Can Roper disaffirm this contract?

4. Gruscho, owner of London Bridge Men's Store, sold a tuxedo to Robbins. Robbins, who was only 17, claimed to be 20. He agreed to pay the $250 purchase price in 30 days. After the 30 days passed, Robbins returned the tuxedo, which he had worn twice, and disaffirmed the purchase. Gruscho refused to accept the tuxedo. He sued Robbins, claiming that Robbins lied about his age and that a used tuxedo has no value. Can Gruscho legally refuse to take back the tuxedo and sue Robbins?

## ACTIVITY: ETHICAL DILEMMA

Should a retail merchant prevent a sale from occurring to a customer he or she (the merchant) knows lacks capacity?

# Chapter 10

# Legal Purpose

## CHAPTER OUTLINE

**The Nature and General Effect of Illegal Agreements**
**Agreements Forbidden by State Statute**
    Agreements That Violate Civil and Criminal Statutes
    Agreements That Violate Licensing Statutes
    Agreements That Violate Gambling Statutes
    Agreements That Violate Usury Statutes
    Agreements That Violate Sunday Statutes
**Agreements Opposed to Public Policy**
    Agreements That Disclaim Liability for Negligence
    Agreements That Interfere with the Administration of Justice
    Agreements That Interfere with the Performance of a Public Duty
    Agreements That Harm Marriage
    Agreements That Unreasonably Restrain Competition and Trade
    Agreements That Are Unconscionable
**Partially Illegal Agreements**

## CASE PROBLEMS

Read the case problems below. For each problem, answer yes or no, and then explain your answer in the space provided.

1. In return for his daughter's promise never to marry, Wesson agreed to give her $25,000. Is this an enforceable agreement?

   _____
   _____
   _____

2. Lane promised $5,000 to a state representative if he would influence the legislature to pass a certain law. Is this an enforceable agreement?

3. Quinn agreed to pay Thorpe $500 if she would not testify against him in a court trial. Thorpe did not testify against Quinn. Is she entitled to the $500?

4. Kulp, although not a properly licensed real estate agent, sold a house for Curtis. Can Kulp legally collect for his services?

5. Wenly sold her retail dress shop in Boston to Ryan, agreeing not to engage in a similar business within five blocks of the present location for one year. Is Wenly bound by the agreement?

6. Beaton, the owner of a grocery store, promised to supply Marven, the mayor, with free food for the next year if an ordinance favorable to Beaton was passed by the city council. Is this agreement binding on Beaton?

7. Rissone received a letter from a magazine publisher inviting her to enter the company's $6,000,000 sweepstakes promotion by simply returning a book of certificates with her name already typed on them. In the same envelope was an invitation to buy one of the company's new books, *Eat Better, Live Better*, at a reduced price. She did not have to buy the book in order to enter the sweepstakes, however. Rissone returned the certificates, but she did not win anything. She was so irritated that she called the company and told them that they were carrying on an illegal operation. Is Rissone correct?

## MULTIPLE-CHOICE QUESTIONS

On the line next to each statement, write the letter of the best answer.

_____ 1. Usury laws provide protection in a contract (a) for the loan of money, (b) for the sale of merchandise on credit, (c) to be performed on a Sunday, (d) for the restraint of trade.

_____ 2. A statute that requires a person to obtain a license to practice a certain trade or profession without having to show competence in that trade or profession is a (a) criminal statute, (b) usury statute, (c) prohibiting statute, (d) revenue-raising statute.

_____ 3. An example of a licensing statute is one that (a) requires an attorney to have a permit to practice law, (b) prevents usury, (c) restricts business activity on Sundays, (d) reasonably restricts trade.

_____ 4. Aaron bet Davis that a certain candidate would win the presidential election. Aaron's candidate won the election, but Davis refused to pay the bet. In most states, Aaron could not enforce the agreement legally because (a) a gambling agreement is illegal and void, (b) the agreement involves usury, (c) the bet was not in writing, (d) Aaron and Davis are both professional gamblers.

_____ 5. If an agreement is partially legal and partially illegal, the (a) entire agreement is void in all cases, (b) legal part of the agreement may be enforced if it can be separated from the illegal part, (c) legal part of the agreement is never enforceable, (d) parties to the agreement may choose to enforce the part of the agreement that is beneficial to both of them.

_____ 6. If both parties know that an agreement is illegal, a court probably will (a) enforce the agreement, (b) refuse to hear the case, (c) allow the agreement to be ratified, (d) permit each party to recover any consideration given.

_____ 7. Charging interest in excess of the legal rate is considered (a) a restraint of trade, (b) enforceable, (c) usury, (d) *stare decisis*.

_____ 8. An example of an agreement that ordinarily would be classified illegal is one that (a) is entered into on a weekday after regular business hours, (b) is in reasonable restraint of trade, (c) involves usury, (d) is between an adult and a minor.

_____ 9. A person whose main livelihood is gambling is classified as a (a) professional gambler, (b) semiprofessional gambler, (c) casual gambler, (d) public gambler.

_____ 10. An agreement that is in unreasonable restraint of trade is (a) enforceable, (b) void, (c) voidable, (d) valid.

_____ 11. Billings and Durrick, competing distributors, made an agreement whereby Billings promised not to sell his goods in a specific area and Durrick promised not to sell his goods in another specified area. They made this agreement to keep prices high by eliminating competition. This arrangement is (a) legal because it reasonably restrains trade in order to control prices, (b) legal because a binding contract was made willingly by both parties, (c) illegal because it unreasonably restrains trade by controlling prices and territories, (d) illegal because agreements that allow manufacturers to set prices are void under the UCC.

12. Maile agrees to sell his retail men's shop in Cleveland to Lunger. Lunger wants a clause restricting competition by Maile included in the contract. Which of the following restrictive clauses would be enforceable? (a) Never to engage in a similar business in Cleveland, (b) not to engage in a similar business in Ohio for the next two years, (c) not to engage in any type of business anywhere in Cleveland for the next year, (d) not to engage in a men's shop business within a radius of one mile for the next year.

13. Which of the following actions is opposed to public policy? (a) An offer to pay money to a witness to testify falsely in court, (b) an offer to pay a contractor extra money to speed up a job he already is legally bound to do, (c) an offer to pay money to neighbors to attend your birthday party, (d) an offer to pay a lawyer to represent your civic group at a legislative session on a bill seeking tax reduction.

14. Slater, believing that his daughter was about to marry and leave him, offered to pay her $10,000 if she would promise never to marry. The daughter promised and accepted the $10,000. One year later, she married. Slater sued for breach of contract. A court probably would rule that Slater is entitled to (a) recover nothing, (b) recover the $10,000, (c) recover the $10,000 plus interest, (d) annul the marriage on the basis of fraud.

15. Which of the following agreements ordinarily would be considered illegal? (a) An agreement between two people that one would pay the other $20 depending on the outcome of a football game, (b) a contract made by a married woman who is a minor, (c) a lobbying agreement, (d) none of these.

16. An agreement to rob a bank is an example of a (a) quasi contract, (b) voidable contract, (c) void contract, (d) contract implied in law.

17. Exculpatory clauses are (a) quasi in nature, (b) generally considered to be contrary to public policy, (c) valid in all cases, (d) legal when they involve the lending of money.

18. When a clause in a non-compete contract is too restrictive, the modern view is for courts generally to (a) enforce it as it is written, (b) enforce it as it is written but agree to evaluate the clause over a period of three years, (c) enforce it as it is written but agree to evaluate the clause over a period of twenty years, (d) throw it out, but enforce the remainder of the agreement.

19. An agreement that is grossly unfair or harsh may be declared void by a court as being (a) impossible, (b) unconscionable, (c) in violation of a state statute, (d) in violation of the blue laws.

20. Which of the following businesses would not be able to enforce an exculpatory clause under most circumstances? (a) hospitals, (b) common carriers, (c) public utilities, (d) all of these.

## ACTIVITY: CASE ANALYSIS

Read the case below and then answer the questions that follow.

The Crown Oak Novelty Company (plaintiff) sued the Fun and Games Entertainment Center (defendant) for breach of contract to recover the purchase price of checkers and checkerboards sold to the defendant. At the trial, the defendant's attorney stated that (a) the checkerboards were used as games of chance at the entertainment center and that (b) games of chance are prohibited by state law. The defendant's attorney further stated, "Because the plaintiff knew these facts, the contract with the entertainment center was illegal, void, and unenforceable. Therefore, my client does not have to pay for the merchandise."

The plaintiff's attorney admitted that Crown Oak knew the checkerboards were being used at the entertainment center, but argued that checkers is a game of skill, not chance. In a game of chance (throwing dice, for example), luck is the dominant feature; in a game of skill, ability and skill in playing the game are the dominant features. The plaintiff's attorney pointed out that only players with enough skill in playing checkers could solve the checker problems used at the Fun and Games Entertainment Center. He then introduced a copy of the relevant state law to show that only games of chance, not games of skill, were prohibited. The court ruled in favor of the plaintiff and ordered the defendant to pay for the checkerboards and checkers.

1. On what basis did Crown Oak Novelty sue the Fun and Games Entertainment Center?

   _____
   _____

2. On what basis did the Fun and Games Entertainment Center deny liability?

   _____
   _____
   _____

3. Did the court agree with the Fun and Games Entertainment Center?

   _____
   _____

4. What evidence was introduced to convince the court to rule the way it did?

   _____
   _____

5. Assume that the defendant's argument is correct. What responsibility does the defendant have to pay the plaintiff as the result of this lawsuit?

   _____
   _____

Copyright © Houghton Mifflin Company. All rights reserved.

# Chapter 11

# Contracts That Must Be in Writing

## CHAPTER OUTLINE

The Status of Oral and Written Contracts
Contracts Required to Be in Writing
   A Contract to Pay the Debt of Another Person
   A Contract to Pay the Debt of a Deceased Person
   A Contract for the Sale of Real Property
   A Contract in Consideration of Marriage
   A Contract That Cannot Be Performed Within One Year
The Memorandum
Parol Evidence Rule

## TRUE-FALSE QUESTIONS

Indicate whether each statement below is true or false by circling T or F in the column on the right.

1. In a contract of guaranty, the guarantor's promise to pay is secondary to the debtor's promise.    T   F

2. Except as provided by statute, oral contracts are just as enforceable as written contracts.    T   F

3. The statute of frauds applies only to executory contracts.    T   F

4. One advantage of a written contract over an oral contract is that a written contract needs no witnesses to establish its existence and terms.    T   F

5. An oral promise to pay your own debt is not enforceable.    T   F

6. The parties to a written contract usually are bound by the terms of the agreement.    T   F

7. The courts usually allow oral evidence to change the terms of a written agreement.  T  F
8. Martin agreed to work for Simmons for 13 months. This agreement would be enforceable if made over the phone.  T  F
9. Parol evidence can be admitted in court to explain vague terms in a written contract.  T  F
10. A written contract can be changed by a subsequent oral agreement if the written contract was not required by the statute of frauds to be in writing.  T  F

## CASE PROBLEMS

Read the case problems below. For each problem, answer yes or no, and then explain your answer in the space provided.

1. Marks tried to purchase some goods on credit from Bellows. Bellows refused to sell him the goods because he did not believe Marks would be able to pay. Minks orally promised Bellows that he would pay for the goods if Marks failed to do so. If Bellows sells the goods to Marks, is Minks legally bound by his promise?

2. DeRoller was the executor of his mother's estate. Because there were insufficient funds in the estate to pay all its debts, DeRoller orally promised several creditors that he would pay the balance out of his own funds. Can DeRoller be held legally responsible for his promise?

3. Bain orally agreed to sell some land to Carroll for $10,000 and accepted a deposit of $1,000 to bind the agreement. Later, on learning that another buyer would pay a higher price, Bain refused to honor the contract with Carroll. Carroll sued to enforce the contract. Did Carroll succeed in this suit?

4. On July 15, 1992, Martin orally agreed to work for Stein until June 1, 1993. Is this contract enforceable?

5. Moralle orally promised Hanson that if she agreed to marry him, he would give her a large monthly expense account, a new car every two years, and a vacation trip each year to a destination of her choice. Hanson accepted, and they were married. Moralle, however, did not keep his promises. Hanson sued for damages. Will she succeed in this suit?

___

___

___

## MULTIPLE-CHOICE QUESTIONS

On the line next to each statement, write the letter of the best answer.

_____ 1. Solomon phoned the Ace Pet Store and told the owner to deliver to his fiancée the French poodle he had looked at the day before. Solomon asked that the cost of the dog be charged to his account. The pet was delivered. This agreement was (a) binding on Solomon because it is an oral promise to pay another's debt, (b) binding on Solomon because it is an oral promise to pay his own debt, (c) not binding on Solomon because an oral promise to pay another's debt is not binding, (d) not binding on Solomon because there was no consideration for the oral promise.

_____ 2. Abbot accepted Milligan's oral offer to sell a small parcel of real property. This agreement is (a) illegal because it should have been in writing, (b) illegal because the sale was not arranged by a licensed real estate salesperson, (c) legal but unenforceable by either party, (d) legal but enforceable only by the offeror.

_____ 3. Yockel agreed to work for Schnabel for 18 months. This agreement would be enforceable if made (a) in a face-to-face conversation, (b) over the telephone, (c) through an exchange of telegrams, (d) orally through a friend.

_____ 4. Parol evidence is admissible to show that (a) terms were added to the original contract, (b) the original contract had been changed, (c) one party was persuaded to make the contract by fraud on the part of the other party, (d) the contract does not show the real intentions of the parties.

_____ 5. The type of contract that arises when one person promises to pay another's debt if that person does not pay is a contract (a) of suretyship, (b) of guaranty, (c) for services, (d) under seal.

_____ 6. Long offered to sell Vickers, a neighbor, a 25-foot-wide strip of land between their two lots so that Vickers would have room to build a garage. Vickers accepted the offer. This agreement would be binding on Long if (a) Vickers paid $100 for an option to buy, (b) it was made in the presence of at least two witnesses, (c) it was made in writing, (d) Long promised orally that he would sell.

_____ 7. An example of an agreement that is binding even if it is not in writing is a contract (a) to borrow an automobile, (b) to sell real property, (c) with marriage as a consideration, (d) to pay the debts of another person.

_____ 8. In most states, the written evidence of an agreement required by the statute of frauds is (a) parol evidence, (b) a guaranty, (c) an executor, (d) an informal memorandum.

9. If two parties fully perform an oral contract that should have been in writing, (a) either party can have the contract set aside because it was not in writing, (b) the statute of frauds no longer applies, (c) the contract is illegal, (d) the parties are guilty of fraud.

10. If a contract is required to be in writing under the statute of frauds, modifications to that contract (a) are not binding, (b) can be made orally, (c) must be in writing, (d) require additional consideration.

## SHORT-ANSWER QUESTIONS

Answer each of the following questions in the space provided.

1. Under what circumstances do the courts allow parol evidence to be introduced in a lawsuit relating to the terms of a written contract?

2. Jackson buys a stereo from Riggins, the owner of a stereo shop. What is the difference between a promise to Riggins by Jackson's friend to pay for the stereo if Jackson does not and the friend's telling Riggins to charge the stereo directly to him (the friend)?

3. When do contracts come under the statute of frauds one-year rule?

4. What are two advantages of written contracts over oral contracts?

5. Under what circumstances would a court of law not permit a seller of real property to cancel an oral contract for the sale of the property?

## ACTIVITY: WRITING A CONTRACT

You have worked the past three summers and have saved $2,000. Now you want to buy a used car. In the space below, write your own contract to buy the car. You are buying the car from an owner rather than a used-car dealer. Be sure to include all the elements of a valid contract in the contract you write.

# Chapter 12

# Transfer of Contract Rights and Obligations

## CHAPTER OUTLINE

**Transfer of Rights and Obligations**
   Transfer of Rights
   Transfer of Obligations
   Rights and Obligations That Cannot Be Transferred
**Form of Assignment**
**Notice of Assignment**
**Assignment by Law**
**Rights of the Assignee**

## MINI-CASE

Read the following notification of assignment. Then, on the line next to each statement, write the letter of the best answer.

    DATE:    September 25, 19—
    TO:       Jane Lu, 189 Factor Road, Cleveland, OH 44112
    FROM:  Brendon Associates, 1334 Duncan Avenue, Cleveland, OH 44112

We have purchased from Hyland Fence Company of Cleveland, Ohio, its entire interest in the account it has against you in the amount of one thousand five hundred fifty dollars ($1,550). Any payments or communications in regard to this account should be made to us.

_____ 1. According to this notification of assignment, what right is being assigned? (a) The right to receive payment of money, (b) the right to the delivery of goods, (c) the right to personal services, (d) the right to a personal skill.

_____ 2. Brendon Associates legally is known as the (a) offeror, (b) assignor, (c) assignee, (d) promisee.

_____ 3. The Hyland Fence Company is known as the (a) assignee, (b) offeror, (c) promisee, (d) assignor.

_____ 4. Lu is the (a) obligor, (b) obligee, (c) assignor, (d) creditor.

_____ 5. Before receiving the notification, Lu informed the Hyland Fence Company that fencing worth $500 was damaged and was being returned. If Lu returns the merchandise, she will be liable to Brendon Associates for payment of (a) $1,550, (b) $1,050, (c) $1,000, (d) nothing.

## TRUE-FALSE QUESTIONS

Indicate whether each statement below is true or false by circling T or F in the column on the right.

1. An obligor is a party to a contract who transfers rights and obligations to other people through assignment.    T    F

2. Contract obligations that require a special skill or knowledge cannot be transferred without permission.    T    F

3. There is no time limit on notifying an obligor of an assignment.    T    F

4. A notice of assignment always must be in writing.    T    F

5. Personal services contracts cannot be assigned without the permission of the person providing the service.    T    F

6. State statutes sometimes place restrictions on the assignment of rights.    T    F

7. Past performance of a contract before receiving notice of an assignment does not reduce the obligor's responsibility to the assignee.    T    F

8. Contract rights legally can be transferred by an assignment.    T    F

9. Two rights that can be assigned without permission are the payment of money and the delivery of goods.    T    F

10. Assigning rights under a contract does not entitle the assignee to the same rights that the assignor had before the assignment.    T    F

## MULTIPLE-CHOICE QUESTIONS

On the line next to each statement, write the letter of the best answer.

_____ 1. Reynolds owed Currie $550. Currie transferred the contract to Butts. What step should Butts take in order to make sure Reynolds pays her instead of Currie? (a) Notify Reynolds of the transfer, (b) file the contract in the county clerk's office, (c) have the transfer drawn up by an attorney, (d) have Reynolds's signature witnessed by a notary public.

2. When rights under a contract are assigned, the assignee receives the same rights as the (a) obligor, (b) debtor, (c) assignor, (d) executor.

3. Renault entered into a contract with Craft to have some plumbing work done. Craft later delegated the work to Marsden, another licensed plumber. Which of the following statements is true? (a) Craft cannot legally delegate her contract obligations, (b) Craft is still responsible for making sure the obligation is carried out, (c) Craft can no longer be held liable if the contract is breached, (d) the contract automatically is terminated.

4. Which of the following statements about the assignment of contracts is *false*? (a) Rights to the payment of money and to the delivery of goods can be assigned without consent, (b) some rights are assigned automatically by law, (c) responsibilities to perform skilled work can be assigned without the approval of all parties, (d) the party that delegates a responsibility remains liable for proper performance.

5. Dr. Senour, a successful ophthalmologist, notified her patients that she had sold her practice to Dr. Horner, an equally competent ophthalmologist, and that Horner would now be responsible for their treatment. Which of the following statements best describes this transaction's legal effect on the patients? (a) They legally can refuse to accept Horner's services, (b) they are legally bound to accept Horner's services, (c) they legally can accept the services of another ophthalmologist but only with Senour's consent, (d) they can sue Senour for malpractice.

## CASE PROBLEMS

Read the case problems below. For each problem, answer yes or no, and then explain your answer in the space provided.

1. On May 2, Blacke's Hardware paid $200 of the $1,000 owed to Greene's Wholesalers for a previous purchase of lawn mowers. On May 15, Greene's transferred all customer accounts to the We Get Results Finance Company. Two weeks later, Blacke's Hardware paid Greene's an additional $200 on account. Blacke's did not receive notice of the assignment until June 9. After receiving this notice, is Blacke's Hardware obligated to pay the We Get Results Finance Company anything more?

_____
_____
_____
_____
_____

2. Corey was hired as a pharmacist by the Daw Drug Company under a one-year contract. After six months, Daw sold out to the Freese Drug Company and assigned Corey's contract to Freese. Is Corey obligated to work for Freese for the remainder of the contract period?

_____
_____
_____

Copyright © Houghton Mifflin Company. All rights reserved.

3. Dr. Christen, a well-known physician and cancer expert, was under contract to deliver a major address to a physicians' group in Washington, D.C. A month before the scheduled address, Christen had a heart attack and had to cancel his engagements for at least six months. He notified the physicians' group that he was sending his assistant, also a doctor, who had been working with him. Does the group have to accept the substitute?

_____
_____
_____
_____

4. Cooke sold all the assets of her business, including the accounts receivable, to Nugent. Did Cooke have the right to assign her accounts receivable to Nugent?

_____
_____
_____

5. Victor hired Carbone, a mason, to build a patio in his backyard. Because Carbone took on too many other jobs, he engaged another mason to build the patio for Victor. Can Carbone legally delegate his duty under an existing contract?

_____
_____
_____
_____

6. You arranged to take guitar lessons from a prominent local guitarist. You chose this guitar teacher because you wanted to study his unique playing style. When you arrived for your first lesson, you found that the guitarist's brother would be giving you lessons instead. Can you refuse to accept this arrangement?

_____
_____
_____
_____

7. Your landlord assigned to a third party his rent claim from you of $300. Because you were not notified of the assignment, you paid the landlord the $300. Your landlord then left town. Can the third party demand payment of the $300 from you?

_____
_____
_____
_____

## SHORT-ANSWER QUESTIONS

Answer each of the following questions in the space provided.

1. What do we mean when we say that the assignee "steps into the shoes of the assignor"?

2. Is it possible for a contract to prohibit an assignment of contract rights? Explain your answer.

3. Why is it important for the assignee to notify the obligor about the assignment as soon as possible after the assignment is made?

4. What formalities, if any, are required for an assignment to be valid?

5. Why do you think that a person who transferred his or her obligation under a contract to a third party continues to have the responsibility for making sure that the obligation is carried out?

## ACTIVITY: CASE PROBLEM

On June 10, The First Bank of Georgia loaned RYCOM Construction Company $50,000. RYCOM assigned its right to receive $30,000 due for work performed for Marlan, a contractor. It also assigned its right to receive $20,000 from Pool, another contractor, who was thinking of hiring RYCOM in the near future to complete a $20,000 project. The First Bank of Georgia notified both Marlan and Pool on June 15. What are the rights of the The First Bank of Georgia in each of the following cases?

a. Marlan pays $30,000 directly to RYCOM Construction on July 15.

_____

_____

_____

b. Pool fails to respond to the notice sent by the First Bank of Georgia.

_____

_____

_____

# Chapter 13

# The Termination of Contracts: Discharge

## CHAPTER OUTLINE

How Contracts End
Discharge of Contracts
  Performance
  Agreement
  Impossibility or Impracticability
  Alteration of a Written Contract

## MULTIPLE-CHOICE QUESTIONS

On the line next to each statement, write the letter of the best answer.

_____ 1. Legal impossibility includes (a) strikes, (b) riots, (c) a change in the law, (d) all of these.

_____ 2. When Johnson finished painting Bristol's house as agreed, Bristol paid him in full. Their contract was discharged by (a) accord and satisfaction, (b) legal tender, (c) full performance, (d) operation of law.

_____ 3. Kemp agreed to build a storage shed at the back of Martin's property. Before work began, the city passed an ordinance forbidding the construction of this kind of building in the neighborhood. As a result of this ordinance, (a) the contract was discharged, (b) Kemp was liable to Martin for breach of contract, (c) the city was liable to Martin for damages, (d) the existing contract was not affected.

_____ 4. An offer to fulfill the terms of a contract by completing an act required by the contract or by paying money is known as (a) novation, (b) ratification, (c) mutual agreement, (d) tender of performance.

_____ 5. Vinton was under written contract to work for Rossi. Vinton had to move to another state and received from Rossi a written release from the agreement. This contract was discharged by (a) performance, (b) mutual agreement, (c) breach, (d) subsequent impossibility.

6. Nash, a rock celebrity, is under contract to give a concert in the Warner Theater. Suppose serious illness prevents her from giving the concert on the agreed date. In this situation, (a) Nash would be released from the contract and would not be liable for any damages or losses incurred by the theater, (b) Nash would be released from the contract but would be liable for damages or losses incurred by the theater, (c) Nash would have the right to give the concert when she recovers, (d) the theater would be obligated to accept performance by another celebrity whom Nash sends as a substitute.

7. Gibbons entered into a written agreement with Bensinger to purchase a painting. In the meantime, without the knowledge of either party, the painting was destroyed in a fire. This contract was discharged by (a) performance, (b) breach, (c) mutual agreement, (d) impossibility.

8. The refusal of a tender of payment (a) forces a settlement by arbitration, (b) forces payment with legal tender, (c) does not excuse the debtor from paying interest charges, (d) does not discharge the obligation.

9. The usual manner of discharging a contract is by (a) subsequent impossibility, (b) the death of one of the parties, (c) assignment, (d) full performance.

10. When Rosco was unable to pay the $1,000 he owed Lyden, Lyden agreed to let Rosco paint Lyden's house in payment. When Rosco finished painting the house, his original obligation was discharged by (a) breach, (b) impossibility of performance, (c) accord and satisfaction, (d) disability.

11. A change made in the terms of an executory contract by one party without the knowledge and consent of the other party is called a(n) (a) novation, (b) substitution, (c) accord, (d) alteration.

12. Vasquez contracted to install vinyl siding on O'Grady's house during the first two weeks of August. When Vasquez arrived on August 1 to begin the work, O'Grady told him that the job would have to be postponed for two months. Vasquez's obligation to perform the contract was discharged by (a) tender of performance, (b) operation of law, (c) agreement, (d) delegation of duty.

## ACTIVITY: CASE ANALYSIS

Read the following news story and then answer the question in the space provided.

### COURT PENALIZES ROCK SINGER FOR NOT SINGING

ROCHESTER, N.Y. (AP)—A state supreme court judge placed a $25,000 judgment on Mike Zoe, well-known rock star, for failing to perform in concert at the Community War Memorial Auditorium on three successive nights. The Honorable Richard Bloom ruled yesterday in favor of the owners of the Community War Memorial Auditorium, who complained that Zoe ignored a contractual agreement to perform three concerts.

Under what circumstances could Zoe be excused from paying damages for not appearing?

## TRUE-FALSE QUESTIONS

On the line at the right of each statement, write the word *true* if the statement is true. If the statement is false, write the word or expression that should be substituted for the underlined word or expression to make the statement correct.

1. If one party to a contract makes a material change in its terms without the other party's permission, the contract is discharged by <u>novation</u>. _____

2. A contract is discharged by <u>full performance</u> when a person in good faith fulfills all the major requirements, leaving only minor details incomplete. _____

3. <u>Full performance</u> is the most common method by which contracts are discharged. _____

4. The offer to perform the terms of a contract or to pay money is called <u>substantial performance</u>. _____

5. If the subject matter that is essential to the performance of the contract is destroyed through no fault of either party, the contract is considered <u>discharged</u>. _____

6. A <u>waiver</u> is a mutual agreement to cancel a contract even after one or both parties have performed completely. _____

7. If a new agreement is made before the original contract is breached, this new agreement is called a <u>substitute contract</u>. _____

8. When West finished repairing Thomas's car as agreed, Thomas paid West in full. The contract was discharged by <u>operation of law</u>. _____

9. Lund and Mann entered into a contract. Two months later, they agreed to let Wells perform Mann's obligations with Lund releasing Mann from her agreement. In this case, Mann's obligations are discharged by <u>accord and satisfaction</u>. _____

10. The form of money accepted as lawful payment of debts in the United States is called <u>legal tender</u>. _____

## CASE PROBLEMS

Read the case problems below. For each problem, answer yes or no, and then explain your answer in the space provided.

1. Shaw, a TV news commentator, died before completing his two-year written contract to broadcast news for Station WKLB. Was Shaw's estate liable for damages to Station WKLB for her failure to complete the contract?

_____

_____

_____

2. Santos entered into a written contract to sell her delicatessen to Gluck for $75,000. Later, both parties changed their minds and mutually agreed to cancel the contract. Is the contract discharged?

_____

_____

_____

3. Tyler owed Franks $1,500. When the debt came due, Tyler offered payment by check. Franks refused to accept it. Two months later, Franks asked Tyler for payment. Tyler refused, claiming that because Franks did not accept payment when the check was presented on the due date, the debt had been discharged. Was Tyler right?

_____

_____

_____

4. Hardies agreed to deliver to Davidson 25,000 standard three-ring student notebooks by September 1. On August 1, Hardies' warehouse and its contents were destroyed by fire through no fault of Hardies. Was Hardies liable on the contract?

_____

_____

_____

_____

5. Peters contracted to paint the exterior of Bottom's frame house for $1,000. Before Peters began work, the house burned to the ground. Was the contract terminated?

_____

_____

_____

## ACTIVITY: LEARNING HOW CONTRACTS ARE TERMINATED

Read the following contract and then answer the questions on the next page.

---

**PROPERTY LEASE**

I, Harriet M. Cole, of 242 Marion Street, Denver, Colorado, agree to lease the premises of 1254 Stillmeadow Drive, Denver, Colorado, to Janet L. and William T. Percy, for a period of two (2) years, beginning March 1, 19--. The tenants are to pay rent of six hundred and fifty dollars ($650.00) per month, with rent being due on the first (1st) day of each month. The premises are to be used as a residence for Janet L. and William T. Percy and are not to be used for any other purposes. The tenants may not sublease the premises without the express, written permission of Harriet M. Cole. At the end of this lease, the tenants will give up possession of these premises in as good condition as they now are, excepting normal wear, accidents, fire, and other acts of God.

If the tenants fail to pay rent when due or fail to vacate the premises upon expiration of this lease, it is agreed that the tenants will pay double the rent specified above for the time the rent remains due and unpaid or the time the tenants fail to give up possession.

Signed this third (3d) day of February, 19--.

_Harriet M. Cole_
Harriet M. Cole

_Janet L. Percy_
Janet L. Percy

_William T. Percy_
William T. Percy

1. Does this contract meet the requirements of a valid contract? Why or why not?

   _____
   _____
   _____
   _____

2. In what ways can this contract be terminated?

   _____
   _____
   _____

3. What conditions must occur for this contract to be performed in full?

   _____
   _____
   _____
   _____

4. How could this contract be discharged by impossibility?

   _____
   _____
   _____

5. If the tenants fail to pay rent when due, what action can Cole take?

   _____
   _____
   _____

## ACTIVITY: LEGAL DISTINCTION

How does the common law rule of impossibility of performance differ from the concept of commercial impracticability recognized under modern law?

_____
_____
_____

# Chapter 14

# The Termination of Contracts: Breach of Contract

## CHAPTER OUTLINE

**Breach of Contract**
**Remedies for Breach of Contract**
    Legal Remedies
    Equitable Remedies
**Defenses for a Breach of Contract Suit**
    Fraud
    Duress

    Undue Influence
    Mistake
    Bankruptcy
    Statute of Limitations
**Remedies for Fraud, Duress, and Undue Influence**

## MULTIPLE-CHOICE QUESTIONS

On the line next to each statement, write the letter of the best answer.

_____ 1. In seeking damages, the victim of a breach of contract has a duty to (a) increase the amount of the damages, (b) mitigate the damages, (c) liquidate the damages, (d) rescind the contract.

_____ 2. Aman had a written employment contract with Bagden for one year at a $48,000 salary, payable at the rate of $4,000 a month. Aman worked for five months, collected $20,000, and then was discharged without cause. Within a few days, he found another job at a lower salary and sued Bagden for breach of contract. The greatest amount that Aman can recover legally is (a) $48,000, (b) $28,000, (c) $28,000 minus his earnings on the new job, (d) $20,000 minus his earnings on the new job.

_____ 3. Marriott agreed to do some electrical work for Bastiuk for $500. The terms of the contract called for one half of the contract price to be paid once the work began. When Marriott began work and requested $250, Bastiuk offered only $175. Bastiuk's action would be considered (a) substantial performance, (b) an alteration, (c) a breach of contract, (d) a rescission.

_____ 4. Manix sued Cartright for breach of contract. The court awarded Manix damages of $1. This award is known as (a) liquidated damages, (b) nominal damages, (c) premeditated damages, (c) mitigated damages.

5. Falvo entered into a contract with Mathis to build an addition to Mathis's house. The price agreed on was $25,000. Falvo failed to do the work, so Mathis contracted with Baily to do the work for $24,000. Mathis then sued Falvo for breach of contract and sought $1,000 in damages. The court probably will rule in (a) Mathis's favor for $1,000 because Falvo breached the contract, (b) Mathis's favor but only for nominal damages, (c) Falvo's favor because Mathis did not suffer a loss, (d) Falvo's favor because Mathis saved money as a result of the breach.

6. The statute of limitations (a) specifies the time within which a lawsuit can be filed, (b) requires that certain contracts be in writing, (c) requires the use of written evidence of an action at a trial, (d) contains the same provisions in all of the United States.

7. Feingold contracted to sell Betz an original letter written by George Washington, for $25,000. Both thought the letter was authentic, but it turned out to be a reproduction. Betz now wants to avoid the contract. The most appropriate remedy is (a) punitive damages, (b) compensatory damages, (c) specific performance, (d) rescission of the contract.

8. The basis of fraud is (a) a misrepresentation of opinion, (b) an act of violence, (c) a threat of force, (d) concealment or misrepresentation of a material fact.

9. Perry sold an old ring to Weeks for $10. Later Perry learned that the ring was worth $500. If Perry sues, she legally is entitled to recover (a) $500, (b) the ring, (c) $490, (d) nothing.

10. All of the following are legal reasons for exercising the right to rescind a contract *except* (a) duress, (b) minority, (c) unilateral mistake, (d) fraud.

## TRUE-FALSE QUESTIONS

Indicate whether each statement below is true or false by circling T or F in the column on the right.

1. One of the elements necessary to establish fraud is a false statement or concealment of a material fact.   T   F

2. Money damages awarded to an injured party by law should place the person in the same position he or she would have been in if the contract had been carried out.   T   F

3. Undue influence renders a contract voidable by either party.   T   F

4. A mutual mistake about the identity of the subject matter does not affect the validity of the contract.   T   F

5. Gugel, a used-car dealer, told Billings, a prospective customer, "This is the best used-car value in town." Relying on this statement, Billings bought the car but soon discovered that it had been substantially overpriced. Billings can avoid the contract on the basis of fraud.   T   F

6. When money damages do not adequately and fairly compensate for a loss, the injured party can sue for specific performance or request a court to issue an injunction.   T   F

7. Neilson requested a catalog from Noom Brothers. She used an order form to order some jewelry but entered an incorrect catalog number. As a result, she received jewelry she did not want. Neilson has a legal right to return the jewelry because her mistake voided the contract.   T   F

8. Specific performance generally is granted in contracts for the sale of real property.   T   F
9. A person who conceals a material fact is guilty of fraud if the concealment prevents the victim from discovering the truth.   T   F
10. A court will not enforce a liquidated damages clause if the stated amount appears to be a penalty.   T   F

## ACTIVITY: ANALYZING A CONTRACT

Read the contract below and then answer the questions on the next page.

---

**PROPERTY STORAGE AGREEMENT**

This agreement is made on June 9, 19--, between Robert S. Greeley of 149 East Rossmoyne Street, Troy, Ohio, and Manuel E. Leon of 1910 Harrison Avenue, Troy Ohio.

Manuel Leon agrees to store the following goods in his warehouse at 310 McGrath Road, Troy, Ohio:

> Mahogany dining room furniture consisting of one (1) oval dining table and eight (8) matching chairs
> One (1) three-cushion sofa
> Two (2) reclining lounge chairs
> One (1) 9' x 12' yellow wool carpet
> Two (2) three-drawer walnut chests
> One (1) rotating electric fan
> One (1) glass and walnut table
> Two (2) brass and ceramic table lamps with shades

It is agreed that the above property currently is undamaged and is to be returned on termination of this contract in the same condition as it currently exists, excepting accidents, fire, and other acts of God.

Robert Greeley agrees to pay Manuel Leon the sum of fifty dollars ($50.00) per month to store this property. Payment is to begin July 1, 19--, and end June 1, 19--. Payment is due on the first day of each month. On termination of this contract, Robert Greeley will assume responsibility for having the furniture listed above removed from the warehouse at 310 McGrath Road.

If Robert Greeley fails to make payments as agreed, Manuel Leon has the right to sell, after notifying Robert Greeley of his intent, part or all of the stored property to satisfy any amounts due on this contract.

*Robert S. Greeley*
Robert S. Greeley

*Manuel E. Leon*
Manuel E. Leon

1. When injury is caused by a breach of contract, what remedies generally are available to the injured party?

2. If Greeley breaches his duties under this contract, what specific remedies does Leon have?

3. Would damages for a breach of contract by Greeley be compensatory, liquidated, or nominal? Explain your answer.

4. Could Leon collect money damages from Greeley other than those provided for in the contract? Why or why not?

5. If Greeley breaches this contract by failing to make the last three payments of $50 per month, and Leon sells some of the furniture for $250, how much money does Leon get? If there is any money left after payment of the amount owed to Leon, who gets the remaining money? Why?

## SHORT-ANSWER QUESTIONS

Answer each of the following questions in the space provided.

1. Describe the two major types of remedies allowed by the courts to the victims of a breach of contract.

2. If a breach is material, what rights does the injured party have?

3. Explain the meaning of the following: "As soon as a breach occurs, the injured party has a duty to *mitigate the damages.*"

4. The injured party can waive his or her rights when the other party to the contract breaches the contract. What is the legal effect of this waiver?

5. Under what conditions can an injured party demand specific performance when a contract has been breached?

# Review

# Part II Contracts

## TRUE-FALSE QUESTIONS

Indicate whether each statement below is true or false by circling T or F in the column on the right.

1. In a contract, the value of the consideration given need not be equal in value to the consideration received.     T   F

2. One who has a right to receive money from another may transfer this right to a third person through the process of delegation.     T   F

3. According to the statute of limitations, certain debts are outlawed and the right to legal action is lost if a claim is not filed within a specific period of time.     T   F

4. A contract to answer for the obligations of others must be in writing.     T   F

5. If a debtor makes a voluntary partial payment after the due date, the time limit under the statute of limitations starts over from the date of payment.     T   F

6. Cilino said to Regal, "I'll sell you my video game system for $175 in cash today." Regal replied, "I'll take it by paying you $100 today and the other $75 in 30 days." Regal's reply resulted in an accord and satisfaction.     T   F

7. Nonpersonal rights cannot be transferred without the other party's permission.     T   F

8. When money damages do not compensate adequately for a loss, one remedy is for the injured party to sue for specific performance.     T   F

9. Not all contracts must be in writing to be valid.     T   F

10. A minor's obligation to pay for necessaries is an express contract.     T   F

## MULTIPLE-CHOICE QUESTIONS

On the line next to each statement, write the letter of the best answer.

_____ 1. A contract that is completely enforceable against all parties unless and until a party legally entitled to avoid the contract does so is (a) valid, (b) void, (c) voidable, (d) performed.

_____ 2. On July 8, Varden wrote to Montague offering to sell Montague her used car for $525. The letter stated: "The offer is subject to the actual receipt of your acceptance no later than July 23." Monty mailed a letter of acceptance on July 21, which reached Varden on July 24. A valid contract (a) was made July 21, (b) was made July 23, (c) was made July 24, (d) was never made.

_____ 3. An agreement induced by fraud is (a) valid, (b) void, (c) voidable by the injured party, (d) voidable by either party.

_____ 4. Carter offered to sell Milford a used power lawn mower. Milford accepted the offer. This offer and acceptance are called (a) mutual assent, (b) compromise, (c) ratification, (d) payment of an option.

_____ 5. Paulson borrowed $100 from Best and promised in writing to pay the debt on March 1. On the due date, Paulson could not pay the full amount but offered Best $50 in cash and a watch worth $25. Best accepted. Was the debt discharged? (a) Yes. When a claim is disputed, a compromise figure is binding, (b) Yes. A debt is canceled if the creditor accepts as full payment a part payment in money plus additional property, (c) No. The consideration was inadequate, (d) No. The additional consideration was illegal.

_____ 6. A contract must be in writing to be enforceable if it involves (a) payment of an excessive interest rate, (b) the sale of goods worth more than $350, (c) the sale of real property, (d) restraint of marriage.

_____ 7. Contracts involving personal services can be assigned or delegated (a) under any conditions, (b) with the consent of all the parties involved, (c) under no circumstances, (d) with the consent of only one of the parties.

_____ 8. If a party proves that a contract has been breached but shows damages of only a few dollars, the injured party may be awarded (a) liquidated damages, (b) remote damages, (c) nominal damages, (d) punitive damages.

_____ 9. In a personal services contract, if the person to perform the services dies, the contract is (a) terminated, (b) assigned to a relative, (c) considered breached, (d) ratified.

_____ 10. Agreements in unreasonable restraint of trade are (a) voidable, (b) quasi contracts, (c) illegal, (d) valid.

_____ 11. An agreement in which the offeree gives something of value to the offeror to keep an offer open is called a(n) (a) tender of performance, (b) compromise agreement, (c) option contract, (d) promise.

_____ 12. A minor can disaffirm a contract for the purchase of a stereo (a) during minority or within a reasonable time after reaching majority, (b) only during minority, (c) within one year of the date of the agreement, (d) only after reaching majority.

13. An agreement that would be illegal and therefore void is a contract (a) in reasonable restraint of trade, (b) to pay a usurious rate of interest, (c) to extend the time of payment of a debt, (d) to hold an offer open for a certain time.

14. The purpose of awarding an injured party money damages for breach of contract is to (a) permit the injured party to avoid the contract, (b) punish the party that breached the contract, (c) compensate the injured party for the loss suffered, (d) permit the injured party to make a profit.

15. Carlson had a written contract with Sanchez to purchase some cattle. Unknown to either party, the cattle had died. The contract was discharged by (a) breach, (b) full performance, (c) impossibility, (d) mutual agreement.

16. The statute of frauds applies only to (a) executed contracts, (b) executory contracts, (c) quasi contracts, (d) illegal contracts.

17. Which of the following, at common law, generally constitutes impossibility? (a) fire caused by lightning, (b) strikes, (c) shortage of supplies, (d) none of these.

## ACTIVITY: IDENTIFYING A CONTRACT

Indicate by a checkmark in the columns on the right whether each agreement described below is valid, void, or voidable on the part of the party underlined in each sentence.

|   | Valid | Void | Voidable |
|---|---|---|---|
| 1. A <u>minor</u> contracted to purchase a motorcycle for his personal use. | | | |
| 2. An <u>adult</u> contracted to purchase a VCR from a minor. | | | |
| 3. An <u>adult</u> sold real estate without a license to do so. | | | |
| 4. An <u>adult</u> thought by some people to be mentally ill made a reasonable contract to purchase a necessity. | | | |
| 5. A <u>minor</u> ratified an executory contract when he reached majority. | | | |

## ACTIVITY: ANALYZING A CONTRACT

Study the contract shown on pages 83 and 84. Decide whether this contract meets all the requirements for a valid contract and then answer the questions on page 84.

# BILL OF SALE

*That* Sandra G. Lockwood, a single person, *of* Marion *County, in the State of* Indiana, *has this day bargained and sold, and does hereby bargain, sell, assign, transfer, set over, and deliver to* S. Kathryn Long, a single person, *in* Marion *County, in the State of* Indiana, *for the sum of* One Thousand ($1,000.00)------------------------------------ *Dollars, to* Sandra G. Lockwood *in hand paid, the receipt whereof is hereby acknowledged, the following described Chattels, Goods, and Personal Property in* Marion *County, State of* Indiana, *to-wit:*

One (1) living room suite, consisting of a sofa and two (2) chairs, one (1) Perricle refrigerator, and one (1) Western range.

*In Witness Whereof, The said* Sandra G. Lockwood *has hereunto set* her *hand and seal this* 5th *day of* June 19- -

*Signed, sealed, and delivered in presence of* *Sandra G. Lockwood* (Seal)
Sandra G. Lockwood

*Diane L. Durkee* (Seal)

*Benjamin Elkins* (Seal)

## REVIEW

> STATE OF INDIANA, Marion County, ss:
>
> Sandra G. Lockwood being duly sworn, on oath says she is the grantor in the within bill of sale; that she is the owner of every article of personal property herein described, and in possession of same, and that the same is free of all incumbrances and liens of every kind. And in this affiant makes oath of the purpose of inducing the sale herein stipulated.
>
> *Sandra G. Lockwood* (Seal)
>
> Subscribed and sworn to before me, this **5th** day of **June**, 19--
>
> *Andrea Meehan* Notary Public
>
> My Commission Expires **August, 19--**

1. Has the requirement of offer and acceptance been met for this contract? Explain your answer.

2. What is the consideration for this agreement?

3. Is the consideration adequate?

4. What effect does the adequacy or inadequacy of the consideration have on the agreement? Explain your answer.

5. Who are the parties to this agreement?

6. Assuming that the parties to this agreement were of legal age, does this agreement meet the requirement of competent parties?

7. Does this agreement meet the requirement of legal purpose? Why or why not?

## MATCHING QUESTIONS

Use the following terms to identify the phrases below. On the line next to each phrase, write the letter of the term that most closely relates to it.

a. Agreement
b. Alteration
c. Breach
d. Impossibility of performance
e. Performance
f. Tender
g. Waiver

_____ 1. The voluntary surrender of one's contractual rights

_____ 2. An offer to pay money in satisfaction of a contractual obligation

_____ 3. A termination by mutual consent

_____ 4. A refusal to perform by one of the contracting parties

_____ 5. A material change of the terms of a written contract without the consent of both parties

## COMPLETION QUESTIONS

In the statements below, important words have been omitted. Fill in the blanks to complete each statement.

1. Duress renders a contract _____ by the victim.

2. The most common method by which contracts are discharged is _____.

3. Damages that are agreed on in advance in case of a breach and stated in the contract are known as _____ damages.

4. Coins and currency of the United States are called _____.

5. A contract in which nothing remains to be done by either party is said to be _____.

6. Once an agreement is executed, the presence of _____ is unimportant.

7. The rights of the assignor are the rights of the _____.

8. A promise based on consideration to keep an offer open for a definite period of time is called a(n) _____.

9. An agreement containing illegal subject matter is _____.

10. When one party to a contract fails to do as agreed, a(n) _____ is said to have occurred.

## ACTIVITY: CASE PROBLEMS

Read the case problems below. For each problem, answer yes or no, and then explain your answer in the space provided.

1. Singer Nancy Green was admitted to a Chicago hospital last night after being reported missing for two days. She had failed to make her scheduled appearance at a night club. Mrs. Helen Mangam, owner of Mangam's Chateau in Chicago where Green was appearing, said the singer apparently suffered a heart attack and would not be able to make any scheduled appearances for at least six months. Is Green's contract with Mangam's Chateau discharged?

   _____
   _____
   _____

2. On February 1, 1995, the Burton Manufacturing Co. contracted to make and ship 1,000 men's suits to the Fisher Clothing Co. by March 1. A prolonged breakdown of factory machinery caused an interruption in production, and the Burton Co. informed Fisher Clothing Co. that it could not fulfill contract commitments until June 1. Does the Fisher Clothing Co. have a case for breach of contract under the common law?

   _____
   _____
   _____

3. Deveraux, a noted columnist, was engaged by a newspaper syndicate to prepare manuscript copy and editorials for their papers. Owing to ill health, Deveraux is obliged to retire and assigns his contract to White, also a prominent journalist. When the newspaper syndicate learns of the assignment, they refuse to give their approval. Is the newspaper syndicate obliged to accept White's services?

   _____
   _____
   _____

# PART III

# PURCHASE AND SALE OF GOODS UNDER THE UCC

# Chapter 15

# The Sales Contract: Key Concepts

## CHAPTER OUTLINE

The Legal Setting for a Sale of Goods
The Sales Contract
    Offer and Acceptance
    Consideration
    Statute of Limitations
    Statute of Frauds
    Enforceable Oral Contracts
Unconscionability
The Parol Evidence Rule

## TRUE-FALSE QUESTIONS

Indicate whether each statement below is true or false by circling T or F in the column on the right.

1. Under the UCC, an agreement modifying a contract for the sale of goods needs no consideration to be binding.    T    F

2. A contract for the sale of goods costing under $500 can be oral or written.    T    F

3. Article 2 of the UCC applies to all sellers and buyers of goods regardless of whether they are merchants or nonmerchants.    T    F

4. The UCC requires all parties entering a sales contract to perform their obligations in good faith.    T    F

5. The term *goods* includes intangible personal property such as shares of stock.    T    F

6. An oral contract for the sale of goods costing $500 or more is enforceable if the buyer makes full payment.    T    F

7. Under the UCC, it is important to determine whether buyers and sellers are    T    F

merchants or nonmerchants.

8. An action for breach of a sales contract must be started within four years of the breach.  T  F

9. Minot, a furniture dealer, sold her car to Martino. In this transaction, according to the UCC, Minot is considered a merchant.  T  F

10. Gibbons bought a record from his friend Marks. Marks is considered a merchant.  T  F

## MULTIPLE-CHOICE QUESTIONS

On the line next to each statement, write the letter of the best answer.

_____ 1. Growing crops are (a) considered goods if severed by the seller, (b) considered goods if severed by the buyer, (c) considered goods regardless of who severs them, (d) not considered goods under any circumstances.

_____ 2. Cuomo, owner of a large men's retail store, signed a written contract to purchase 100 dozen ties at $60 a dozen from the Gem Wholesale Company. The ties were shipped, and Cuomo paid the $6,000 due. Gem then sued Cuomo for an additional $300, and at the small claims court hearing testified that Cuomo orally had agreed to pay an additional $3 a dozen. The judge held the evidence inadmissible because (a) all contracts must be in writing to be enforceable, (b) written contracts cannot be modified at the will of the parties, (c) a contract of guaranty must be in writing to be enforceable, (d) evidence of an oral agreement that contradicts a written contract is inadmissible.

_____ 3. Berry entered into an oral agreement over the phone with a book club to purchase a book a month for $19.95 per book. After he had received and accepted one book, he decided to cancel the contract. Under the contract, Berry is liable for (a) the full contract price for one year, (b) none of the contract price, (c) the cost of one book, (d) the cost of two books.

_____ 4. A contract for the sale of goods costing $500 or more can be made orally if the (a) agreement is executory, (b) buyer deposits at least $100, (c) buyer receives and accepts the goods, (d) goods are intangible.

_____ 5. Lopez orally agreed to buy some computer equipment. When the company shipped the equipment, Lopez decided to accept and pay for only two items. Lopez legally is obligated to pay for (a) only the equipment he accepted, (b) all of the equipment he agreed to buy, (c) the equipment he accepted plus half of the remainder of the order, (d) none of the equipment.

_____ 6. Under the UCC, the sale of goods involves (a) real property, (b) real and personal property, (c) personal property, (d) items attached to real property only.

_____ 7. Which of the following contracts is not covered by Article 2 of the UCC? (a) A contract for the sale of goods that have been specially manufactured, (b) a contract for the sale of a computer, (c) a contract for the sale of growing crops, (d) a contract for services.

_____ 8. O'Brien paid $600 cash for a color television at a local retail store. O'Brien did not sign a memorandum for the sale. In this case, he (a) can avoid the agreement because contracts for the sale of goods costing $500 or more must be in writing to be enforceable, (b) can avoid the agreement because a memorandum is required for all sales of merchandise, (c) cannot avoid the agreement because the contract need not be in writing when the buyer has paid in full for the goods, (d) cannot avoid the agreement because it involves specially manufactured goods.

_____ 9. If a merchant makes a firm offer, the time stated in the offer cannot exceed (a) three months, (b) six months, (c) one month, (d) nine months.

_____ 10. The UCC requires that the parties to every contract (a) place their agreement in writing, (b) state a price in their agreement that is acceptable to both the buyer and the seller, (c) act in good faith, (d) be merchants.

## SHORT-ANSWER QUESTIONS

Answer each of the following questions in the space provided.

1. A motorcycle dealer in your town sells you a new motorcycle. Under the UCC, would this be classified as a sale? Why or why not?

2. A repair shop fixed the turntable on your stereo. Under the UCC, would this be classified as a sale? Why or why not?

3. Lemond orally agreed to purchase three pairs of prescription eyeglasses for a total cost of $550. Can Lemond later claim that because the oral agreement involved goods costing more than $500, she is not bound by it?

## ACTIVITY: ANALYZING A SALES CONTRACT

Study the bill of sale shown on page 91 and then answer the questions on page 92.

# BILL OF SALE

*That* Beverly B. Richards, a single person, of Marion County, in the State of Indiana, *has this day bargained and sold, and does hereby bargain, sell, assign, transfer, set over, and deliver to* Herschel Clifford Simpson, a single person, in Marion County, in the State of Indiana, *for the sum of* One Thousand ($1,000.00)------------------------------------ *Dollars,* to Beverly B. Richards *in hand paid, the receipt whereof is hereby acknowledged, the following described Chattels, Goods, and Personal Property in* Marion County, State of Indiana, *to-wit:*

One (1) antique cherry bedroom suite, consisting of bed, dresser, night stand, and mirror.

*In Witness Whereof, The said* Beverly B. Richards *has hereunto set* her *hand and seal this* 5th *day of* June 19--

*Signed, sealed, and delivered in presence of* **Beverly B. Richards** (Seal)
Beverly B. Richards

........................................ ........................................ (Seal)

........................................ ........................................ (Seal)

1. Is the seller most likely a merchant or a nonmerchant? Why?

   _____
   _____

2. Why is it necessary to know whether the seller is a merchant or a nonmerchant?

   _____
   _____
   _____

3. Would this contract be enforceable if it had been made orally? Why or why not?

   _____
   _____
   _____

4. What type of property is the subject of this sales contract?

   _____
   _____

5. If the money paid for this property had been $10 instead of $1,000, could this contract be set aside because it was unconscionable? Explain your answer.

   _____
   _____
   _____

## ACTIVITY: COMPARISON OF RULES

Distinguish between the common law's mirror image rule and the UCC's provisions for dealing with the acceptance of an offer.

_____
_____
_____
_____

# Chapter 16

# The Sales Contract: Transfer of Title and Risk of Loss

## CHAPTER OUTLINE

**Relevance of Title and Risk of Loss in Sales Law**
**Present Sale Versus Contract to Sell**
**Risk of Loss**
    Sale by Merchant at Merchant's Place of Business
    Sale by Nonmerchant at Nonmerchant's Location
    Free-on-Board Sales
    Delivery to Shipping Point
    Delivery to Destination
**Sale on Approval or Return**
**Auction Sales**
**Bulk Transfers**
**COD Sales**
**Rights of Third Parties**
    Stolen Goods
    Where the Seller Had a Voidable Title
    Where a Merchant Was Given Temporary Possession

## MULTIPLE-CHOICE QUESTIONS

On the line next to each statement, write the letter of the best answer.

_____ 1. Goods that are not in existence and not yet identified are called (a) personal goods, (b) real goods, (c) future goods, (d) unsatisfactory goods.

_____ 2. Mincer bought an electric saw from Brown's Hardware Store. Because the saw needed minor adjustments, he left it with the dealer. Risk of loss passed to Mincer when he (a) made the agreement, (b) picked up the saw, (c) felt that the saw was satisfactory, (d) accepted the risk of loss.

3. Figmont, of Albany, New York, ordered fifty calculators from Mund Calculator Company, terms FOB Atlanta, Georgia. The calculators were damaged in transit from Atlanta to Albany. Who suffers the loss? (a) Figmont, (b) Figmont and Mund Calculator equally, (c) Figmont suffers 25%, and Mund 75%, (d) Mund Calculator.

4. Lannigan bought an onyx ring and left it with the jeweler to be sized. Before it was sized, Tanzer came into the store to purchase an onyx ring. Because Lannigan's ring was the only onyx ring Tanzer liked, the jeweler sold it. Can Tanzer keep the ring? (a) Yes. A merchant who has temporary possession of goods can transfer a valid title, (b) Yes. A merchant who has temporary possession of goods can transfer a voidable title, (c) No. A buyer obtains no better title to goods than the seller, (d) No. A buyer with a voidable title cannot transfer a valid title.

5. Barnes went to Caines Furniture Store to buy a sofa. The store was sold out but agreed to call the factory and have one made up. This transaction is (a) a present sale, (b) void, (c) a contract to sell, (d) a sale of identified goods.

6. If the requirements of the bulk transfer law under Article 6 of the UCC are not met, creditors may have the right to declare a bulk sale (a) void, (b) voidable, (c) inadequate, (d) performed.

7. Johnson bought a portable radio from Hughes without realizing that the radio was stolen. Johnson received (a) a valid title, (b) no title, (c) a voidable title, (d) an informal title.

8. A bill of sale is (a) a storage document, (b) used in a sale or return, (c) written proof of ownership of goods, (d) a document that shows a person is keeping goods beyond the approval date.

9. When he bought a new boat, Johnson was given the choice of delivery FOB shipping point or FOB destination. Of these terms, delivery FOB destination is to Johnson's legal advantage because (a) risk of loss passes to him when the boat is delivered to the carrier, (b) shipping expenses are paid by the buyer on delivery, (c) Johnson will not sustain a loss if the boat is damaged in transit, (d) all losses caused by damage to the boat will fall on the carrier.

10. Kimball charged a lamp at the Ames Department Store and asked that it be delivered to her house on the next delivery run. The lamp was damaged while being loaded onto the company's delivery truck. Which of the following statements best describes Kimball's legal position? (a) The risk of loss has not yet shifted to Kimball, so Ames must bear the loss of the lamp, (b) the risk of loss shifted to Kimball at the moment the Ames employees were loading the lamp onto the truck, so Kimball must bear the loss, (c) Kimball must accept delivery of the lamp even though it is damaged because she charged it, (d) Kimball does not have to pay because the lamp is considered to be future goods.

## MATCHING QUESTIONS

Use the following terms to identify the phrases below. On the line next to each phrase, write the letter of the term that most closely relates to it.

a. Identified goods
b. Sale or return
c. Contract to sell
d. COD
e. Title
f. FOB
g. Future goods
h. Sale on approval
i. Present sale
j. Risk of loss

_____ 1. A promise to transfer title to a buyer at some time in the future

_____ 2. A method of shipping that allows the seller to retain possession of the goods until the buyer pays the price and any delivery charges

_____ 3. Goods to be sold that have been selected by the seller and the buyer

_____ 4. A sale of goods in which title passes from the seller to the buyer at the time the parties make the contract

_____ 5. A burden assumed by either the buyer or seller in a sales contract for damage or destruction of the goods

## CASE PROBLEMS

Read the case problems below. For each problem, answer yes or no, and then explain your answer in the space provided.

1. Rogers ordered some electrical equipment from Cobb in Dayton, Ohio. The equipment was shipped to Utica, New York, terms FOB Utica. An accidental fire destroyed the equipment soon after it left Dayton. Must Rogers bear the loss in this case?

_____
_____
_____

2. Gornig bought a dozen sport shirts from Rock's Men's Shop, paid for them, and asked the merchant to hold the shirts in the store until he could pick them up the next day. During the night, a fire destroyed the store and its contents. Gornig demanded his money back, claiming that he had not yet taken physical possession of the shirts. Is Gornig entitled to the money?

_____
_____
_____

3. Roman, a consumer, purchased a VCR from a merchant on ten days' approval. Five days later, the VCR was stolen. Was Roman responsible for the loss?

_____
_____
_____

4. Otterman purchased an oriental rug in good faith from a house-to-house salesperson. Later he sold the rug to Redstone. Philips proved that the rug had been stolen from her before it was sold to Otterman. Did Philips have a legal claim to the rug?

_____
_____
_____

5. Klein sold his entire ice cream business—merchandise and equipment—to Hartman. Hurst, a creditor of Klein, sought to have the sale set aside, claiming that as a creditor, he was entitled to notice of the sale. Was Hurst correct?

___

## ACTIVITY: CASE PROBLEM

Tomari, a manufacturer's representative, and Gould, a real estate agent, entered into a written contract for the sale of Tomari's minivan to Gould for $8,000 cash. Tomari agreed to tune up the motor on the van, which he did, and on the night of August 1 phoned to tell Gould that the van was ready for pick up. Upon pick up, Gould was to make payment. Gould replied to Tomari by saying: "I'll be there in the morning to pick up the van and to pay you the $8,000." The next morning, however, Gould held an unexpected meeting with a potential client and decided to pick up the van later in the week. On the night of August 2, the van was destroyed by fire of unknown origin. Neither Tomari nor Gould had any comprehensive insurance (which would have included protection from fire) on the van. Who must bear the loss?

# Chapter 17

# The Sales Contract: Performance, Breach, and Remedies for Breach

## CHAPTER OUTLINE

**Performance of the Sales Contract**
    Delivery of Goods
    Inspection of Goods
    Acceptance and Payment
**Breach of the Sales Contract**
**Remedies for Breach Available to the Buyer**
    Sue for Breach of Warranty
    Cancel the Contract and Cover
    Cancel the Contract and Sue for Damages
    Sue to Obtain the Goods

**Remedies for Breach Available to the Seller**
    Cancel the Contract
    Resell the Goods and Sue for Damages
    Sue to Recover the Purchase Price
    Sue to Recover Damages for Nonacceptance
    Withhold Delivery of the Goods
    Reclaim the Goods from the Buyer

## COMPLETION QUESTIONS

In the statements below, important words have been omitted. Fill in the blanks to complete each statement.

1. The first obligation of the seller is to tender (offer) _____ goods.

2. A buyer can sue for breach of warranty only after _____ is given to the seller that there is a problem with the goods.

3. If the seller breaches the sales contract, one remedy available to the buyer is to buy substitute goods elsewhere to replace those originally due from the seller. This remedy is called the right to _____.

4. The buyer has the right to _____ the goods within a reasonable time before accepting delivery to determine if they conform to the contract.

5. Assuming that the goods have been delivered properly and that they conform to the contract, the buyer has a duty to _____ the goods and pay for them according to the terms of the contract.

6. Damages for the breach of a sales contract by a seller generally are set at the difference between the contract price and the _____ price at the time the buyer learns of the breach, plus any expenses.

7. In the case of a breach of contract by a buyer, a seller who still has possession of the goods but who is unable to resell them elsewhere can hold the goods for the buyer and sue for the _____.

8. A seller legally can withhold the delivery of goods purchased on credit if the seller discovers before delivery that the buyer is _____.

9. Under the UCC, a breach of contract allows the injured party to pursue more than one _____.

10. The UCC allows a seller who gives up possession of goods to the buyer to reclaim them on discovering a buyer's insolvency if a demand is made within _____ days after the buyer receives the goods.

## SHORT-ANSWER QUESTIONS

Answer each of the following questions in the space provided.

1. List three remedies available to the buyer if the seller breaches the sales contract.

   _____
   _____
   _____

2. List three remedies available to the seller if the buyer breaches the sales contract.

   _____
   _____
   _____

## MULTIPLE-CHOICE QUESTIONS

On the line next to each statement, write the letter of the best answer.

1. If, while the goods are in transit with a common carrier, the seller learns that the buyer has become insolvent, the seller can (a) stop the goods in transit, (b) sue for nonacceptance, (c) sue the buyer for fraud, (d) sue the buyer for conversion.

2. Snyder sold some standard-sized sheets of plywood on credit to Robinson, promising delivery within ten days. Five days later, Snyder wrongfully refused to deliver the goods to Robinson. Robinson legally is entitled to (a) sue for the purchase price, (b) exercise a right of lien on the goods, (c) sue for specific performance, (d) purchase similar goods elsewhere and sue for damages.

3. Franklin, owner of Best Buy Department Store, accepted and paid for twenty-five dozen ballpoint pens from the Perkins Stationery Company. After selling some of the pens, Franklin began to get complaints that the pens would not write. What action can Franklin take against the Perkins Company? (a) None, (b) resell the goods and sue for damages, (c) sue for specific performance, (d) sue Perkins for breach of warranty.

4. A seller who is notified that the buyer is not going through with a contract can (a) cancel the contract, (b) obtain specific performance, (c) sue for breach of warranty, (d) cover.

5. One remedy that is not available to a seller is (a) rescinding the contract, (b) reclaiming the goods, (c) stopping the goods in transit, (d) suing for breach of warranty.

6. Which of the following is not available to the buyer? (a) cover, (b) cure, (c) replevin, (d) specific performance.

7. If the contract provides for delivery C.O.D., (a) the buyer must pay prior to inspection, (b) the buyer has the right to pay after inspection, (c) the buyer has no right of inspection, (d) none of these answers.

8. The remedy that enables the buyer to obtain goods that have been identified and ordered but wrongfully detained by the seller is called (a) curing, (b) covering, (c) replevin, (d) restitution.

9. When a seller breaches a warranty, the measure of damages is generally the difference between (a) the value of the warranty and the contract price, (b) the value of the warranty and the cover price, (c) the value of the goods accepted and their value had they conformed to the warranty, (d) the cover price and the contract price.

10. Under Article 2 of the UCC, cure involves (a) the right of the seller to correct defective performance, (b) the duty of the seller to provide additional goods, (c) the right of the buyer to reject a shipment of goods for no reason at all, (d) the duty of the buyer to accept goods without first inspecting them.

## CASE PROBLEM

Read the case problem below and then answer the questions that follow.

The Morgan Company, a manufacturer of men's clothing, entered into a contract to send twenty dozen shirts a month between September and December to the Best Wholesale Clothing Company. In November, the Morgan Company discovered that Best Wholesale Clothing was insolvent. What action can the Morgan Company take under the following circumstances?

1. The September and October shipments were delivered to Best Wholesale Clothing.

   _____
   _____
   _____

2. The November shipment had been placed in the hands of a common carrier for delivery to Best Wholesale Clothing.

   _____
   _____
   _____

3. The December shipment had been manufactured but was in Morgan's warehouse awaiting shipment.

   _____
   _____
   _____

# Chapter 18

# Product Liability: Negligence, Warranties, and Strict Liability

## CHAPTER OUTLINE

What Product Liability Is
Negligence
Warranty Liability
    Express Warranties
    Implied Warranties
    Warranty of Title
    Exclusion of Warranties
    Breach of Warranty
    Magnuson-Moss Warranty Act
Strict Liability
Misuse of Product by Injured Party

## TRUE-FALSE QUESTIONS

Indicate whether each statement below is true or false by circling T or F in the column on the right.

1. The trend today is to allow anyone harmed by a defective product to sue whoever is in any way responsible.  T  F

2. The Magnuson-Moss Warranty Act requires that all express warranties given by manufacturers be full warranties.  T  F

3. Product liability cases all are based on breach of warranty.  T  F

4. Statements by salespersons expressing their opinions about the quality of the goods they sell constitute express warranties.  T  F

5. Even though it is not written, an implied warranty imposes obligations on a seller.  T  F

6. If a buyer purchases goods after inspecting a model, there is an implied warranty that the goods will conform to the model.   T   F

7. The implied warranty of merchantability can be excluded either orally or in writing.   T   F

8. Both merchants and nonmerchants can make implied warranties of fitness for a particular purpose.   T   F

9. Under the UCC, it is not necessary that a warranty be given at the time of a sale.   T   F

10. In making an express warranty to a buyer, the seller does not have to actually use the word *warranty*.   T   F

## MULTIPLE-CHOICE QUESTIONS

On the line next to each statement, write the letter of the best answer.

_____ 1. In selling an electronic game to a customer, the salesperson stated that "the game is made of a durable plastic and will not crack or break even when dropped on the floor." The salesperson's statement (a) is sales puffing, (b) is an implied warranty, (c) is an express warranty, (d) creates a warranty of merchantability.

_____ 2. Martins bought an automotive diagnostic analyzer for $59.95. A one-year warranty covering original factory defects in materials and workmanship came with the analyzer. The consideration given by Martins for the warranty was (a) part of the purchase price, (b) giving up the right to sue the store, (c) acceptance of the offer to buy the analyzer, (d) the entire sales contract.

_____ 3. *Product liability* describes the liability that manufacturers and sellers have to those harmed because of (a) products they place on the market that are defective or do not work right, (b) their lack of privity of contract, (c) their lack of negligence, (d) their lack of knowledge about warranties.

_____ 4. Montgomery cut her mouth on a piece of glass that was in a bowl of chili at Piper's Restaurant. If Montgomery sues the restaurant, she can base her action on the (a) express warranty of title, (b) express warranty of description, (c) implied warranty of merchantability, (d) express warranty of merchantability.

_____ 5. Under the UCC, a warranty, oral or written, given by the seller following the sale (a) becomes part of the original sales contract without additional consideration, (b) must be accompanied by additional consideration, (c) is illegal, (d) is a breach of the sales contract.

## CASE PROBLEMS

Read the case problems below. For each problem, answer yes or no, and then explain your answer in the space provided.

1. Santos called Chicken Delight and ordered several buckets of chicken for a party. Following the party, two guests became seriously ill because some of the chicken was spoiled. The sick guests missed several days of work while they were under a doctor's care. Because they had

used up their sick time, they were not paid for the days they missed. Could the guests sue Chicken Delight for damages resulting from their medical bills and their lost pay?

2. Horton entered into a written contract to sell and install a central air conditioning system in Cordero's house. A week after the system was installed, Cordero asked Horton about a warranty, and Horton warranted the system in writing against all defects for one year. Eight months later, the system broke down because of a defective switch. Could Cordero enforce the warranty?

3. When he ordered a water pump by mail, Banks specified that he wanted one that would pump 25 gallons a minute. When the pump arrived and was installed, Banks found that it pumped only 20 gallons a minute. Was there a breach of warranty?

4. Sims bought a 50-amp battery charger from Newcomb. A short time later, Cole recognized the battery charger as one that had been stolen from him, and he took the charger back from Sims. When Sims demanded that Newcomb refund his money, Newcomb claimed that because he never stated that he had title to the charger, Sims had no rights against him. Is Newcomb legally correct?

5. Marvin was using a power press manufactured by United Press. While operating the press, Marvin's hand was caught in the mechanism and severely injured. The press was manufactured without a guard device to prevent injuries such as the one suffered by Marvin. Marvin sued United Press for defective design and for producing an unreasonably dangerous product. At trial Marvin's attorney made two important points: The press was only six months old, and United sold the guard as an optional piece of equipment rather than as a standard part of the press. Is United Press liable to Marvin for the injuries he sustained?

## ACTIVITY: UNDERSTANDING PRODUCT WARRANTIES

Study the warranty below and then answer the questions that follow.

---

### FULL ONE-YEAR WARRANTY

Fulton Electric Company warrants this product to be free of manufacturing defects for a **one-year** period after the original date of consumer purchase or receipt as a gift. This warranty does not include damage to the product resulting from accident or misuse.

If the product should become defective within the warranty period, we will elect to repair or replace it free of charge, including free return transportation provided it is delivered prepaid to any Fulton Electric authorized service facility. There is a nationwide network of authorized service facilities whose names and addresses are included with this product. Any questions regarding warranty service can be directed to Manager-Consumer Counseling, Fulton Electric Company, Housewares & Audio Business Division, 1285 Stoughton Avenue, Bridgeport, Connecticut 06602.

This warranty gives you specific legal rights, and you also may have other rights that vary from state to state.

---

1. Is this warranty an express warranty or an implied warranty? Explain your answer.

2. Does this warranty meet the requirements of the Magnuson-Moss Warranty Act discussed in the textbook? Why or why not?

3. Could the manufacturer include a statement eliminating all implied warranties?

PRODUCT LIABILITY: NEGLIGENCE, WARRANTIES, AND STRICT LIABILITY | 105

4. If the electric motor in the product covered by this warranty wears out after fifteen months of use, what liability does Fulton Electric Company have to replace or repair the motor?

5. If the buyer of this product left it outside in the open for seven months and then found it unusable because of rust, is the company liable for replacement of the product? Why or why not?

6. If this product is returned to Fulton Electric Company for repair during the warranty period, who must pay the cost of postage to and from the company's repair facility?

7. If the buyer has this product repaired during the warranty period by a local repair service, must Fulton Electric Company pay for the repair? Explain your answer.

8. Assume that the product covered by this warranty is a clock radio. If the radio had deep scratches on the case at the time of purchase, is the manufacturer obligated under this warranty to replace the radio? Why or why not?

9. If this product stopped working properly during the warranty period and the company offered to repair it, could you insist that the company replace it with a new product? Explain your answer.

10. Suppose a friend bought this product on June 10 and gave it to you as a gift on July 13. On what date would the warranty period start? Explain your answer.

Copyright © Houghton Mifflin Company. All rights reserved.

# Review

## Part III
## Purchase and Sale of Goods Under the UCC

### TRUE-FALSE QUESTIONS

Indicate whether each statement below is true or false by circling T or F in the column on the right.

1. Under the UCC, an agreement modifying a contract for the sale of goods needs no consideration to be binding.  T  F

2. When a merchant sells to a consumer at the merchant's place of business, risk of loss does not pass until the buyer actually receives the goods.  T  F

3. In a sale of goods FOB shipping point, risk of loss passes to the buyer when the goods are properly delivered to the carrier at the shipping point.  T  F

4. A buyer with a voidable title can transfer a valid title to a third party who obtains the goods for value and in good faith.  T  F

5. A sale or return is a present sale in which risk of loss passes to the buyer when the buyer accepts the goods.  T  F

6. Part of the purchase price of goods purchased under a sales contract is consideration for any express warranty given with those goods.  T  F

7. A warranty of title can be express or implied.  T  F

8. Express warranties cannot be excluded from sales contracts even if clear, specific language is used.  T  F

9. Under the UCC, courts can refuse to enforce an entire contract or any particular clause in a contract it finds unconscionable at the time the agreement was made.  T  F

10. A bill of sale can be an informal document, such as a sales slip from a store, or a formal document.  T  F

## MULTIPLE-CHOICE QUESTIONS

On the line next to each statement, write the letter of the best answer.

_____ 1. The bulk sales law pertains to (a) the sale of an entire stock of goods outside the ordinary course of a merchant's business to one person, (b) the sale of bulky goods, (c) the sale of land, (d) none of these.

_____ 2. Which of the following statements made by a salesclerk at the time of a sale is a warranty? (a) "This coat is an unusual bargain," (b) "This coat will be in style for many years," (c) "This coat has an all-silk lining," (d) "This coat will wear like iron."

_____ 3. A warranty implied in every sale of goods is that the (a) goods are of high quality, (b) seller has title to the goods, (c) seller will refund the purchase price if the goods are unsatisfactory, (d) purchase price is reasonable.

_____ 4. If the buyer possesses and holds title to goods but is found to be insolvent, within ten days the seller can (a) place a lien on the goods, (b) reclaim the goods, (c) rescind the transfer of the title, (d) resell the goods to a third party.

_____ 5. If a buyer wrongfully refuses to accept goods when a seller makes proper delivery, the seller is entitled to (a) keep the goods for his or her own use and sue for the purchase price, (b) sue the buyer for damages for not accepting the goods, (c) sue the buyer for specific performance, (d) sue the buyer for breach of warranty.

_____ 6. Young purchased a 50-foot length of garden hose at a hardware store. When she tried to use it, the hose pulled apart in several places. Was there any breach of warranty by the store? (a) Yes. There was an implied warranty that the goods were of the finest quality, (b) Yes. There was an implied warranty that the goods were merchantable, (c) No. No warranties were expressed by the store clerk, (d) No. Unless the store states a definite warranty, there is none.

_____ 7. When goods are shipped from Buffalo, New York, to Columbus, Georgia, terms FOB Columbus, risk of loss passes to the buyer when the (a) contract is made, (b) goods are delivered to the common carrier, (c) goods reach their destination, (d) goods leave the seller's warehouse.

_____ 8. The McCracken Garment Company sold one hundred clown suits to Getz for $2,000. Getz inspected the goods and paid for ten suits at the time of the sale. Getz later refused to receive and accept the rest of the suits, claiming that because the goods cost over $500, the oral agreement was unenforceable. Can Getz get his money back for the ten suits he paid for, even though the contract was oral? (a) Yes. There was no written memorandum of the sale, (b) No. Acceptance of the ten clown suits made the entire agreement enforceable, (c) Yes. The agreement was unenforceable under the statute of frauds, (d) No. When the buyer has made a partial payment, the contract can be enforced for those goods covered by the partial payment.

_____ 9. Goods not yet in existence and not yet identified are called (a) nonexisting goods, (b) real goods, (c) future goods, (d) personal goods.

_____ 10. Unless a contract for the sale of a stereo states otherwise, the place of delivery is the (a) seller's residence, (b) buyer's residence, (c) buyer's place of business, (d) seller's place of business.

_____ 11. Which of the following types of property would be classified as goods under Article 2 of the UCC? (a) growing trees, (b) shares of stock, (c) a bathtub in a house that could not easily be removed without doing substantial damage, (d) a mobile home.

_____ 12. If a merchant (offeror) makes a "firm offer" to sell goods but does not specify a time in which the offeree must accept (a) the merchant can revoke the offer at any time, (b) the merchant can revoke the offer at any time before it is accepted, (c) the merchant cannot revoke the offer for one year, (d) the merchant cannot revoke the offer until after a reasonable time has passed.

_____ 13. Which of the following people would *not* be considered a merchant under the UCC? (a) a person who regularly sells the type of goods involved, (b) a person who occasionally sells the type of goods involved, (c) a person who claims to have specialized knowledge of the type of goods involved, (d) a person who is considered a commercial expert in the type of goods involved.

_____ 14. Under the UCC, an action for breach of a sales contract must be started by the nonbreaching party within (a) four years of the breach, (b) six years of the breach, (c) eight years of the breach, (d) one year of the breach.

_____ 15. The "mirror image rule" relating to offer and acceptance (a) remains a fundamental cornerstone of the UCC, (b) is no longer relevant under the UCC, (c) applies only to merchants, (d) applies only to consumers.

## ACTIVITY: UNDERSTANDING WARRANTIES

Base your answers to Questions 1 through 5 on the following information.

McDonnell purchased an electric razor from the Sibley Department Store for $79.95. He took the razor home when he made the sales agreement on December 10, and he paid for the razor at the end of the 30-day credit period. The following statement appeared on a tag attached to the razor:

**LIMITED WARRANTY**

Warranted for one year from the date of purchase against original factory imperfections in materials and workmanship. During this time, Excello will elect to repair or replace the product without charge for parts or labor, provided the product is returned to the manufacturer with the warranty card.
Excello Razor Company

_____ 1. The warranty statement on the tag represents an (a) express warranty, (b) implied warranty, (c) express and an implied warranty, (d) exclusion of warranties.

_____ 2. McDonnell would benefit from the warranty if (a) he left the razor out in the rain on a camping trip and the razor was damaged, (b) he gave the razor to a friend for Christmas and the friend did not like it enough to use it, (c) the cutting edges of the razor became dull after McDonnell used it for one month, (d) the razor did not give him as good a shave as his old razor.

_____ 3. The consideration given by McDonnell for the warranty was (a) his reputation, (b) his acceptance of the electric razor, (c) part of the purchase price, (d) money paid in addition to the purchase price.

_____ 4. McDonnell brought the razor back for an adjustment two weeks after he bought it. He questioned the clerk about the razor's quality. The clerk replied that in addition to the manufacturer's warranty, the store guaranteed all razors for two years against all defects and, if necessary, would replace the razor with a new one. The clerk's statement is (a) binding because a warranty made after a sales contract is completed needs no additional consideration, (b) binding because it is based on common usage in the trade, and most razors carry this kind of guarantee, (c) not binding because it is based on past consideration, (d) not binding because it was simply sales talk or "puffing."

5. Risk of loss passed to McDonnell on (a) January 10, (b) December 10, (c) January 9, (d) December 11.

## CASE PROBLEMS

Read the case problems below. For each problem, answer yes or no, and then explain your answer in the space provided.

1. Briggs wanted to buy a computer for his home-based business. He went to the Harvard Computer Supply Company and signed a written memorandum to purchase one for $2,500. However, Briggs refused to accept delivery of the computer the next day, saying he had changed his mind. He claimed that the memorandum he signed was not enforceable because the salesperson had not signed it. Is Briggs liable for breach of contract?

2. Friske, of Boston, Massachusetts, placed an order with Kevin Supply Company in Dayton, Ohio, for office furniture he had seen in a catalog. If, after the furniture is received in Boston, Friske finds that it does not conform to the description in the catalog, does he have a legal claim against the Kevin Supply Company?

3. In the case described in Question 2, the shipping terms were FOB Dayton. If the furniture is damaged en route to Boston, through no fault of the common carrier, should Friske bear the loss?

4. Jayson purchased a power lawn mower from the American Department Store on 30 days' approval. Before the 30-day period expired, a thief broke into Jayson's garage and stole the mower. Must Jayson bear the loss in this case?

## SHORT-ANSWER QUESTIONS

Answer each of the following questions in the space provided.

1. Compare the three theories of liability that a buyer who is injured can use in a product liability action. How do these theories differ?

   _____
   _____
   _____
   _____
   _____
   _____
   _____
   _____
   _____

2. Explain why it is difficult for a merchant to completely avoid making any type of express warranty.

   _____
   _____
   _____
   _____
   _____
   _____

# PART IV

# COMMERCIAL PAPER

# Chapter 19

# Nature and Types of Commercial Paper

## CHAPTER OUTLINE

**What Commercial Paper Is**
**Types of Commercial Paper**
**Commercial Paper as a Negotiable Instrument**
    Written Form
    Signature
    Promise or Order to Pay
    Unconditional Promise or Order
    A Sum Certain in Money
    Payable on Demand or at a Definite Time
    Payable to Order or Bearer
    Drawee Named with Certainty
**Added Language and Omissions Not Affecting Negotiability**

## MULTIPLE-CHOICE QUESTIONS

On the line next to each statement, write the letter of the best answer.

_____ 1. A check is issued by the (a) maker, (b) payee, (c) drawee, (d) drawer.

_____ 2. A promissory note must contain (a) words indicating a promise to pay, (b) the word *IOU*, (c) a certificate of deposit, (d) a date.

_____ 3. The signature on a negotiable instrument must (a) be printed or stamped on the instrument, (b) be that of the maker or drawer, (c) appear in the body of the instrument, (d) appear in the lower right-hand corner.

_____ 4. A written order by one person on a second person to pay a third person is a (a) promissory note, (b) certificate of deposit, (c) draft, (d) receipt.

_____ 5. The omission of the word *order* or *bearer* on a promissory note can render it (a) voidable, (b) void, (c) negotiable, (d) nonnegotiable.

## NATURE AND TYPES OF COMMERCIAL PAPER | 113

_____ 6. The term *nonnegotiable* means (a) void, (b) not cash, (c) not readily transferable from one person to another, (d) not payable.

_____ 7. An instrument is payable on demand or at a definite time if it is payable (a) at someone's death, (b) under a certain condition, (c) on, before, or after a specified date, (d) at a bank.

_____ 8. A check that contains the words *three hundred fifty dollars* and the figures *$3.50* is (a) payable in the amount of $350, (b) illegal, (c) payable in the amount of $3.50, (d) void.

_____ 9. An instrument is not payable in a sum certain in money and thus is not negotiable if (a) it is payable in a foreign currency that is a legal currency, (b) it is payable with interest, (c) the amount in figures is omitted, (d) the person required to pay the instrument has the option to pay something in addition to money.

_____ 10. A check is (a) a written promise, (b) usually payable at a certain time, (c) payable immediately, (d) not a substitute for cash.

_____ 11. Which of the following contains the necessary words of negotiability? (a) Pay to Mary Roe, (b) Please pay Mary Roe, (c) Pay to holder, Mary Roe, (d) Pay to the order of Mary Roe.

_____ 12. Brown signed a document unconditionally promising to pay a certain sum of money on a definite day to the order of Nevarez. Nevarez is called the (a) maker, (b) payee, (c) drawer, (d) drawee.

_____ 13. A promissory note is not negotiable if it is (a) not dated, (b) payable thirty days after the death of the maker, (c) signed by two people, (d) payable thirty days after the date of the note.

_____ 14. A note or check payable in a foreign currency that is a legal currency is (a) nonnegotiable, (b) fully negotiable, (c) not payable in the dollar equivalent of that currency, (d) void.

_____ 15. If the day of issue is omitted from a note or check, its negotiability is (a) restricted, (b) voided, (c) not affected, (d) postponed.

## ACTIVITY: DETERMINING NEGOTIABILITY

Indicate whether each of the following is a negotiable or nonnegotiable instrument by circling N or NN in the column on the right.

| | | | |
|---|---|---|---|
| 1. | An unsigned check | N | NN |
| 2. | A note signed with an X | N | NN |
| 3. | An instrument payable to "Bearer" | N | NN |
| 4. | A promissory note payable 10 days before February 8, 1993 | N | NN |
| 5. | A check that is not dated | N | NN |
| 6. | An oral promise to pay $1,000 | N | NN |
| 7. | A check on which the name of the payee has been omitted | N | NN |
| 8. | A signed promissory note containing the words "I promise to pay 500 pounds of scrap iron to the order of Merle Thomas" | N | NN |
| 9. | A draft payable at sight | N | NN |
| 10. | A draft in which the drawee's name has been omitted | N | NN |

## TRUE-FALSE QUESTIONS

Indicate whether each statement below is true or false by circling T or F in the column on the right.

1. A person to whom a negotiable instrument is transferred obtains special privileges.  T  F
2. A check is an instrument that is payable on demand.  T  F
3. The drawee of a check is always a bank.  T  F
4. An instrument that places conditions on the promise or order to pay is negotiable.  T  F
5. A draft is a negotiable instrument that is a written promise to pay money.  T  F
6. The party who promises to pay a promissory note is called the drawee.  T  F
7. A promissory note need not be in writing.  T  F
8. A promissory note is an order to pay.  T  F
9. An instrument made payable to "Myself" is considered payable to the bearer.  T  F
10. An instrument that is payable "fifteen days after I paint my house" is negotiable.  T  F

## SHORT-ANSWER QUESTIONS

Answer each of the following questions in the space provided.

1. What test is used to determine whether an instrument is payable in money?

2. What kind of writing is required for a negotiable instrument?

3. If the words and figures in an instrument differ, which controls?

4. If an instrument is made payable to cash, to whom is it payable?

5. What is the effect of making an instrument payable in the event of something—even something certain—happening?

# Chapter 20

# Issue, Transfer, and Discharge of Commercial Paper

## CHAPTER OUTLINE

The Issue and Transfer of Commercial Paper
    Negotiation of Order Instruments
    Negotiation of Bearer Instruments
Types of Indorsements
How Commercial Paper Is Discharged
    Payment
    Alteration
    Statute of Limitations
    Bankruptcy
    Cancellation

## TRUE-FALSE QUESTIONS

Indicate whether each statement below is true or false by circling T or F in the column on the right.

1. A payee of commercial paper can transfer that instrument to someone by negotiation.     T   F

2. An indorsement that limits the liability ordinarily undertaken by an indorser is called a restrictive indorsement.     T   F

3. An indorsement that states the name of the person to whom the instrument is being transferred is a special indorsement.     T   F

4. A check payable to "Cash" must be negotiated by indorsement and delivery.     T   F

5. The purpose of an indorsement is to transfer ownership of commercial paper.     T   F

6. An accommodation indorsement often is used to help someone who does not have good credit.     T   F

7. A person who has a negotiable instrument containing a blank indorsement legally can change the indorsement to a special indorsement.     T   F

8. A blank indorsement makes the instrument payable to the bearer.  T  F
9. The use of a qualified indorsement makes an instrument nonnegotiable.  T  F
10. Marking a promissory note "void" is one way of canceling the instrument.  T  F
11. "For deposit only" is a special indorsement.  T  F
12. An instrument with a blank indorsement can be transferred from one person to another by delivery alone, without further indorsement.  T  F
13. Bearer paper can be negotiated by voluntary delivery alone.  T  F
14. An instrument with a blank indorsement should not be mailed because if the instrument is lost, anyone can collect without proving ownership of the instrument.  T  F
15. A special indorsement must contain the word *order* or *bearer*.  T  F

## MULTIPLE-CHOICE QUESTIONS

On the line next to each statement, write the letter of the best answer.

_____  1. Barbara Allen indorses her paycheck "For deposit only—Barbara Allen." This indorsement is (a) blank, (b) restrictive, (c) special, (d) qualified.

_____  2. Which of the following indorsements by Walter Bly, the payee of a check, makes the check payable to bearer? (a) Walter Bly, (b) Pay to the order of Herb Winthrop, (signed) Walter Bly, (c) Pay to Herb Winthrop, (signed) Walter Bly, (d) Pay to Herb Winthrop or Order, (signed) Walter Bly.

_____  3. Varden wanted to make a bank deposit by mail. The safest indorsement for her to use on checks deposited this way is a(n) (a) special indorsement, (b) blank indorsement, (c) accommodation indorsement, (d) restrictive indorsement.

_____  4. Barron negotiated a check that she received from Cleary by making the following indorsement: "Pay to the order of Blythe Love—Jane Barron." Legally, Love now can negotiate this check by (a) delivery only, (b) indorsement only, (c) either indorsement or delivery, (d) both indorsement and delivery.

_____  5. To be valid, an indorsement (a) must be typed, (b) must be handwritten, (c) can be typed or handwritten, (d) must be printed.

## CASE PROBLEMS

Read the case problems below. For each problem, answer yes or no, and then explain your answer in the space provided.

1. Falvo made a check payable to "Cash" and gave the check to Gamber. Gamber left the check on his desk while he attended a meeting. When Gamber returned, he discovered that the check had been stolen. Did the thief receive the check by negotiation?

_____
_____
_____

2. Freeman's house was burglarized, and several checks were stolen, one of which was made out to "Cash." The thief who stole the check passed it on to another party. Did the transfer by the thief to the other party constitute a negotiation of the check?

_____
_____
_____

## SHORT-ANSWER QUESTIONS

Answer each of the following questions in the space provided.

1. James Tuttle wrote a check drawn on the Friendly Trust Bank, payable to Rachel Fellows in the amount of $500. Fellows owed $500 to Timothy Blanchard, so she indorsed the check and gave it to Blanchard.

   a. Who is the drawer? _____
   b. Who is the drawee? _____
   c. Who is the payee? _____
   d. Who is the indorser? _____
   e. Who is the indorsee? _____

2. Identify each type of indorsement in the illustrations below.

   a. _____

   *Pay to Robyn Regan*
   *May Schwartz*

   b. _____

   *Without Recourse*
   *Beth Griffin*

   c. _____

   *For Deposit Only*
   *Arnold Johnson*

# Chapter 21

# Rights and Duties of Parties to a Negotiable Instrument; Holder in Due Course Status

## CHAPTER OUTLINE

**Liability of Parties to Negotiable Instrument**
   Presentment for Payment
   Dishonor of Instrument
   Notice of Dishonor
**Holder in Due Course Status**
   For Value
   In Good Faith
   Without Knowledge of Overdue or Dishonored Paper
   Without Knowledge of Defenses
**Defenses Against Holders of Negotiable Instruments**
   Personal (Limited) Defenses
   Universal (Real) Defenses
   Defense of Consumers Against Holders in Due Course
**Liability of Accommodation Parties**

## TRUE-FALSE QUESTIONS

Indicate whether each statement below is true or false by circling T or F in the column on the right.

1. Under the UCC, the holder of a check has 30 days after the date of issue to present it for payment or the drawer is not liable.  T  F

2. If presentment of a promissory note is late, the maker is discharged from any liability.  T  F

3. A person whose name is forged to an instrument has a personal defense against all holders.  T  F

4. If a promissory note falls due on January 8, proper presentment can be made on January 9.  T  F

5. Kuhn, the payee of a promissory note, changed the amount due from $60 to $600. The maker can be held liable for $600.   T   F

6. Nonnegotiable instruments are subject to the rules of ordinary contracts and can be transferred by assignment.   T   F

## CASE PROBLEMS

Read the case problems below. For each problem, answer yes or no, and then explain your answer in the space provided.

1. Blair wanted to make a gift to his son Eric but did not have enough cash on hand. Instead, he gave Eric a $5,000 promissory note, payable in 30 days. Eric negotiated the note 10 days later to his friend Tompkins. When Tompkins tried to collect on the note from Blair, Blair refused to pay, claiming that there was no consideration for the execution of the note. Is this a valid defense against payment to Tompkins?

   _____
   _____
   _____

2. Curran bought a new car from Superior Motors. He paid $1,000 in cash and gave a promissory note for the balance of the purchase price. Superior negotiated the note to Calumet Bank and received cash in return. Curran then found the car's transmission was defective, and he refused to make any payments to Calumet Bank. If it had no knowledge of the defective transmission, is Calumet Bank considered a holder in due course?

   _____
   _____
   _____

3. Hackman was the holder of a time draft payable on July 8, 19___. However, Hackman discovered that July 8, 19___ fell on a Sunday, which is not a business day. Can Hackman require payment on July 8?

   _____
   _____
   _____

## MATCHING QUESTIONS

Use the following terms to identify the phrases below. On the line next to each phrase, write the letter of the term that most closely relates to it.

a. Secondary party
b. Real defense
c. Primary party
d. Notice of dishonor
e. Presentment
f. Improper presentment
g. Unauthorized completion
h. Ordinary holder
i. Holder in due course
j. Accommodation parties who sign as indorsers

_____ 1. Notification of a secondary party that can be given orally or in writing

_____ 2. A party who can enforce payment despite personal defenses

_____ 3. A demand for payment that discharges the liability of secondary parties

_____ 4. A party who has secondary liability

_____ 5. A personal defense

_____ 6. Makes a negotiable instrument void from the time of its creation

_____ 7. A demand for payment made by the holder of commercial paper

_____ 8. Has unconditional liability for the payment of commercial paper

_____ 9. Has conditional liability for the payment of commercial paper

_____ 10. The holder of a nonnegotiable instrument

## ACTIVITY: ANALYZING COMMERCIAL PAPER

The promissory note below was given to Erica Karvelos by Maria Schmidt as evidence of a $350 loan made by Karvelos to Schmidt. Karvelos indorsed the note and gave it to her niece as a wedding present. Study the note and then answer the questions that follow.

```
$ 350.00                          June 25,      19--
  Thirty days     after date   I   promise to pay
to the order of  Erica Karvelos
  Three hundred fifty                            Dollars
at The First National Bank of Boston, Boston, Massachusetts
Value received

No. _____    Due July 25, 19--      Maria A. Schmidt
```

1. Who is primarily responsible for the payment of this note? _____

2. Is Karvelos an ordinary holder or a holder in due course? _____

3. Is the niece a holder or a holder in due course? _____

4. What are the conditions that determine whether a person to whom commercial paper has been transferred is an ordinary holder or a holder in due course?

_____

_____

_____

# Chapter 22

# Checks, Electronic Fund Transfers, and the Banking System

## CHAPTER OUTLINE

The Importance of Checks
Relationship Between a Bank and Its Depositor
Duty of a Bank to Pay Checks
    Postdated Checks
    Stop-Payment Order
Obligations of a Depositor
Special Types of Checks
    Certified Checks
    Money Orders
    Cashier's Checks
    Traveler's Checks

Bank's Liability for Wrongful Payment of a Check
    Alteration of a Check
    Forgery of a Drawer's Signature
    Forgery of an Indorsement
    Missing Indorsement
    Death of the Depositor
The Collection Process
Check Processing
Electronic Banking

## TRUE-FALSE QUESTIONS

Indicate whether each statement below is true or false by circling T or F in the column on the right.

1. A stop-payment order can be telephoned to the bank.     T   F

2. A depositor has a duty to advise the bank promptly of any mistakes found in the monthly statement of bank transactions.     T   F

3. Writing a bad check is a criminal act.     T   F

4. If the drawer's negligence contributes to the alteration of a check, any loss resulting from the bank's payment of the altered check is borne by the bank.     T   F

5. A bank is liable to the drawer for paying a check on which the payee's indorsement has been forged, but may recover from the holder who presented the check to the bank.     T   F

6. A bank is in no way liable for any loss that results from its cashing a check that lacks an indorsement.    T   F

7. Some banks, by express agreement, allow certain customers to write checks for more than the amount on deposit.    T   F

8. A bank can be held liable to a drawer if it pays a postdated check before it is due and such action harms the drawer.    T   F

9. A bank can be held liable to the payee for wrongfully refusing to pay a check when sufficient funds are on deposit in the bank.    T   F

10. The drawer of a certified check can issue a stop-payment order on the check.    T   F

11. If, after checking a holder's identification, the bank is suspicious of the holder, it can refuse to honor the check without liability to the drawer.    T   F

12. A drawer who writes a check that a bank dishonors for lack of funds remains liable to the holder.    T   F

13. A cashier's check is drawn by a bank on its own funds.    T   F

14. If a bank pays a check that has been materially altered, the bank is not liable to the drawer for the amount of the alteration.    T   F

15. A bank can pay a check up to 10 days after the death of the drawer.    T   F

## MULTIPLE-CHOICE QUESTIONS

On the line next to each statement, write the letter of the best answer.

_____ 1. A written stop-payment order is effective for (a) 14 days, (b) 7 days, (c) 6 months, (d) 90 days.

_____ 2. A check that a bank draws on its own funds, payable to a certain party, is a (a) cashier's check, (b) certified check, (c) personal check, (d) money order.

_____ 3. A personal check that a bank guarantees to pay is a (a) cashier's check, (b) money order, (c) certified check, (d) traveler's check.

_____ 4. The relationship between a bank and a depositor who opens a checking account at the bank is one of (a) bailor and bailee, (b) debtor and creditor, (c) bailor and independent contractor, (d) assignor and assignee.

_____ 5. If a drawer has a check certified, the drawer (a) remains primarily liable for payment, (b) is relieved of secondary liability, (c) is discharged, (d) remains secondarily liable for payment.

_____ 6. To hold a bank liable for a forged signature, how long after the canceled check has been returned does the drawer have to report the forgery? (a) 90 days, (b) 6 months, (c) 1 year, (d) 60 days.

_____ 7. If a bank pays a check that has been materially altered, the bank (a) has no liability for the alteration, (b) is liable to the drawer for the amount of the alteration only if the drawer notifies the bank within one year after the altered check is returned to the depositor, (c) is liable only for the original amount of the check, (d) is liable only if notice of the alteration is received by the drawer within one year after the check is returned.

_____ 8. The electronic funds transfer system allows depositors to (a) make deposits and withdrawals using a computer terminal, (b) obtain traveler's checks quickly, (c) postdate checks, (d) locate a missing indorsement on a check quickly.

_____ 9. A bad check is one written by a (a) maker who has insufficient funds in a savings account, (b) drawer who has insufficient funds in a checking account, (c) drawee who has insufficient funds in a checking account, (d) depositor who has insufficient funds in a savings account.

_____ 10. After a drawer's death, a bank legally can pay or certify checks drawn before the drawer's death for (a) 90 days, (b) 60 days, (c) 5 days, (d) 10 days.

_____ 11. When a depositor tells the bank not to pay a particular check, the procedure is called (a) dishonoring the check, (b) forging the check, (c) negotiating the check, (d) stopping payment on the check.

_____ 12. A postdated check is (a) payable on demand, (b) invalid, (c) payable on its due date, (d) payable 30 days after its due date.

_____ 13. A draft issued by a bank, a private company, or the U.S. Postal Service that is used to transfer funds to a named payee is a (a) money order, (b) certificate of deposit, (c) certified check, (d) stock certificate.

_____ 14. When a check is certified, the certifying bank (a) dishonors the check, (b) draws on its own funds, (c) guarantees payment of the check, (d) draws on the funds in another bank.

_____ 15. If the name of a fictitious payee is put on a check and that name then is indorsed, the bank that pays the check (a) is liable for the full amount of the check, (b) is not liable to the drawer, (c) shares liability with the drawer, (d) shares liability with the payee.

_____ 16. An oral stop-payment order is binding on a bank for (a) 30 days, (b) 14 days, (c) 6 months, (d) 3 months.

_____ 17. A stale check is one that is more than (a) 6 weeks old, (b) 3 months old, (c) 1 year old, (d) 6 months old.

_____ 18. If a bank dishonors a check for no good reason, the customer can collect from the bank (a) only the service fee charged by the bank, (b) all damages the customer suffers, (c) any damages that cause injury to the customer's reputation resulting from a bad credit rating or from being arrested and prosecuted, (d) nothing.

_____ 19. An overdraft occurs when a (a) bank allows a customer to write checks for more than the amount of money on deposit, (b) customer writes a bad check, (c) bank cashes a check that is more than 3 months old, (d) bank cashes a check dated after its actual date of issue.

_____ 20. When a customer presents a merchant with a debit card to purchase goods, the transaction is called a(n) (a) EFTS transfer, (b) ATM transaction, (c) POS transaction, (d) VISA transaction.

## SHORT-ANSWER QUESTIONS

Answer each of the following questions in the space provided.

1. What responsibilities does a bank have to a depositor for the payment of checks written by the depositor?

   _____
   _____
   _____
   _____

2. What liability does a bank have to a depositor for wrongfully refusing to pay a holder the amount of a check written by the depositor?

   _____
   _____
   _____
   _____

3. What obligations does a depositor have to the bank in which the depositor maintains a checking account?

   _____
   _____
   _____
   _____

4. What effect does the electronic funds transfer system have on the use of checks as a method of paying bills?

   _____
   _____
   _____
   _____

5. What happens if a bank pays a check by mistake over a valid stop-payment order?

   _____
   _____
   _____
   _____

# CHAPTER 22

## MATCHING QUESTIONS

Use the following terms to identify the phrases below. On the line next to each phrase, write the letter of the term that most closely relates to it.

a. Signature card
b. Postdated check
c. Predated check
d. Traveler's check
e. Certified check
f. Material alteration
g. Stale check
h. Forged check
i. Overdraft
j. Cashier's check
k. POS transaction
l. Stop-payment order
m. COD transaction

_____ 1. A check used primarily by tourists who want a safe method of carrying funds while traveling

_____ 2. Raising the amount on the face of a check

_____ 3. A personal check that a bank guarantees to pay

_____ 4. A check that is dated after its actual date of issue

_____ 5. A check written, with the bank's permission, for more than the amount of money on deposit

_____ 6. A contract between the bank and its customer

_____ 7. A purchase transaction in which no money or checks change hands

_____ 8. An order to a bank to refuse payment of a check

_____ 9. A check drawn by a bank against its own funds

_____ 10. A check in which the drawer's signature is made without authorization

## ACTIVITY: ANALYZING CHECKS

The completed check below contains at least five errors. Study the check carefully. In the space on the next page, describe the errors.

## ACTIVITY: CASE PROBLEM

Read the case problem below. Answer yes or no, and then explain your answer in the space provided.

Frontier Phone Company issued a check in the amount of $1,000 to Hanson Manufacturing Company, one of its major customers. The check was presented for payment eleven months later to the First National Bank, which made payment on the check and charged the Frontier Phone Company's account. Frontier now seeks to recover the payment from the bank, claiming that the check was "stale." Can Frontier collect?

# Review

## Part IV Commercial Paper

**MULTIPLE-CHOICE QUESTIONS**

On the line next to each statement, write the letter of the best answer.

_____ 1. If only the signature of the indorser is written on the back of a check, it is known as a(n) (a) bearer indorsement, (b) blank indorsement, (c) order indorsement, (d) special indorsement.

_____ 2. To be a holder in due course, a person must take an instrument (a) before its due date, (b) the day after its due date, (c) 30 days after its due date, (d) 10 days after its due date.

_____ 3. The party to a draft who is ordered to make payment to the payee is called the (a) drawer, (b) maker, (c) payer, (d) drawee.

_____ 4. The defense that a person was a minor when he or she signed a note is a(n) (a) real defense, (b) invalid defense, (c) bearer defense, (d) personal defense.

_____ 5. Defenses that are not good against a holder in due course are called (a) holder defenses, (b) real defenses, (c) instrument defenses, (d) personal defenses.

_____ 6. An indorsement that limits the indorser's liability is called (a) limited, (b) restrictive, (c) qualified, (d) special.

_____ 7. To be negotiable, an instrument must be payable in (a) services or money, (b) money only, (c) money or goods, (d) U.S. currency only.

_____ 8. The maker of a draft is called the (a) drawee, (b) payor, (c) drawer, (d) payee.

_____ 9. A check that a bank draws on its own funds, payable to a certain party, is called a (a) money order, (b) draft, (c) letter of credit, (d) cashier's check.

_____ 10. A check written by a depositor, with the bank's permission, for more than the amount on deposit is called a(n) (a) presentment, (b) overdraft, (c) postdated check, (d) promissory note.

11. When the maker's name on a promissory note has been forged, the maker has a defense that is good against (a) all holders, (b) only ordinary holders, (c) only holders in due course, (d) none of these.

12. If there is a discrepancy between the amount written in words and the amount indicated in figures on a check, the amount is (a) the amount indicated in figures, (b) the difference between the two amounts, (c) the amount written in words, (d) none of these.

13. A promissory note payable in merchandise is (a) negotiable, (b) nonnegotiable, (c) illegal, (d) payable in the dollar equivalent of the merchandise.

14. The maker of a promissory note is a (a) primary party, (b) secondary party, (c) payee, (d) drawee.

15. If a primary party dishonors an instrument, notice of dishonor must be given to the secondary party within (a) 90 days, (b) 60 days, (c) a reasonable time, (d) 3 business days.

16. A check that is more than six months old is called a(n) (a) overdraft, (b) stale check, (c) bad check, (d) postdated check.

## TRUE-FALSE QUESTIONS

Indicate whether each statement below is true or false by circling T or F in the column on the right.

1. A promissory note must contain the word *IOU*.     T   F
2. A negotiable instrument can be readily transferred from one person to another.     T   F
3. *Payable on demand* means payable when the payee presents it to the person obligated to pay it.     T   F
4. A bearer instrument can be negotiated by voluntary delivery alone.     T   F
5. An alteration of commercial paper discharges the obligation of any party whose liability is changed by the alteration.     T   F
6. Delivery of a note back to the maker cancels the note.     T   F
7. The liability of secondary parties is unconditional.     T   F
8. Personal defenses are not good against holders in due course.     T   F
9. Real defenses make an instrument void from the time of its creation.     T   F
10. Without exception, a bank must honor all checks written by its depositors.     T   F
11. A bank can be held liable if it pays a postdated check before its due date.     T   F
12. A cashier's check is a personal check that a bank guarantees to pay.     T   F
13. A bank can pay checks for up to 10 days after the drawer's death.     T   F
14. Presentment is a demand for payment made by or on behalf of a holder.     T   F
15. A note or check payable in merchandise is a negotiable instrument.     T   F

## MATCHING QUESTIONS

Use the following terms to identify the phrases below. On the line next to each phrase, write the letter of the term that most closely relates to it.

a. Draft
b. Promissory note
c. Accommodation indorsement
d. Primary parties
e. Dishonor
f. Commercial paper
g. Restrictive indorsement
h. Real defenses
i. Holder in due course
j. Personal defenses

_____ 1. A written promise by one party to pay a certain amount of money to another party

_____ 2. Fraud, lack of consideration, and other defenses that are not good against holders in due course

_____ 3. An indorsement by a person who helps another by adding her or his signature to guarantee payment

_____ 4. A holder who has special rights that can be enforced against a party who is obligated to pay

_____ 5. Defenses that exist on creation of an instrument and that are good against all holders

_____ 6. Those persons who are first obligated to make payment on an instrument

_____ 7. An indorsement that limits what a party can do with an instrument

_____ 8. The different types of written instruments that can be used as a substitute for money

_____ 9. The refusal of the primary party to pay or accept an instrument when it is presented for payment

_____ 10. An order by one party to a second party to pay a certain amount of money to a third party

## SHORT-ANSWER QUESTION

Answer the following question in the space provided.

What are the advantages of paying for goods and services by check rather than with cash?

_____
_____
_____
_____

## CASE PROBLEM

On March 8, Antes writes a check for $300 payable to Goodsen in payment for goods to be received later in the month. Before the close of business on the eighth, Antes notifies the bank by telephone to stop payment on the check. On Monday, March 18, Goodsen gives the check to Bingo for value. On the nineteenth, Bingo deposits the check in his account at the First National Bank. On the twentieth, the First National Bank sends the check to its correspondent, Key Bank. On the twenty-first, Key Bank presents the check through the clearinghouse to Chase Bank. On the twenty-second, Chase Bank presents the check to Manhattan Bank, the payor bank. On March 27, the payor bank makes payment of the check final. Antes sues the payor bank for the amount of the check. Can Antes recover?

# PART V
# AGENCY, EMPLOYMENT, AND LABOR LAW

# Chapter 23

# Employer-Employee Relationship

## CHAPTER OUTLINE

**The Employment Process**
**Creation of the Employer-Employee Relationship**
**Rights of Employers**
**Rights of Employees**
   Access to Personnel Records
   Labor-Management Relations
**Terminating the Employer-Employee Relationship**
   Termination in Violation of Law
   Termination that Goes Against a Well-Defined Public Policy
   Termination Prohibited Based on an Implied Contract Term
   Discharge Affected by Employee Policies and Practices

**Legislation Affecting Employer-Employee Relations**
   Labor-Management
   Employment Discrimination
   Sexual Harassment
   Defenses
   Health and Safety
   Privacy
   Employee Protection: The Disabled, Retired, and Unemployed
   Pension Protection
   Wages, Hours, and Minors
**The Hiring of Aliens**

## TRUE-FALSE QUESTIONS

Indicate whether each statement below is true or false by circling T or F in the column on the right.

1. An employment contract for more than one year must be in writing.     T   F

2. An employee can be forced to join a union as a condition for being hired.     T   F

3. Employers have a legal right to tell employees what tasks are to be performed and how the tasks are to be performed.     T   F

4. The Fair Labor Standards Act requires certain employers to provide employees a legal minimum hourly wage plus one and a half times their regular hourly wage for all hours worked over 40 hours a week.   T   F

5. The Occupational Safety and Health Act requires employers to provide employees with safe working conditions in the buildings where they work.   T   F

6. An invention produced by the employee on the job always belongs to the employer.   T   F

7. An employer can end a contract with an employee at any time without liability.   T   F

8. If a contract does not specify a length of employment, an employee can quit a job at any time.   T   F

9. An employer has no right to dismiss an employee who consistently fails to perform.   T   F

10. Extreme negligence by an employee would prevent recovery under workers' compensation laws.   T   F

11. The federal government may not require a lie detector test of a potential employee.   T   F

12. The Civil Rights Act of 1964 prohibits discharge of an employee because of a handicap.   T   F

## CASE PROBLEMS

Read the case problems below. For each problem, answer yes or no, and then explain your answer in the space provided.

1. The Disco Roller Skating Rink advertised in a local newspaper for a male floor guard. Schantz, a female, applied for the job and was turned down by the rink manager, who claimed that she could not handle the job because it was for a "tough man." Can Schantz legally be turned down for this reason?

___

2. Steeper was hired under a 3-year contract as head accountant for the Alliance Tool Company. When the owner discovered that Steeper was giving a competing tool company confidential information about Alliance, he fired Steeper. Steeper sued for breach of contract, claiming that because his contract had not expired, he could not be fired. Was Steeper correct?

___

3. Tydings Garage was required by state law to provide ventilating equipment to protect its workers. Because this equipment was not installed, one mechanic suffered carbon monoxide poisoning and was unable to work for several weeks. Was the mechanic entitled to benefits under workers' compensation?

___

4. Baxter was employed by Veteran Motors as a mechanic. He worked from 8:00 a.m. to 5:00 p.m., with an hour for lunch. After many warnings, Baxter continued to take much more than an hour for lunch. Would Veteran Motors be justified in discharging Baxter?

___

5. Marston, who is 70 years old, applied for a job at Acme Steel but was turned down because of his age. Marston claims that Acme cannot discriminate against him because of his age. Is Marston correct?

___

6. Barstow entered the United States on a tourist visa. She was offered a good job and decided to remain here Is she permitted to accept the offer of employment?

___

7. Curtis believed that his personnel file contained reference letters that might be unfavorable to him. He claims that he has an absolute right to examine his file. Is he correct?

___

## MULTIPLE-CHOICE QUESTIONS

Read the information below. Then, on the line next to each statement, write the letter of the best answer.

Curran was employed by Bond Wholesale Foods to deliver food supplies to grocery stores.

_____ 1. Curran legally is known as a(n) (a) assignee, (b) employee, (c) merchant, (d) employer.

_____ 2. After Curran had been employed for some time, he tried to organize his fellow workers into a union. Curran was allowed to organize his fellow workers, without interference from Bond Wholesale Foods, under the provisions of the (a) National Labor Relations Act, (b) Fair Labor Standards Act, (c) Wage and Hour Law, (d) Occupational Safety and Health Act.

_____ 3. As a result of Curran's efforts, the workers formed a union that was recognized by Bond Wholesale Foods. Curran, as the union's representative, negotiated a contract with higher wages and improved working conditions. Because both the employees and the company approved the contract, it is called a(n) (a) workers' agreement, (b) collective bargaining agreement, (c) equal pay agreement, (d) workers' compensation agreement.

_____ 4. Curran, while making a delivery, fell and broke his leg. As a result, he could not work for several weeks. Curran's medical bills, as well as a weekly income while he could not work, were paid under (a) unemployment insurance, (b) the Fair Labor Standards Act, (c) the Occupational Safety and Health Act, (d) state workers' compensation laws.

_____ 5. Bond Wholesale Foods prohibits its employees from conducting anything other than company business during working hours. Curran runs a part-time storm window business on the side. While making deliveries for Bond, he often meets with customers for his storm window business. If Bond discovers what Curran is doing, it could (a) report Curran to the EEOC, (b) report Curran to OSHA, (c) fire Curran, (d) have Curran arrested.

_____ 6. The burden of proving that a discriminatory labor practice is necessary for the proper performance of a job is on the (a) union, (b) employer, (c) U.S. Department of Labor, (d) employee.

# Chapter 24

# Principal-Agent Relationship

## CHAPTER OUTLINE

The Agency Concept
Classification of Agents
    General Agents
    Special Agents
    Gratuitous Agents
Who May Serve as Principal and Agent
Relationships Similar to Agencies
    Employer-Employee
    Independent Contractor
Creation of the Principal-Agent Relationship
    By Contract
    By Appearance
    By Ratification
    By Necessity
Obligations of the Agent to the Principal
    Obedience
    Loyalty
    Reasonable Skill
    Accurate Accounting
    Communication

Obligations of the Principal to the Agent
    Compensation
    Reimbursement
    Indemnity
    Safe Working Conditions
    Cooperation
Termination of the Principal-Agent Relationship
    Fulfillment of Purpose
    Mutual Agreement
    Revocation of Authority
    Renunciation by the Agent
    Operation of Law
    Subsequent Destruction or Illegality
Notifying Third Parties of the Termination

## MULTIPLE-CHOICE QUESTIONS

On the line next to each statement, write the letter of the best answer.

   \_\_\_\_   1. The right of an agent to require the principal to pay for personal losses incurred by the agent while the agent is performing business for the principal is called (a) rebate, (b) reimbursement, (c) indemnification, (d) recovery.

2. Browning hired Barrett to paint her house for the sum of $2,500. Barrett would be classified as a(n) (a) general agent, (b) special agent, (c) independent contractor, (d) employee.

3. All profits that result from an agency (a) belong solely to the agent, (b) belong solely to the principal, (c) are divided equally between the principal and the agent, (d) are divided according to the agreement between the principal and the agent.

4. A real estate agent hired to sell a house is considered a(n) (a) independent contractor, (b) employee, (c) general agent, (d) special agent.

5. A principal legally can appoint an agent by (a) a written contract only, (b) an oral contract only, (c) putting a notice in a newspaper, (d) either a written or an oral contract.

6. A person can act (a) both as an employee and an independent contractor, (b) both as an employee and an agent, (c) both as an employer and an employee, (d) all of the above.

7. Agents who do not receive compensation are called (a) free agents, (b) special agents, (c) gratuitous agents, (d) general agents.

8. In an emergency, an agency relationship can be created by (a) ratification, (b) appearance, (c) duress, (d) necessity.

9. The major difference between a special agent and a general agent is the (a) amount of compensation paid, (b) way in which the agency is created, (c) authority given to the agent, (d) type of work the principal does.

10. A formal written document authorizing one person to act for another is called a(n) (a) appointment, (b) power of attorney, (c) employment contract, (d) bailment agreement.

11. When an agent makes a contract for a deceased principal, the contract is (a) binding on the agent, (b) binding on the principal's estate, (c) voidable, (d) void.

12. Doan authorized Marple to sell Doan's car for not less than $2,000 for a commission of 10%. Marple sold the car for $2,400. How much must Marple give Doan? (a) $2,000, (b) $2,000 less the commission, (c) $2,200, (d) $2,400 less the commission.

13. An agent is given formal written authority to sign checks for her principal. This formal written authorization is called a(n) (a) affidavit, (b) power of attorney, (c) notary, (d) certification.

14. Morales, a general agent for the Kincaid Manufacturing Company, was notified of the company's bankruptcy. Which of the following statements about the principal-agent relationship is *true*? (a) Contracts made by an agent after the bankruptcy of the principal are binding on the principal, (b) a general agent is liable as a guarantor of the bankrupt principal's unpaid accounts, (c) the principal's bankruptcy has no effect on the principal-agent agreement, (d) the bankruptcy of the principal terminates the agency agreement.

15. A principal-agent relationship can be terminated by (a) the death of a third party, (b) the request of a third party, (c) mutual agreement between principal and agent, (d) the bankruptcy of a third party.

## MATCHING QUESTIONS

Use the following terms to indicate the way in which the agency relationship was created. On the line next to each description, write the letter of the term that most closely relates to it.

a. Agency created by contract
b. Agency created by appearance
c. Agency created by ratification
d. Agency created by necessity

_____ 1. Arlis left Marvin, a friend, at her fruit and vegetable stand with instructions only to tell customers that the stand would open two hours late because of an emergency. While Arlis was gone, Marvin sold fruit and vegetables to several customers.

_____ 2. Calkins used Green's car to drive Green's parents to a family reunion 50 miles away. The car developed engine trouble, and Calkins had to have it repaired in order to reach the destination. Calkins presented the repair bill to Green.

_____ 3. Beaty signed a 3-year written contract to manage Richard's Tour Guide Agency in New York City.

_____ 4. Downs asked Erlman to purchase a stereo and charge it to her (Downs's) account with her credit card. She asked Erlman to pay no more than $750. Erlman charged a stereo that cost $1,000. When the bill arrived, Downs paid it in full.

_____ 5. Count is employed under a 5-year contract as a sales representative for Arnold's Clothes Unlimited. Count sold merchandise on credit to Barnes's Department Store, which must pay the bill in 30 days.

## CASE PROBLEMS

Read the case problems below. For each problem, answer yes or no, and then explain your answer in the space provided.

1. Todd was a salesperson for the Marcum Textbook Company. The company provided her with a car to travel to various high schools within a specific territory in Wyoming. While she was driving within the speed limit on a highway, the car was struck by a hit-and-run driver, causing $200 in damages. Todd paid for the repairs out of her own pocket, but Marcum refused to repay Todd, claiming it had no legal obligation to do so. Was the company correct?

_____

_____

_____

2. O'Brien, a retiree, decided to invest in a fast-growing company that was selling its stock for $20 a share. He appointed Walford, a person with a good business background, as his agent to buy 50 shares of Xeon stock. Unknown to O'Brien, Walford already had purchased 100 shares of Xeon stock for himself when it was being offered at $10 a share. Walford then sold 50 of his shares to O'Brien for $20 a share and kept the profit. When O'Brien found this out, he demanded that Walford take the stock back, stating that what Walford did was a breach of trust. Did Walford have to comply?

3. DiFabio, an adult, hired Nichols, a minor, as general manager of a service station and authorized him to buy supplies. Nichols contracted to buy some supplies that were not needed. DiFabio claimed that the contract was not valid because Nichols was a minor and therefore could not act as an agent. Was DiFabio legally correct in claiming that he was not bound by Nichols's contract?

4. As purchasing agent for the Delton Company, Millson often bought materials from the Howard Supply Company. After he was discharged by Delton, Millson bought something for himself from Howard Supply but charged it to Delton. Howard Supply knew nothing about Millson's dismissal. Was Howard Supply able to hold the Delton Company liable for Millson's purchase?

5. Fox, who was going into the army, contracted with Scutti Auto Sales to sell his car for a commission. Scutti Auto Sales advanced $500 to Fox, with the understanding that the advance would be paid back out of the proceeds of the sale. Three weeks later, before the car was sold, Fox changed his mind and tried to terminate the agency. Was Fox legally able to terminate the agency?

## ACTIVITY: IDENTIFYING VIOLATIONS

In each of the following situations, the underlined party is liable for violating a specific principal or agent obligation. In the space provided, identify the obligation that has been violated.

1. <u>Conte</u> collected credit payments from Nill's dry cleaning customers. Because he put the money from the collections into his regular bank account, he could not determine the correct amount to send Nill.

2. <u>Mendon</u> sent Roberts, one of his traveling salespersons, to investigate sales possibilities in a distant city. Mendon later refused to pay Roberts for his trip expenses.

3. <u>Baskin</u> told Robbins, his salesperson, to sell door to door in a neighboring town. While carrying out his work, Robbins was arrested and fined for not having a license required by town ordinance. Baskin refused to pay Robbins the amount of the fine.

4. <u>Burley</u> agreed to sell Arno's boat for a commission. Burley previously had been hired to purchase a boat for Fisher. Without disclosing either agreement, Burley bought Arno's boat, sold it to Fisher, and tried to collect a commission from both.

5. <u>Thayer</u>, a sales clerk for Quarrels Card Shop, was told to place a certain brand of greeting card on sale. Thayer placed all of the greeting cards in the shop on sale, resulting in a considerable loss to Quarrels.

## ACTIVITY: FINDING THE FACTS

Read the following paragraph. Then, in the space provided, answer the questions below.

Vonnie Everard owned several apartment buildings in Providence, Rhode Island. Because she planned to take a European trip during June, she composed and signed a power of attorney designating Carmen Longo, also of Providence, as her agent. The power of attorney read, in part, as follows: "I, Vonnie Everard, hereby appoint Carmen Longo to collect rent from tenants in all my apartment buildings and to pay all bills connected with these apartments by signing and executing checks as my agent." Everard set up a special checking account at the Lincoln Alliance Bank in Providence. Longo was directed to place all rent money collected in that account and to write any necessary checks on that account.

1. Is every agency created by means of a power of attorney like the one in the example above?

2. Is Longo classified as a general or a special agent? _____

3. Could the authority given to Longo have been given orally? _____

4. According to the power of attorney, does Longo have the authority to authorize repairs to any of the apartments? _____

5. Longo did not follow Everard's instructions for paying bills. As a result, Everard had to pay a late charge to many companies. Can Everard collect from Longo the amount of the late charge? _____

# Chapter 25

# Principal-Agent, Employer-Employee, and Third-Party Relationship

## CHAPTER OUTLINE

**Liability of Principal and Employer to Third Parties**
  Contract Liability of Principal
  Tort Liability of Principal and Employer
**Liability of Agent to Third Parties**
  Contract Liability of Agent
  Tort Liability of Agent and Employee
**Criminal Liability of Principal, Agent, Employer, and Employee**

## COMPLETION QUESTIONS

In the statements below, important words have been omitted. Fill in the blanks to complete each statement.

1. The direct authority that an agent is given by a principal is called _____ authority.

2. A principal whose identity is unknown to a third party is called a(n) _____ principal.

3. A principal can be held liable for a(n) _____ committed by an agent while the agent is pursuing agency business.

4. A principal can approve the actions of an unauthorized agent by _____ them.

5. A power of attorney is an example of _____ authority in a principal-agent relationship.

6. The authority that a principal leads third parties to believe that an agent has is called _____ authority.

7. If an agent acts within the scope of his or her authority, the agent is not considered a(n) _____ to a contract with a third party.

8. An agent can be held personally liable if the agent fails to disclose the principal's identity to a(n) _____.

9. The authority that an agent has to perform duties not expressly given by the principal is called _____ authority.

10. A principal or employer is not liable for a _____ committed by an agent or employee.

## MULTIPLE-CHOICE QUESTIONS

On the line next to each statement, write the letter of the best answer.

____ 1. Frost was hired as general manager of Casey's snow plowing business. As general manager, Frost has (a) implied authority to hire and fire people to help clear snow, (b) implied authority to sell the snow plowing business, (c) implied authority to purchase new equipment, (d) express authority to cancel equipment orders placed by Casey.

____ 2. A principal generally is not liable for her or his agent's (a) torts, (b) contracts, (c) criminal acts, (d) false statements.

____ 3. A principal whose identity is not known to a third party with whom the agent makes a contract is called a(n) (a) independent contractor, (b) fiduciary, (c) undisclosed principal, (d) irrevocable principal.

____ 4. Apparent authority is (a) express authority, (b) implied authority, (c) the extent of the agent's authority, (d) authority that a principal leads third parties to believe the agent has.

____ 5. When a principal approves of an agent's unauthorized act, the principal has (a) ratified the act, (b) rejected the act, (c) elected to either ratify or reject the act, (d) acted in the scope of authority.

____ 6. A principal generally is bound by contracts an agent makes with third parties on behalf of the principal if the agent acts (a) quickly, (b) within the scope of authority, (c) to the principal's advantage, (d) on commission.

____ 7. When a third party discovers the identity of an undisclosed principal, the third party can hold (a) both the principal and the agent liable on the contract, (b) only the principal liable on the contract, (c) only the agent liable, (d) either the principal or the agent liable but not both.

____ 8. If the agent does not include the principal's name on a written contract, (a) both the principal and the agent are bound by the contract, (b) only the agent is bound by the contract, (c) only the principal is bound by the contract, (d) the contract is not binding.

9. A person who pretends to be an agent (a) is personally liable to a third party, (b) binds the principal, (c) binds the third party, (d) has the power of ratification.

10. The proper signature by an agent, R. M. Figs, on behalf of a principal, Norman Corner, is (a) R. M. Figs, (b) Norman Corner by R. M. Figs, Agent, (c) R. M. Figs, Agent, (c) Norman Corner, Principal.

## CASE PROBLEMS

Read the case problems below. For each problem, answer yes or no, and then explain your answer in the space provided.

1. While she was away on a business trip, Martin, a store owner, left Maxim, one of her salesclerks, in charge of the store. During this time, a heavy rainstorm flooded the basement. Maxim hired two men to remove some merchandise from the basement to save it from water damage. Was Martin legally obligated to pay the two men?

2. Lerner, a sales agent for Burke, sold jewelry to Polk, stating that it was platinum. Later, when Polk learned that the jewelry was white gold, he sued Burke. Burke claimed that he was not liable because he had not authorized Lerner to make the statement about the jewelry. Was Burke liable for damages?

3. Hammer was employed as a salesperson by the Outgoing Merchandise Company. In the company's name, with a view to boosting sales, she entered into a contract with a TV station for a series of spot announcements. The Outgoing Company refused to pay for the advertising, claiming that Hammer did not have the authority to buy TV spots. Was Outgoing liable to the TV station?

4. Folwell, a plumber, needed a certain wrench to complete a job. He asked Burns, his employee, to buy one at a local hardware store. Finding the store closed, Burns broke into it and stole the wrench. Is Folwell liable for Burns' crime?

5. ABC Motor Lines held a company party at a restaurant and used one of its buses to transport some employees to the party. The bus driver was speeding and hit a taxi, injuring its passengers. Is ABC liable for the injuries?

_____
_____
_____

# Review

## Part V
## Agency, Employment, and Labor Law

### TRUE-FALSE QUESTIONS

Indicate whether each statement below is true or false by circling T or F in the column on the right.

1. One obligation of an agent to a principal is indemnification.     T  F
2. Implied authority is a type of actual authority.     T  F
3. If a principal terminates an agent's actual authority, the agent's apparent authority automatically is terminated as well.     T  F
4. If an agent refuses to continue to work for the principal, the principal-agent relationship automatically is terminated.     T  F
5. A person can be an employee and also act as an agent for the employer.     T  F
6. A principal-agent relationship is created only through an oral or written contract.     T  F
7. Under the Occupational Safety and Health Act, employers must provide employees with safe working conditions.     T  F
8. An employee who is covered by workers' compensation laws is entitled to certain benefits if injured on the job, regardless of whether the employee was at fault.     T  F
9. A person can act as an agent for both parties to a transaction even if neither party is aware of the agent's dual status.     T  F
10. An agent who makes a secret profit is entitled to keep the money even if the principal discovers it and demands its return.     T  F

## MULTIPLE-CHOICE QUESTIONS

Read the information below. Then, on the line next to each statement, write the letter of the best answer.

Whitmore, a used-car dealer, hired Chambers as a sales representative for six months at a weekly salary of $200 plus commission.

_____ 1. Chambers paid for some repairs that were required when she was demonstrating a car to a customer. Her right to collect this amount from Whitmore is called the right of (a) accounting, (b) compensation, (c) indemnification, (d) reimbursement.

_____ 2. If, after Chambers had sold several used cars, Whitmore found that she was a minor, (a) Chambers's contracts still would be valid, (b) Chambers's contracts would be voidable, (c) Chambers's contracts would be invalid, (d) Chambers could not legally make any more contracts.

_____ 3. After a customer purchased a used car on the basis of Chambers's remark that the car was "a bargain at $1,500," the customer found that the engine was in very bad condition. The customer can hold Whitmore legally liable for (a) fraud, (b) undue influence, (c) deceit, (d) nothing.

_____ 4. Chambers is a(n) (a) general agent, (b) special agent, (c) implied agent, (d) public agent.

_____ 5. If a customer is injured in an accident caused solely by Chambers's careless driving, that customer can sue Whitmore because the principal (a) has a duty to live up to the terms of the contract, (b) is bound by any knowledge acquired by the agent, (c) is liable for torts of an agent acting within the scope of the agency, (d) has a duty to compensate the agent for any loss or damage.

## CASE PROBLEMS

Read the case problems below. For each problem, answer yes or no, and then explain your answer in the space provided.

1. Bauman agreed to act as general manager of the Furniture Mart for 3 years. Is it necessary for this agreement to be in writing?

_____

_____

_____

2. Franklin worked as a cook in the Little Chef Restaurant. Melanson, the owner of the restaurant, did not anticipate the large Thanksgiving Day business, and so authorized Franklin to buy several food items at a local food market where Melanson often shopped. Was Franklin a special agent?

_____

_____

_____

3. Drake, the owner of Rent-A-Car, hired Pincus to purchase five new cars for the business. On the day that Pincus made the purchase, Drake, who was on vacation, died in a hotel fire. Was the contract made by Pincus valid?

4. Pitnell authorized her office manager to employ an additional bookkeeper. The office manager hired a bookkeeper and a clerk typist. Pitnell refused to pay the clerk typist's salary, claiming she was not liable because the office manager had exceeded her authority. Was Pitnell correct?

5. Jackson hired Ames, a minor, to manage a store. Without Jackson's knowledge, Ames bought merchandise for the store from the Rustic Supply Company. Jackson later refused to pay for the merchandise on the grounds that he was not bound by a minor's contract. Was Jackson bound by the contract?

# PART VI

# BUSINESS ORGANIZATION AND REGULATION

# Chapter 26

# Sole Proprietorships and Partnerships

## CHAPTER OUTLINE

Forms of Business Ownership
The Sole Proprietorship
The Partnership
    Types of Partners and Partnerships
    Forming a Partnership
    Operation of a Partnership
    Termination of the Partnership
Limited Partnership
    Forming a Limited Partnership

Role and Liability of the Partners
Dissolution
Limited Liability Company
Other Forms of Business Organization
    Joint Venture
    Syndicate
    Cooperative

## TRUE-FALSE QUESTIONS

Indicate whether each statement below is true or false by circling T or F in the column on the right.

1. The sole proprietorship is the most flexible form of business organization.     T    F
2. In most states, certain formalities are required to establish a sole proprietorship.     T    F
3. A sole proprietor who uses a trade name must register that name in a public office.     T    F
4. Lawyers or doctors can practice their professions in partnerships.     T    F
5. To establish a partnership, there always must be a partnership agreement.     T    F
6. If a partnership is formed by an agreement, the agreement must be in writing.     T    F
7. In the absence of an agreement, a partnership can be implied from the actions of the partners.     T    F

8. If a partnership wants to admit new partners, all of the existing partners must agree to the change.  T  F

9. All partners in a partnership can share equally in the profits even if they do not share equally in management responsibilities.  T  F

10. If there are three equal partners in a business, one of them can sell a third of the assets to someone else.  T  F

## SHORT-ANSWER QUESTIONS

Answer each of the following questions in the space provided.

1. Explain the difference between a trading and a nontrading partnership.
   _____
   _____

2. List and briefly explain five different types of partners.
   _____
   _____
   _____
   _____
   _____

3. Explain the basic difference between a general partnership and a limited partnership.
   _____
   _____
   _____

4. Explain the difference between a limited partnership and a limited liability company.
   _____
   _____
   _____
   _____

## MULTIPLE-CHOICE QUESTIONS

On the line next to each statement, write the letter of the best answer.

_____ 1. The most common form of business organization is the (a) corporation, (b) limited partnership, (c) sole proprietorship, (d) partnership.

_____ 2. An inactive partner known by the public to be a partner is called a (a) limited partner, (b) silent partner, (c) secret partner, (d) dormant partner.

_____ 3. The liability of partners as a group and individually is called (a) collective liability, (b) general liability, (c) group liability, (d) joint and several liability.

4. Unless otherwise agreed, the partners' shares of the profits are (a) equal, (b) based on the amount each partner invested, (c) based on the partners' ages, (d) based on the partners' salaries.

5. The termination of a partnership is called (a) disassociation, (b) cessation, (c) dispartnership, (d) dissolution.

6. When two or more persons conduct a business as a formal partnership without making a partnership agreement, they have formed a(n) (a) express partnership, (b) partnership by implication, (c) illegal partnership, (d) corporation.

7. One disadvantage of a sole proprietorship is (a) lack of flexibility, (b) the difficulty of setting it up, (c) the expense of setting it up, (d) the owner's risk.

8. A medical partnership is classified as a (a) trading partnership, (b) limited partnership, (c) joint venture, (d) nontrading partnership.

9. A partnership formed to last six months (a) can be made with an agreement, (b) must be formed with a written agreement, (c) is invalid, (d) is unconstitutional.

10. Termination of a partnership can result from (a) the death of a partner, (b) the bankruptcy of a partner, (c) the retirement of a partner, (d) all of these.

## CASE PROBLEMS

Read the case problems below. For each problem, answer yes or no, and then explain your answer in the space provided.

1. Hill and Doan became partners in an automobile business. Their partnership agreement contained no provision for dividing profits and losses. At the end of the year, Hill claimed that he was entitled to more of the profits than Doan because he spent more time managing the business than Doan did. Was Hill correct?

2. Jansen and Johnson operated a grocery store as partners. Jansen told Johnson not to buy a certain product because it was not selling well. Johnson disregarded Jansen's request and bought a large quantity of the product. Jansen refused to pay the bill, claiming that her orders had been disregarded. Was the partnership obligated to pay for the product?

3. Fain and Warner were partners in a service station. Because of personal business problems, Fain had to file a petition in bankruptcy. Warner claimed that the partnership could continue. Was Warner correct?

# ACTIVITY: ANALYZING A PARTNERSHIP AGREEMENT

Study the partnership agreement below and then answer the questions on the next page.

---

PARTNERSHIP AGREEMENT

This agreement, made June 20, 19--, between Penelope Wolfburg of 783A South Street, Hazelton, Idaho, and Ingrid Swenson of RR 5, Box 96, Hazelton, Idaho.

1. The above named persons have this day formed a partnership that shall operate under the name of W-S Jewelers, located at 85 Broad Street, Hazelton, Idaho 83335, and shall engage in jewelry sales and repairs.

2. The duration of this agreement will be for a term of fifteen (15) years, beginning on June 20, 19--, or for a shorter term if agreed on in writing by both partners.

3. The initial investment by each partner will be as follows: Penelope Wolfburg, assets and liabilities of Wolfburg's Jewelry Store, valued at a capital investment of $40,000; Ingrid Swenson, cash of $20,000. These investments are partnership property.

4. Each partner will give her time, skill, and attention to the operation of this partnership and will engage in no other business enterprise unless permission is granted in writing by the other partner.

5. The salary for each partner will be as follows: Penelope Wolfburg, $40,000 per year; Ingrid Swenson, $30,000 per year. Neither partner may withdraw cash or other assets from the business without express permission in writing from the other partner. All profits and losses of the business will be shared as follows: Penelope Wolfburg, 60 percent; Ingrid Swenson, 40 percent.

6. On the dissolution of the partnership due to termination of this agreement, or to written permission by each of the partners, or to the death or incapacitation of one or both partners, a new contract may be entered into by the partners or the sole continuing partner has the option to purchase the other partner's interest in the business at a price that shall not exceed the balance in the terminating partner's capital account. The payment shall be made in cash in equal quarterly installments from the date of termination.

7. At the conclusion of this contract, unless it is agreed by both partners to continue the operation of the business under a new contract, the assets of the partnership, after the liabilities are paid, will be divided in proportion to the balance in each partner's capital account on that date.

_Penelope Wolfburg_
Penelope Wolfburg

_Ingrid Swenson_
Ingrid Swenson

_June 20, 19--_
Date

_June 20, 19--_
Date

1. Under the statute of frauds, could this agreement have been oral?

2. What restriction does this agreement place on the partners' ability to pursue other business enterprises?

3. How will the partners share the profits and losses of the business?

4. If Swenson wants to borrow $2,000 from the assets of the business, does the partnership agreement allow her to do so?

5. Wolfburg learned that a large jewelry collection was to be auctioned off at an estate sale. She bought several items at the auction and then resold them at a considerable profit. Was Wolfburg correct in claiming that she was not required to share the earnings from this transaction with Swenson?

6. What provisions does the agreement list for terminating the partnership?

# Chapter 27

# Corporations and Franchising

## CHAPTER OUTLINE

Nature of a Corporation
    Profit Corporations
    Nonprofit Corporations
Forming a Corporation
    Articles of Incorporation
Ownership of a Corporation
Rights of Stockholders
Liabilities of Stockholders
Financing a Corporation
    Equity—Stock: Common and Preferred
    Debt—Bonds and Loans
Managing a Corporation
    Powers of a Corporation

Powers and Duties of Directors
Powers and Duties of Officers
Terminating a Corporation
Purchase of Assets and Stock
    Purchase of Assets
    Purchase of Stock
Advantages and Disadvantages of
    Corporations
    Investor Protection
Franchising

## CASE PROBLEMS

Read the case problems below. For each problem, answer yes or no, and then explain your answer in the space provided.

1. The directors of the Brennan Corporation were negligent in handling the corporation's business, and the company lost money. The stockholders then voted to dissolve the corporation. Did the common stockholders have first claim against the assets?

_____
_____
_____

2. The Rogers Corporation was organized to manufacture electronic equipment. The board of directors voted (a) to borrow $1,000,000 to expand the company and (b) to go into the plumbing business. Neither action was authorized by the charter and bylaws. Were the stockholders able to invalidate both these actions?

_____
_____
_____
_____

3. Segal and Finch owned a pizza shop. Business was good and they decided to expand. What would be the advantages of expanding by franchising their business?

_____
_____
_____
_____

## MATCHING QUESTIONS

Use the following terms to identify the phrases below. On the line next to each phrase, write the letter of the term that most closely relates to it.

a. Board of directors
b. Preferred stock
c. Dividend
d. Proxy
e. Ultra vires
f. Common stock
g. Stock certificate
h. Stockholder
i. Merger
j. Articles of incorporation
k. Tender offer

_____ 1. The written permission given by stockholders to someone else to vote for them
_____ 2. A type of stock entitled to receive dividends provided profits are earned
_____ 3. The joining of two corporations, with one surviving
_____ 4. Stock having a prior right to receive a dividend
_____ 5. Exceeding the powers of the corporation
_____ 6. The application for permission to incorporate
_____ 7. A person having an interest in a corporation
_____ 8. The group that sets corporate policy
_____ 9. A document showing part ownership of a corporation
_____ 10. The part of corporate profits paid to a stockholder
_____ 11. A public offer to stockholders to purchase their shares

## MULTIPLE-CHOICE QUESTIONS

On the line next to each statement, write the letter of the best answer.

_____ 1. To organize a private corporation, permission first is required from (a) the courts, (b) the state government, (c) a judge, (d) the federal government.

_____ 2. A corporation that is organized in one state and does business there is known in that state as a (a) local corporation, (b) foreign corporation, (c) regional corporation, (d) domestic corporation.

_____ 3. The first formal step in incorporating a corporation is drafting and filing the (a) articles of incorporation, (b) company bylaws, (c) stock certificates, (d) minutes of incorporation.

_____ 4. The number, type, and nature of stocks issued by a corporation are known collectively as its (a) liquidity factor, (b) stock composition, (c) capitalization, (d) no-par factor.

_____ 5. Corporate stock that has a prior claim to dividends over all other classes of stock is called (a) cumulative stock, (b) participating stock, (c) no-par stock, (d) preferred stock.

_____ 6. General policy for a corporation is determined by the (a) stockholders, (b) legislature, (c) directors, (d) New York Stock Exchange.

_____ 7. Officers of a corporation are hired by (a) the directors, (b) the stockholders, (c) the state, (d) other officers.

_____ 8. Most corporations are incorporated for a(n) (a) term of 10 years, (b) term of 100 years, (c) indefinite term, (d) term of 75 years.

_____ 9. When two corporations join together and a new one is formed, the result is called a(n) (a) merger, (b) joint venture, (c) amalgamation, (d) consolidation.

_____ 10. All of the following terminate corporate existence *except* (a) the end of the corporate term, (b) stockholder agreement, (c) revocation of the corporate charter, (d) a change in ownership.

_____ 11. When one corporation buys another corporation, the purchase is called a(n) (a) consolidation, (b) merger, (c) amalgamation, (d) proxy.

_____ 12. A corporation organized to operate a state hospital is an example of a (a) public corporation, (b) nonprofit corporation, (c) common stock corporation, (d) municipal corporation.

_____ 13. If a corporation organized to build homes began selling used cars instead, the action would be considered (a) sua sponte, (b) de bonis non, (c) ultra vires, (d) inter vivos.

_____ 14. In Ohio, an Idaho corporation that does business in Ohio is called a(n) (a) domestic corporation, (b) foreign corporation, (c) public corporation, (d) common stock corporation.

_____ 15. Directors of a corporation are elected by the (a) stockholders, (b) state, (c) officers, (d) federal government.

_____ 16. A stockholder's written authorization allowing another person to cast her or his vote is called (a) ultra vires, (b) a stock certificate, (c) a pre-emptive right, (d) a proxy.

_____ 17. Nonprofit corporations can be organized to (a) provide charitable services, (b) earn money, (c) operate without a charter, (d) issue stock.

18. The board of directors of a corporation usually is elected for a period of (a) 1 year, (b) 2 years, (c) 5 years, (d) 10 years.

19. Two types of private corporations are (a) stock and nonstock, (b) profit and nonprofit, (c) limited and general, (d) common and preferred.

20. All stockholders in a corporation have the right to (a) receive dividends, (b) vote on corporate matters, (c) sell their stock, (d) all of the above.

## SHORT-ANSWER QUESTIONS

Read the following paragraph, and then answer the questions in the space provided.

Salerno and Peterson are organizing a corporation in Indiana to manufacture and market solar heating panels. They have chosen the name Icarus, Inc., even though there already is a company in Indiana named Icarus, Ltd., which manufactures sunglasses. They plan to issue 200,000 shares of stock in the corporation. In drawing up the bylaws, Salerno wants to include a provision that in the event of his death, the corporation will be dissolved.

1. Will Salerno and Peterson be allowed to use the name Icarus, Inc.? Why or why not?

2. What are the advantages of organizing this company as a corporation rather than as a partnership?

3. Can Salerno insist that in the event of his death the corporation be dissolved?

4. Like most corporations, this company will be subject to double taxation. Explain double taxation.

5. Cortillo buys 1,500 shares of stock in the corporation. After one year, the company declares an annual dividend of $1.25 per share. How much will Cortillo receive?

   _____

6. Describe the ways in which this corporation can be dissolved.

   _____
   _____
   _____
   _____

# Chapter 28

# Government Regulation of Business

## CHAPTER OUTLINE

The Need for Government Regulation
The Authority of Government to Regulate Business
Areas of Government Regulation
    Preventing Monopolies
    Maintaining Fair Competition
    Taxation

Regulating Crucial Industries
Securities Regulation
Preserving the General Welfare and the Environment
**How Government Regulations Are Enforced**
Licensing and Liability of Professionals

## MULTIPLE-CHOICE QUESTIONS

On the line next to each statement, write the letter of the best answer.

_____ 1. Government regulation of business is designed to protect (a) consumers, (b) employees, (c) stockholders, (d) all of these.

_____ 2. The basic power of governments to regulate business is called the (a) commerce power, (b) police power, (c) regulatory power, (d) public power.

_____ 3. Business activity that is conducted solely within the boundaries of a state is called (a) domestic commerce, (b) interstate commerce, (c) intrastate commerce, (d) foreign commerce.

_____ 4. The power to regulate interstate commerce comes from (a) the individual states, (b) the U.S. Constitution, (c) local governments, (d) the United Nations Charter.

_____ 5. Antitrust regulation at the federal level is based on the (a) Sherman Act, (b) Jackson Act, (c) Nixon Act, (d) Reagan Act.

_____ 6. The Federal Trade Commission Act of 1914 prohibits (a) monopolies, (b) mergers, (c) price discrimination, (d) unfair competition.

_____ 7. The antitrust laws apply to all the following organizations *except* (a) labor unions, (b) railroads, (c) steel companies, (d) lumber companies.

_____ 8. Most governmental regulations of business are enforced by (a) the police, (b) local government, (c) administrative agencies, (d) the U.S. Congress.

_____ 9. The sale and trading of securities is regulated by the (a) Federal Reserve Board, (b) New York Stock Exchange, (c) Securities and Exchange Commission, (d) Bank of the United States.

_____ 10. Laws prohibiting the sale of certain products on certain days of the week are called (a) sunshine laws, (b) closing laws, (c) common laws, (d) Sunday laws.

_____ 11. Federal legislation prohibiting practices that lessen competition is known as (a) The Sherman Act, (b) The First Trade Act, (c) The Miller-Tydings Act, (d) The Carter-Glass Act.

_____ 12. Competitors who divide a market among themselves to lessen competition are engaging in an illegal restraint of trade known as (a) a tying agreement, (b) market allocation, (c) an exclusive dealing arrangement, (d) a monopoly.

## SHORT-ANSWER QUESTIONS

Answer each of the following questions in the space provided.

1. List five important areas in which government regulates business to protect the public.

   _____
   _____
   _____
   _____
   _____

2. Administrative agencies have legislative, executive, and judicial powers. Give a brief explanation of each type of power.

   _____
   _____
   _____

## CASE PROBLEMS

Read the case problems below and then state which agency or agencies you would consult for help in each situation.

1. You operate a retail store selling musical instruments. A large chain store that also sells musical instruments opens for business a few blocks from your store. The owners of that store spread a rumor that your pianos are made of inferior materials and will not last more than six months.

   Agency: _____

2. You work for a machine tool company and operate a lathe. It is common practice for employers to provide employees with safety glasses to prevent injury caused by pieces of metal thrown from the machines. Your employer, however, refuses to provide you with this type of safety equipment.

   Agency: _____

3. You buy 50,000 shares of stock in a uranium mining company and then discover that the company did not disclose the fact that uranium has never been found in the area in which the company plans to do business. You want to return the stock and get your money back, but the company refuses.

   Agency: _____

4. You are the chairperson of the federal agency that is responsible for protecting those who borrow money from banks. You learn that a certain bank has been charging its borrowers an interest rate that is double the maximum permitted by federal law.

   Agency: _____

5. You live in a city in which there are four TV stations. One company purchases all four stations and broadcasts the same news on all the stations. You feel that the public interest is not being served by this monopolistic practice.

   Agency: _____

6. You live in a residential area that is zoned for one-family houses. A local manufacturer buys the three homes next to yours and announces that it plans to demolish them and build a factory.

   Agency: _____

7. You go to a doctor for treatment of a skin condition. Two weeks later you discover that your doctor never graduated from medical school and is not licensed to practice medicine in your state.

   Agency: _____

8. You apply for telephone service and are advised that a $200 deposit is required before you can obtain service. You believe that the deposit is excessive and unfair, but the phone company refuses to provide you with service unless you pay the deposit.

   Agency: _____

9. Your local television station broadcasts programs that you feel are not appropriate to be viewed by minors.

   Agency: _____

10. Your bank refuses to cash your checks unless you pay a fee of $5.00 per check, even though you have an account at that bank.

    Agency: _____

11. You discover that an industrial plant in your area is dumping toxic waste into a nearby stream.

    Agency: _____

# Review

## Part VI
## Business Organization and Regulation

**MINI-CASE**

The announcement below appeared in the Rochester (New York) *Times Union*, December 10 through December 17. Use the information in the announcement to answer the questions that follow. On the line next to each statement, write the letter of the best answer.

TO ALL PROSPECTIVE CREDITORS OF THE FIRM
OF SINK AND BOWL, PLUMBING CONTRACTORS,
ROCHESTER, NEW YORK

TAKE NOTICE, that the above-named partnership, by agreement dated December 1, 1991, with Certificate filed in the Monroe County Clerk's Office on May 28, 1981, has been dissolved. Fuller Sink shall continue the said business as a sole proprietor, under his own name.

Dated: December 1, 1991                Hill & Dale
                                       Attorneys for Fuller Sink
                                       Rochester, New York

_____ 1. The partnership of Sink and Bowl was dissolved by the (a) bankruptcy of the firm, (b) death of a partner, (c) admission of a new partner, (d) mutual consent of the partners.

_____ 2. The announcement constitutes (a) an act of bankruptcy, (b) proper notice to new creditors, (c) actual notice to old creditors, (d) the formation of a partnership.

_____ 3. Bowl is liable for (a) all debts contracted by the partnership before proper notice was given, (b) half of the debts of the partnership contracted before proper notice was given, (c) the debts of his former partner, now operating as a sole proprietor, (d) none of the partnership's debts.

Copyright © Houghton Mifflin Company. All rights reserved.

___ 4. After the dissolution of the partnership, Sink orally offered Plummer, an employee, 25% of the profits of the business as wages. Plummer is not a partner because (a) there is no charter, (b) the agreement was not made in writing, (c) partners share the ownership of a business, (d) Bowl did not give his consent before the dissolution.

___ 5. For Sink, one advantage of a proprietorship is (a) limited liability, (b) the freedom to conduct business as he wants to within the limits of the law, (c) increased capital, (d) the advice of the members of his board of directors.

## MULTIPLE-CHOICE QUESTIONS

On the line next to each statement, write the letter of the best answer.

___ 1. The most easily started form of business organization is the (a) general partnership, (b) corporation, (c) limited partnership, (d) sole proprietorship.

___ 2. In most states, a sole proprietor must register a business or trade name with (a) the local chamber of commerce, (b) a local bank, (c) a public office, (d) Washington, D.C.

___ 3. A partner who is neither active in a partnership nor known to the public as a partner is called (a) silent, (b) dormant, (c) general, (d) secret.

___ 4. The major difference between a general partnership and a limited partnership is the partners' (a) degree of liability, (b) degree of management, (c) investment, (d) percentage of ownership.

___ 5. A business corporation can (a) borrow money in its own name, (b) sue and be sued in its own name, (c) own property in its own name, (d) do all of these.

___ 6. Public utilities are chartered by (a) city or town governments only, (b) state governments only, (c) the federal government only, (d) both state and federal governments.

___ 7. Officers of a corporation are chosen by the (a) stockholders, (b) directors, (c) previous officers, (d) trustees.

___ 8. The life of a corporation is not affected by (a) mergers, (b) the death of a stockholder, (c) a court decree, (d) consolidation.

___ 9. Laws enacted to prevent monopolies are called (a) ultra vires laws, (b) merger laws, (c) antitrust laws, (d) OSHA laws.

___ 10. A local zoning board is an example of a(n) (a) corporation, (b) monopoly, (c) administrative agency, (d) public utility.

## MATCHING QUESTIONS

Use the following terms to identify the phrases below. On the line next to each phrase, write the letter of the term that most closely relates to it.

a. Joint and several liability
b. Joint venture
c. No-par stock
d. Treble damages
e. Police power

____ 1. Stock with no stated value
____ 2. The liability of partners as a group and individually
____ 3. The power of a state to protect the welfare of its citizens
____ 4. An association of two or more companies engaged in a common venture
____ 5. Damages payable for violation of the antitrust laws

## CASE PROBLEMS

Read the case problems below. For each problem, answer yes or no, and then explain your answer in the space provided.

1. Curry, Davis, and Ivy were partners operating a motel. Davis died, and Ivy and Curry decided to continue to operate the business. Was it legally necessary for them to make a new partnership agreement?

2. Pillson, a partner in a retail drug business, was responsible for purchasing drugs from wholesalers. One wholesaler gave Pillson a 5% commission in appreciation for the order placed for the partnership. Was Pillson entitled to keep the commission for personal use?

3. Granby was treasurer of Eagle Electric Corporation. The company owed $10,000 for electric cable purchased by the corporation for use in its business. An action was brought against Granby for payment of the $10,000. Was Granby liable?

4. Hill and Fox each owned 50% of the shares of stock of the Ames Corporation. Hill died and left the stock to her family. Was it necessary for Fox to set up a new corporation to be able to continue in business?

5. Polcin believed that her accountant had prepared her income tax returns improperly, causing her to be fined by the IRS. In what way or ways may the accountant be held liable to Polcin?

# PART VII

# REAL AND PERSONAL PROPERTY

# Chapter 29

# Basic Legal Concepts of Property

## CHAPTER OUTLINE

**The Nature of Property**
   Personal Property
   Real Property
   Easements, Licenses, and Profits
**Acquiring Real and Personal Property**
   Purchase
   Gift or Inheritance
   Abandonment
   Lost Property
   Mislaid Property
   Adverse Possession
   Accretion
   Condemnation
**Acquiring Rights in Personal Property**
   Patents
   Trademarks
   Copyrights
   Protection Against Infringement
**Forms of Ownership of Property**
   Tenancy
   Community Property
   Cooperative Ownership
   Condominium Ownership
   Time Sharing
**Restrictions on the Use of Real Property**
   Restrictive Covenants
   Easements
   Zoning Laws and Regulations
   Wills

## COMPLETION QUESTIONS

In the statements below, important words have been omitted. Fill in the blanks to complete each statement.

1. A stock certificate is an example of _____ property.

2. An item of personal property so attached to real property that it cannot be removed without damage to the structure is called a(n) _____.

3. A public utility that wants a permanent right to cross someone's property with a power line must obtain a(n) _____.

4. A(n) _____ is a formal document that transfers title to real property.

5. A gift of personal property can be made by document or _____.

6. A person who occupies another person's land for a certain period of time can claim title to that land under a right known as _____.

7. The distinguishing feature of a joint tenancy is the right of _____.

8. The process by which a state government obtains title to abandoned or unclaimed property is called _____.

9. A joint tenancy by a husband and wife usually is called a tenancy by _____.

10. The use of land can be restricted by municipalities through _____ ordinance.

## MULTIPLE-CHOICE QUESTIONS

On the line next to each statement, write the letter of the best answer.

_____ 1. Patent and copyright protection is granted by (a) state governments, (b) warranty, (c) the chamber of commerce, (d) the federal government.

_____ 2. A patent protects an invention for (a) 10 years, (b) 17 years, (c) 35 years, (d) 37 years.

_____ 3. Ownership of property by one person is called (a) tenancy in common, (b) tenancy by the entirety, (c) a cooperative, (d) sole tenancy.

_____ 4. On the death of a joint tenant, the property automatically belongs to the (a) surviving joint tenants, (b) state, (c) spouse, (d) heirs.

_____ 5. The use of land can be restricted by (a) the state government, (b) the federal government, (c) the city government, (d) all of these.

_____ 6. The process by which the state can obtain title to abandoned or unclaimed property is called (a) presumption, (b) adverse possession, (c) condemnation, (d) escheat.

_____ 7. An example of a fixture is a(n) (a) refrigerator, (b) elevator, (c) typewriter, (d) couch.

_____ 8. The temporary right to use a portion of another person's land is called a(n) (a) profit, (b) easement, (c) permit, (d) license.

_____ 9. Ownership of a condominium unit is shown by a (a) stock certificate, (b) mortgage, (c) bill of sale, (d) deed.

_____ 10. A restrictive covenant is binding on (a) the seller, (b) the original buyer, (c) all subsequent buyers, (d) both b and c.

## MATCHING QUESTIONS

Use the following terms to identify the phrases below. On the line next to each phrase, write the letter of the term that most closely relates to it.

a. Condominium
b. Easement
c. Escheat
d. Adverse possession
e. License
f. Restrictive covenant
g. Trademark
h. Fixture
i. Deed
j. Patent

_____ 1. The right to use someone's property perpetually or for a specific period of time

_____ 2. The process by which a state government obtains title to private property that is abandoned or unclaimed

_____ 3. A word or symbol used to identify a product or a business

_____ 4. A temporary right to use someone's property

_____ 5. Ownership of a specific unit in an apartment project

_____ 6. A clause in a deed that limits the use of property

_____ 7. Occupying another person's land without that person's permission

_____ 8. A grant to a person of an exclusive right to manufacture and sell, or to license others to manufacture and sell, an invention

_____ 9. An item of personal property that is attached to and treated as real property

_____ 10. A formal document that transfers title to real property

## SHORT-ANSWER QUESTIONS

Answer each of the following questions in the space provided.

1. Explain the difference between a joint tenancy and a tenancy in common.

   _____
   _____
   _____

2. Explain the nature of patents, trademarks, and copyrights and the type of protection each affords.

   _____
   _____
   _____
   _____
   _____

BASIC LEGAL CONCEPTS OF PROPERTY | 173

3. List six ways in which real property can be acquired.

_____
_____
_____
_____
_____
_____

# Chapter 30

# Renting Real Property

## CHAPTER OUTLINE

The Landlord-Tenant Relationship
Types of Tenancies
    Tenancy for Years
    Periodic Tenancy
    Tenancy at Will
    Tenancy at Sufferance

Nature and Elements of a Lease
    Unconscionability
    Factual Information
    Rights and Duties
How a Lease Is Terminated
Obligations to Third Parties

## MULTIPLE-CHOICE QUESTIONS

On the line next to each statement, write the letter of the best answer.

_____ 1. Under the statute of frauds, a lease of real property must be in writing if it is for (a) residential property, (b) commercial property, (c) more than one year, (d) less than one year.

_____ 2. The major difference among the various types of tenancies is the (a) relationship between the parties, (b) length of the lease term, (c) type of property being leased, (d) rent paid under the lease.

_____ 3. If you want to be able to cancel a lease at any time, you should get a (a) tenancy at will, (b) holdover tenancy, (c) tenancy at sufferance, (d) periodic tenancy.

_____ 4. When a lease is assigned by a tenant, the (a) original tenant has no further obligations, (b) the landlord assumes all responsibility, (c) the new tenant assumes all responsibility, (d) the original tenant is still liable.

_____ 5. Most leases provide that if the leased property is totally destroyed by fire or other casualty, (a) rent continues, (b) the tenant pays half the original rent, (c) the lease terminates, (d) the tenant pays the cost of repairs.

_____ 6. Graber is renting an apartment to Brill. Graber can require Brill to pay a security deposit to be used to pay (a) the first month's rent, (b) for damage caused during Brill's lease term, (c) the last month's rent, (d) property taxes.

7. Under most leases, permanent fixtures installed by the tenant (a) can be removed by the tenant when the lease ends, (b) become the property of the landlord and cannot be removed, (c) must be purchased by the landlord when the lease ends, (d) belong to the next tenant.

8. If a tenant fails to pay the rent when it becomes due, the landlord can (a) sue to evict the tenant, (b) sue the tenant for the rent due, (c) have the tenant arrested, (d) evict or sue the tenant.

9. A constructive eviction occurs when the (a) landlord wants to repair the property, (b) tenant redecorates the property without the landlord's permission, (c) landlord makes the property uninhabitable, (d) tenant intentionally damages or destroys the property.

10. A person who leases residential property can (a) be restricted in the type of furniture placed on the property, (b) restricted from having visitors, (c) use the property only for the purpose described in the lease, (d) use the property for any purpose.

11. A landlord's promise in a lease that the tenant will have undisturbed possession of the property is called a (a) covenant of quiet enjoyment, (b) tenancy at sufferance, (c) constructive eviction, (d) warranty of habitability.

12. A lease that omits the names of the landlord or tenant is (a) enforceable, (b) a sublease, (c) unenforceable, (d) a covenant.

## SHORT-ANSWER QUESTIONS

Answer each of the following questions in the space provided.

1. Explain the difference between a lease and a sublease.

2. List seven important terms that every lease should contain.

3. Describe six ways in which a lease can be terminated.

## CHAPTER 30

## ACTIVITY: ANALYZING A LEASE

Read the following lease and then answer the questions on the next page.

---

### LEASE

THIS INDENTURE WITNESSETH, That **Mark and Anna Essex** of the County of **Marion** in the State of Indiana has this day leased to **Brent J. and LeeAnn McDowell**, of said County and State, and to **their** executor/executrix, administrator/administratrix, and assigns the following premises in said County and State, to-wit:

Condominium #15A located in Valley Vista Estates, 2062 West Park Drive, Southport, Indiana, consisting of five (5) rooms plus bath, garage, and patio,

together with the right, privileges, and appurtenances to the same belonging, to have and to hold the same for and during the term of **one (1) year** from the **1st** day of **April**, 19 **--**. And the said **Brent J. and LeeAnn McDowell** hereby agree to pay as rent for said premises, the sum of **Two Hundred Fifty Dollars ($250.00)** per **month**, the said rent to be paid on the **2d** day of **each month** in advance without relief from valuation or appraisement laws. THE CONDITIONS of this lease are: That the premises are to be used and occupied by **Brent J. and LeeAnn McDowell** for a **residence** and for no other purpose. That no waste be allowed to accumulate on the premises. That the premises are not be be sub-leased by said **Brent J. and LeeAnn McDowell** or occupied by other persons or for other purposes than herein expressed, or this lease assigned by the said **Brent J. and LeeAnn McDowell** without the written consent of the said **Mark and Anna Essex**. And the said lessee hereby further agree, at the expiration of this lease to deliver up the possession of said premises, peaceable and in as good condition and repair as the same is now in, or in as good condition and repair as the said lessor may at any time during this lease put the same in. The natural wear, accidents, fire, and other acts of God excepted.

At the expiration of this lease, or on the failure to pay the rent when the same is due, or on a failure to comply with any of the conditions of this lease, the same shall terminate at once without notice, and the said **Mark and Anna Essex** representatives and assigns may enter upon and take possession of said premises and expel the occupants thereof, without in anywise being a trespasser; and the failure of the said **Mark and Anna Essex** to take possession of said premises at the times aforesaid, shall not estop **them** from afterwards asserting said rights, and the occupation of said premises by the said tenant, after the expiration of said lease, or the forfeiture thereof, shall give **them** no rights as a tenant but **they** may be expelled at any time without notice. On failure to pay rent at maturity, or to give possession at the expiration of this lease and as liquidated damages for failure, it is agreed that double the rent above specified shall be paid for the time the rent remains due or unpaid or said tenant holds possession without right, and should suit be instituted to collect rent, or obtain possession of the said premises, the said **Brent J. and LeeAnn McDowell** agrees to pay attorney's fees therefor.

Witness our hands, this **10th** day of **March**, 19 **--**

*Mark Essex*
Mark Essex

*Anna Essex*
Anna Essex

*Brent J. McDowell*
Brent J. McDowell

*LeeAnn McDowell*
LeeAnn McDowell

THIS DOCUMENT PREPARED BY **Anthony E. Santos, QUIMBY, SANTOS & LOUIS**

1. Who is the landlord?
   _____

2. Who is the tenant?
   _____

3. What is the term of this lease?
   _____

4. What type of tenancy is provided for in this lease?
   _____
   _____

5. What are the restrictions on the use of this property outlined in the lease?
   _____
   _____
   _____

6. If the tenants fail to pay the rent, what damages are provided for in the lease?
   _____
   _____

7. Under this lease, who is responsible for paying the real estate taxes? Why?
   _____
   _____

8. Under this lease, how can the tenants sublease the property?
   _____

9. What are the obligations of the tenants at the end of the term of this lease?
   _____
   _____

10. If a fire destroys part of the kitchen during the term of this lease, who is responsible for having the damages repaired? Why?
    _____
    _____
    _____

11. If the tenants are sued for failure to pay the rent or to vacate the property at the end of the term of the lease, who must pay the attorneys' fees?
    _____
    _____

# Chapter 31

# Buying and Selling Real Property

## CHAPTER OUTLINE

**The Buying and Selling Process**
Contract of Sale
Financing
Title Examination
The Closing

**Transfer of Title**
The Quitclaim Deed
The Bargain and Sale Deed
The Warranty Deed

## TRUE-FALSE QUESTIONS

Indicate whether each statement below is true or false by circling T or F in the column on the right.

1. A contract for the sale and purchase of a home need not be in writing if the purchase price is under $25,000.     T  F

2. A homeowner and a potential buyer can negotiate directly, without using the services of a real estate broker.     T  F

3. Once a contract of sale is executed, it is binding on both seller and buyer.     T  F

4. Contingencies in a contract protect the buyer but not the seller.     T  F

5. A person buying a house that already is mortgaged automatically can assume the mortgage without the mortgagee's consent.     T  F

6. The seller can give a buyer a mortgage in the same way that a lending institution can give a mortgage.     T  F

7. Every mortgage gives the mortgagor the right to pay the balance due on the mortgage without penalty before the end of the mortgage term.     T  F

8. When a house is sold, the buyer pays the real estate agent's commission.     T  F

9. Title insurance protects the buyer against financial loss if the title proves to be defective.  T  F
10. Title to real estate passes from seller to buyer when the deed is recorded in the appropriate public office.  T  F

## MATCHING QUESTIONS

Use the following terms to identify the phrases below. On the line next to each phrase, write the letter of the term that most closely relates to it.

a. Abstract of title
b. Counteroffer
c. Covenant
d. Escrow
e. Grantee
f. Mortgage commitment
g. Purchase money mortgage
h. Quitclaim deed
i. Title
j. Warranty deed

_____ 1. A mortgage used to finance the purchase of real property

_____ 2. The holding of closing documents and purchase funds until a final title search is made

_____ 3. A summary of transactions concerning the title to real property

_____ 4. The legal interest an owner has in real property

_____ 5. A counterproposal made by a seller to the offer made by a buyer to purchase real property

_____ 6. A deed given by the seller to the buyer that guarantees good title

_____ 7. A promise made by a grantor in a warranty deed

_____ 8. A deed that gives the buyer whatever title the seller had

_____ 9. An agreement by a lending institution to give a mortgage to the mortgagor

_____ 10. The person to whom title is transferred by the owner of real property

## MULTIPLE-CHOICE QUESTIONS

On the line next to each statement, write the letter of the best answer.

_____ 1. A contract entered into between a property owner and a real estate broker for the sale of real property is called a(n) (a) oral contract, (b) listing contract, (c) title contract, (d) deed contract.

_____ 2. Ownership of real property is transferred by means of (a) a mortgage, (b) title insurance, (c) a deed, (d) a bond.

_____ 3. A provision in a contract of sale that makes the sale subject to obtaining financing is called a(n) (a) covenant, (b) restriction, (c) easement, (d) contingency.

____ 4. When a buyer takes over and agrees to pay an existing mortgage, the process is called (a) a prepayment privilege, (b) escrow, (c) mortgage assumption, (d) a purchase offer.

____ 5. A survey that shows the approximate measurement of property is called a(n) (a) tape location map, (b) instrument survey, (c) plot, (d) transit.

____ 6. A person who transfers real estate to another is known as the (a) grantor, (b) mortgagor, (c) mortgagee, (d) grantee.

____ 7. The most complete interest in real property is obtained by receiving a (a) mortgage, (b) warranty deed, (c) quitclaim deed, (d) bargain and sale deed.

____ 8. To ensure that title to real property is good, a buyer can purchase (a) mortgage insurance, (b) homeowners' insurance, (c) title insurance, (d) liability insurance.

____ 9. To determine whether title to property is good, an attorney usually uses a(n) (a) computer, (b) deed to the property, (c) abstract of title, (d) survey.

____ 10. Claims against property for unpaid taxes, claims of a mortgagee, and the like are called (a) covenants, (b) prescriptions, (c) escrows, (d) encumbrances.

____ 11. Conditions included in a contract of sale that, if not met, can void the agreement are called (a) contingencies, (b) covenants, (c) encumbrances, (d) escrow.

____ 12. A lien held by a bank or other lender as security until a loan for the purchase of property is repaid is called (a) a title, (b) a mortgage, (c) escrow, (d) a deed.

____ 13. A property survey made by a surveyor that shows exact angles and distances is called (a) a tape location map, (b) the Torrens system, (c) a title search, (d) an instrument survey.

____ 14. A copy or condensed summary of all transactions relating to a particular piece of property over a period of years is called a(n) (a) deed, (b) abstract of title, (c) closing statement, (d) listing contract.

____ 15. Promises and guarantees transferred by a warranty deed are called (a) covenants, (b) contingencies, (c) escrow, (d) surveys.

## ACTIVITY: TYPES OF DEEDS

The following statements contain language taken from various deeds. In the space provided, state the type of deed used.

1. The grantor hereby gives to the grantee whatever title the grantor may have in and to the following property.

    Type of deed: _____

2. The grantor hereby gives to the grantee whatever title the grantor may have in and to the following property and covenants that the grantor is in possession of the property and has done nothing to harm or disturb the title to the property.

    Type of deed: _____

3. The grantor hereby gives to the grantee all of the rights to the following property and covenants to forever warrant the title to the property.

    Type of deed: _____

# Review

## Part VII
## Real and Personal Property

**MULTIPLE-CHOICE QUESTIONS**

On the line next to each statement, write the letter of the best answer.

_____ 1. A promissory note is an example of (a) real property, (b) intangible personal property, (c) fixed property, (d) tangible personal property.

_____ 2. A trailer is considered (a) personal property, (b) real property, (c) real and personal property, (d) none of these.

_____ 3. If you want a permanent right to cross your neighbor's land to have access to a lake, you want a(n) (a) license, (b) profit, (c) patent, (d) easement.

_____ 4. Real property, but not personal property, can be transferred by (a) gift, (b) deed, (c) purchase, (d) inheritance.

_____ 5. A bill of sale would be used to transfer title to a (a) cottage and lakefront lot, (b) car, (c) farm, (d) home.

_____ 6. A covenant restricting the use of land can be imposed by (a) local or state government, (b) the federal government, (c) local, state, or federal government, (d) none of these.

_____ 7. Allowing your neighbor to store her sailboat on your property for a certain period of time is considered a(n) (a) license, (b) easement, (c) profit, (d) tenancy.

_____ 8. The law that requires that a lease of real property for more than one year be in writing is called the (a) statute of limitations, (b) law of 1879, (c) statute of writings, (d) statute of frauds.

_____ 9. An escalator clause in a lease is designed to protect the (a) tenant, (b) state government, (c) federal government, (d) landlord.

_____ 10. At the end of a lease term, a security deposit usually is returned to the (a) tenant, (b) landlord, (c) new tenant, (d) housing authority.

_____ 11. To lease property for a specific period of time and have the lease continue automatically unless you or your landlord cancels it, you would get a (a) tenancy at will, (b) joint tenancy, (c) periodic tenancy, (d) tenancy at sufferance.

12. When government condemns property for public use, it must pay the owner (a) the property's fair market value, (b) whatever the owner paid for the property, (c) double the market value, (d) half the market value.

13. A lease can be terminated by (a) agreement between the parties, (b) the passage of time, (c) destruction of the property, (d) all of these.

14. A landlord can allow a tenant to secure another occupant for the premises leased by means of a(n) (a) eviction, (b) sublease, (c) novation, (d) accord and satisfaction.

15. Title to real property passes to the buyer when (a) a mortgage is obtained, (b) the deed is recorded, (c) a deposit is given, (d) the deed is delivered.

16. At the closing, the buyer and seller and their attorneys meet for the purpose of (a) surveying the property, (b) considering a purchase offer, (c) transferring title, (d) conducting a title search.

## TRUE-FALSE QUESTIONS

Indicate whether each statement below is true or false by circling T or F in the column on the right.

1. A patent protects an invention for the inventor's lifetime. T F
2. A copyright protects any form of expression except musical compositions. T F
3. To transfer real property as a gift, a deed must be signed and delivered. T F
4. An appliance usually can be removed from a home before a sale, provided it does not damage real property. T F
5. Title to public property can be acquired through adverse possession. T F
6. A landowner can control the use of the land through purchase of the property. T F
7. The purchaser of a cooperative apartment receives a deed indicating ownership of the unit. T F
8. Government can restrict the use of land to aid the public welfare. T F
9. Under certain circumstances, the state can claim ownership of property if it has been abandoned or unclaimed for a certain period of time. T F
10. In most states, title to property held in the names of two or more persons is a tenancy by the entirety. T F
11. The landlord's and tenant's obligations in a lease are called *warranties*. T F
12. If leased premises are partially destroyed by fire and can be repaired, the lease continues while the repairs are made. T F
13. If the entire leased premises are taken by condemnation, the tenant is entitled to finish out the remainder of the lease. T F
14. A bargain and sale deed transfers whatever title the seller has in the property but does not guarantee that the seller has done nothing to disturb the title. T F
15. When a lease is assigned, the assignee becomes a tenant of the assignor. T F

16. If a guest is injured on leased premises, the landlord and tenant can be held liable for the guest's injuries.  T  F

17. A buyer of real estate can always assume an existing mortgage.  T  F

18. A husband and wife who own property as tenants by the entirety cannot sell their individual interests without the consent of their spouse.  T  F

19. A buyer can refuse to complete the purchase of a house if it is discovered that there are flaws in the title.  T  F

20. A guarantee of title is one of the covenants in a bargain and sale deed.  T  F

## MATCHING QUESTIONS

Use the following terms to identify the phrases below. On the line next to each phrase, write the letter of the term that most closely relates to it.

a. Purchase money mortgage
b. Sublease
c. Encumbrance
d. Escheat
e. Escrow
f. Tenancy at will
g. Title
h. Constructive eviction
i. Profit
j. Sole tenancy

_____ 1. The process by which the state obtains title to abandoned property

_____ 2. The right to remove water, gas, minerals, and wood from someone else's property

_____ 3. Ownership by one person

_____ 4. A lease of real property for an indefinite period

_____ 5. A transfer by a tenant of a portion of an unexpired lease term

_____ 6. Conduct by a landlord that makes the leased premises uninhabitable

_____ 7. A mortgage obtained by a buyer to finance the purchase of real property

_____ 8. The holding of closing documents and funds in trust until it is determined the title is clear

_____ 9. The interest a person has in real property

_____ 10. An interest in real property that conflicts with the owner's title

# PART VIII

# BAILMENTS

# Chapter 32

# Nature and Creation of Bailments

## CHAPTER OUTLINE

What a Bailment Is
Requirements for a Valid Bailment
    Personal Property
    Retention of Title by the Bailor
    Possession of Property by the Bailee
    Return of Bailed Property
How a Bailment Is Created
    Bailment Implied in Fact
    Bailment Implied by Law

How a Bailment Ends
    Completion
    Mutual Agreement
    Acts of the Parties
    Destruction of the Bailed Property
    Operation of Law
Situations Similar to Bailments

## YES-NO QUESTIONS

Read each statement to determine whether it is an example of a bailment. Indicate your answer by circling Y (yes) or N (no) in the column on the right.

1. You buy a TV set, agreeing to pay for it over a two-year period.     Y   N
2. You lend your sister a tennis racket that you borrowed from a friend.     Y   N
3. A friend lets you use a tape recorder in the basement of his home.     Y   N
4. Your cousin lets you use her cottage for the weekend.     Y   N
5. A friend asks you to take his snowmobile in for repairs.     Y   N
6. A neighbor leaves a raincoat on the back seat of your car without telling you about it.     Y   N
7. A neighbor asks you to watch his child while he is in the store.     Y   N
8. You accept delivery of a TV set on behalf of a friend who is away.     Y   N
9. You see someone else's wallet on the ground but do not pick it up.     Y   N

| | | |
|---|---|---|
| 10. You store a radio and some clothing in a rented locker at a bus station. | Y | N |
| 11. You place some jewelry and legal documents in a safe-deposit box at a bank. | Y | N |
| 12. Your friend keeps your guitar for you while you go on vacation. | Y | N |
| 13. You ask a salesperson in a store to watch your coat while you go to a different department in the store. | Y | N |
| 14. You find a briefcase that has been stolen and attempt to return it to its owner. | Y | N |
| 15. You borrow a library book and agree to return it in two weeks. | Y | N |

## SHORT-ANSWER QUESTIONS

Answer each of the following questions in the space provided.

1. List and briefly explain four characteristics of a valid bailment.

   _____
   _____
   _____
   _____

2. Give two examples of bailments you have entered into. Do not use the ones mentioned in the textbook.

   _____
   _____

3. Explain the difference between a bailment and a sale.

   _____
   _____

4. Explain why depositing money in a bank is not considered a bailment.

   _____
   _____

5. List five ways a bailment ends.

   _____
   _____
   _____
   _____
   _____

## MULTIPLE-CHOICE QUESTIONS

On the line next to each statement, write the letter of the best answer.

_____ 1. A bailment involves the transfer of (a) title to, but not possession of, personal property, (b) title to, but not possession of, real property, (c) possession of, but not title to, personal property, (d) possession of, but not title to, real property.

_____ 2. A bailment that arises because of the actions of the parties, without any oral or written agreement, is (a) illegal, (b) implied by law, (c) an express bailment, (d) implied in fact.

_____ 3. Bailments implied by law often are created (a) through express agreements, (b) through implied agreements, (c) through mutual agreement, (d) when people find and take possession of lost or stolen property.

_____ 4. If bailed property is lost or damaged as a result of the bailee's negligence, the (a) bailee has no liability, (b) bailee is liable to the bailor for the value of the property, (c) bailment ends by mutual agreement, (d) bailment ends by operation of law.

_____ 5. All of the following can be the subject of a bailment *except* a(n) (a) stock certificate, (b) automobile, (c) garage, (d) motorcycle.

## COMPLETION QUESTIONS

In the statements below, important words have been omitted. Fill in the blanks to complete each statement.

1. A person who takes possession of a bailed item is the _____.

2. Only _____ property can be the subject of a bailment.

3. The transfer of personal property for a specific time and purpose is called a(n) _____.

4. Land and buildings are examples of _____ property.

5. A bailment in which the agreement is stated in words, either oral or written, is a(n) _____ agreement.

# Chapter 33

# Bailments: Types, Rights, and Responsibilities

## CHAPTER OUTLINE

**Classification of Bailments**
**Mutual Benefit Bailments**
    Renting
    Work and Services
    Pledging
    Consigning
    Storage and Parking

**Gratuitous Bailments**
    Bailments for the Sole Benefit of the Bailor
    Bailments for the Sole Benefit of the Bailee
**Constructive Bailments**
    Bailments of Lost Property
    Bailments by Necessity
**Limiting Liabilities—Disclaimers**

## TRUE-FALSE QUESTIONS

On the line at the right of each statement, write the word *true* if the statement is true. If the statement is false, write the word or expression that should be substituted for the underlined word or expression to make the statement correct.

1. A <u>mutual benefit bailment</u> is one in which both parties benefit. _____

2. In a <u>constructive bailment</u>, only one party to the bailment benefits. _____

3. The standard of care required in a mutual benefit bailment is <u>extraordinary</u> care. _____

4. A bailee who is not paid for work done can exercise a <u>bailee's lien</u>. _____

5. A deposit of personal property as security for a loan is called a <u>pledge</u>. _____

6. Bailments for the sole benefit of a bailor require a <u>reasonable</u> degree of care. _____

7. Storing your friend's tractor as a favor is an example of an <u>implied</u> bailment. _____

8. Receiving goods on approval for purchase is an example of a <u>pledge</u>. _____
9. A bailment for the sole benefit of the bailor is a <u>gratuitous</u> bailment. _____
10. A person who takes possession of someone else's property by mistake has a <u>bailment by necessity</u>. _____

## SHORT-ANSWER QUESTIONS

Answer each of the following questions in the space provided.

1. List the five types of mutual benefit bailments. Give an example of each, but do not use the examples in the textbook.

   _____
   _____
   _____
   _____
   _____

2. Give two examples of gratuitous bailments. Do not use the examples in the textbook.

   _____
   _____
   _____

## MATCHING QUESTIONS

Use the following terms to identify the phrases below. On the line next to each phrase, write the letter of the term that most closely relates to it.

a. Consignment
b. Pledgor
c. High degree of care
d. Warehouse receipt
e. Bailment by necessity
f. Slight care
g. Consignor
h. Bailee's lien
i. Consignee
j. Bailor

_____ 1. A bailee's rights, before being paid, in the property bailed
_____ 2. A bailment that occurs when property comes into someone's possession by mistake
_____ 3. The person who delivers personal property to a bailee
_____ 4. The bailor in a consignment
_____ 5. One who transfers property to make a pledge
_____ 6. A receipt given by one who stores goods for another

_____ 7. The bailee in a consignment

_____ 8. The degree of care required of a bailee in a bailment solely for the bailor's benefit

_____ 9. A bailment for the purpose of purchase or sale by the bailee

_____ 10. The degree of care required of a bailee in a bailment for the sole benefit of the bailee

## CASE PROBLEMS

Read the case problems below. For each problem, answer yes or no, and then explain your answer in the space provided.

1. Sloan was going on vacation and asked Brown to keep his guitar while he was away. While Sloan was away, excessive humidity warped the guitar's neck and ruined it. When Sloan returned, he insisted that Brown pay him for the damaged guitar. Was he entitled to collect?

   _____
   _____
   _____

2. Monteiro, a high school senior, placed a camera in his high school locker and locked the door. When he returned from class, he discovered that the door had been broken and the camera stolen. Can he hold the school authorities liable for the loss on the grounds that a bailment had been created?

   _____
   _____
   _____

3. By mistake, Andrews received in the mail a book her neighbor ordered. Not wanting to be bothered with it, she left it on her front porch. Two months later, the book was stolen. Was Andrews liable to her neighbor for the loss?

   _____
   _____
   _____

# Chapter 34

# Special Bailments

## CHAPTER OUTLINE

The Nature of Special Bailments
Exceptions to the Rule of Strict Liability
   Agreement to Limit Liability
   Act of God
   Act of a Public Enemy
   Act of Public Authorities
   Fault of the Bailor or Guest
   Nature of the Bailed Goods
Duties, Liabilities, and Rights of Hotelkeepers
   Duties of a Hotelkeeper
   Liabilities of a Hotelkeeper
   Rights of a Hotelkeeper
Duties, Liabilities, and Rights of Common Carriers
   Duties of a Common Carrier
   Liabilities of a Common Carrier
   Rights of a Common Carrier

## MULTIPLE-CHOICE QUESTIONS

On the line next to each statement, write the letter of the best answer.

_____ 1. An example of a special bailment is the liability imposed on a (a) person who rents a car, (b) trucking company, (c) parking garage, (d) service station.

_____ 2. The degree of care imposed on a special bailee is (a) reasonable care, (b) slight care, (c) a high degree of care, (d) extraordinary care.

_____ 3. Under common law, the liability of special bailees was (a) absolute, (b) minimal, (c) based on the status of the parties, (d) based on the property bailed.

_____ 4. A special bailee's liability can be limited by all of the following *except* (a) an act of God, (b) agreement between the bailor and the bailee, (c) the actions of rioters, (d) the actions of public authorities.

5. A special bailee is not liable for losses resulting from a typhoon because (a) a typhoon is a natural disaster that could not have been anticipated, (b) special bailments require only a reasonable level of care, (c) special bailees are exempt from all liabilities, (d) special bailees always have agreements with bailors to limit their liability.

6. A person who enters a hotel solely for the purpose of having dinner is a (a) hotel guest, (b) transient, (c) bailor by implication, (d) business guest.

7. A hotelkeeper can refuse to accept a person as a guest because of that person's (a) inability to pay, (b) religion, (c) race, (d) gender.

8. A carrier that transports goods for certain customers only is a (a) limited carrier, (b) common carrier, (c) contract carrier, (d) mutual carrier.

9. The liability of a common carrier is that of a(n) (a) special bailee, (b) ordinary bailee, (c) constructive bailee, (d) bailee by necessity.

10. A common carrier whose equipment is detained by a customer for an unreasonable period of time can make a special charge called (a) containerage, (b) detonage, (c) a bailee's charge, (d) demurrage.

## SHORT-ANSWER QUESTIONS

In the space below, list four exceptions to the rule of absolute liability of hotelkeepers and common carriers. Give an example of each exception.

1. _____

2. _____

3. _____

4. _____

## CASE PROBLEMS

Read the case problems below. For each problem, answer yes or no, and then state the rule of law that supports your answer in the space provided.

1. Berger checked into a motel and left a valuable stamp collection in his room because the motel did not provide safe-deposit boxes. The stamps were stolen. Was the motel liable for the value of the collection?

_____
_____

2. Corrida Corporation shipped a large quantity of gold bars via Ajax Trucking Lines. The shipment was hijacked by a gang of escaped prisoners. Could Corrida hold Ajax responsible for the loss?

___

3. Thurston moved to a nearby city to start a new job. She rented a suite in a hotel for a two-year period. Would the hotelkeeper be absolutely liable to Thurston if any of her belongings are stolen?

___

4. Allingham checked her coat in a theater and was told that the liability for loss was limited to $100. The coat, which was worth $500, was stolen. Did Allingham collect that amount from the theater?

___

5. The Grange Company stored a large quantity of apples in a warehouse owned by Storage, Inc. The warehouse roof was defective, and the apples were ruined when a freak storm resulted in a large amount of water leaking through the roof. Was Storage, Inc., liable for the loss?

___

6. Melons Ltd. shipped a quantity of overripe melons by Freight Carriers, Inc. The carrier was aware of the condition of the fruit and took every precaution to prevent spoilage. Still, the melons spoiled en route. Was Freight Carriers responsible for the loss?

___

7. Cruise checked his coat at the Ultimate Hotel while having dinner there. The coat was stolen despite the reasonable care of the check room attendant. Can Cruise recover the value of his coat?

___

8. Golden checked out of the Acme Motel and left his suitcase with an attendant while he went to get his car. When he returned, he discovered that the suitcase had been stolen. Was the motel liable for the loss if it was not at fault?

___

9. The Comfort Motel refused to permit Regis to register as a guest because Regis was just 15 years old. Was the motel liable for discrimination?

_____

_____

10. Western Express agreed to transport a valuable painting provided its liability did not exceed $5,000. Can a carrier limit its liability in this way?

_____

_____

# Review

# Part VIII
# Bailments

## TRUE-FALSE QUESTIONS

Indicate whether each statement below is true or false by circling T or F in the column on the right.

1. If a bailment has no specific time limit, it cannot be terminated by either party.  T  F
2. A bailment can involve land and other real property.  T  F
3. An illegal transaction cannot be the subject of a bailment.  T  F
4. The bailor does not have to be the owner of the property being bailed.  T  F
5. The standard of care required in a bailment depends on the amount of the consideration paid for the bailment.  T  F
6. A bailee can be held liable to a bailor for failing to observe the terms of a bailment.  T  F
7. The lease of a car for a two-year period is considered a bailment.  T  F
8. Parties to a bailment can agree to limit the liability of the bailee.  T  F
9. A hotel has a greater responsibility toward a hotel guest than it does toward a business guest.  T  F
10. The consignor gives the consignee a bill of lading.  T  F

## MULTIPLE-CHOICE QUESTIONS

On the line next to each statement, write the letter of the best answer.

____ 1. Renting a public locker is not considered a bailment because (a) it does not involve personal property, (b) the owner of the locker never actually accepts delivery of the articles in the locker, (c) no consideration is given, (d) the agreement is not in writing.

2. The subject of a bailment can be (a) twenty shares of corporate stock, (b) a sailboat, (c) a sweater, (d) all of these.

3. For a bailment to exist there must be (a) a transfer of possession, (b) a transfer of title, (c) a written lease, (d) real property of any type.

4. In a gratuitous bailment, (a) both parties benefit, (b) only the bailor or the bailee benefits, (c) no one benefits, (d) only a third party benefits.

5. The relationship between a bank and one of its depositors is that of (a) bailor-bailee, (b) trustor-trustee, (c) debtor-creditor, (d) none of these.

6. Grimm picked up a wallet that had been left on a bus. This is an example of a(n) (a) express bailment, (b) constructive bailment, (c) bailment implied in fact, (d) mutual benefit bailment.

7. Curtis wanted to borrow money from a bank. The bank wanted collateral for the loan, so Curtis deposited some of her stock with the bank as security. This is an example of a (a) consignment, (b) pawn, (c) pledge, (d) bailee's lien.

8. The standard of care required in a bailment for the sole benefit of the bailor is that of (a) minimal care, (b) extraordinary care, (c) slight care, (d) ordinary care.

9. Renting an item is an example of a (a) mutual benefit bailment, (b) bailment by necessity, (c) constructive bailment, (d) bailment implied in fact.

10. A bailee's right to keep bailed property as security until paid for the work performed is called the (a) bailee's mortgage, (b) bailee's lien, (c) consignment right, (d) pledge.

Read the information below and then answer the questions that follow.

Bell, an onion farmer, shipped four hundred sacks of onions from Jones, Long Island, to the Farmers' Market in Detroit, Michigan. The onions were shipped via Long Island Railroad, terms FOB Jones, Long Island.

11. The Long Island Railroad, which accepted the onions from Bell, transports goods for anyone who requests its services. This railroad is a (a) consignee, (b) consignor, (c) common carrier, (d) private carrier.

12. The rates charged by the Long Island Railroad for shipping goods from Jones, Long Island, to Detroit, Michigan, are subject to the regulations of the (a) Federal Trade Commission, (b) Public Service Commission, (c) Interstate Commerce Commission, (d) Intrastate Commerce Commission.

13. The onions were shipped according to the railroad's regular shipping conditions and without any unusual delay. When they reached their destination, however, the onions in several of the bags had spoiled. The railroad was liable for (a) the value of the spoiled onions, (b) negligence in not speeding delivery to prevent spoilage, (c) negligence in accepting goods that were subject to spoilage, (d) no part of the loss because of the nature of the goods.

14. When the onions arrived in Detroit, the Farmers' Market was unable to unload them for 2 days. The carrier levied a charge for this delay. This charge is called (a) demurrage, (b) fee simple, (c) a tariff, (d) a lien.

## CASE PROBLEM

Read the case problem below and then answer the questions that follow.

Blake drove her car into a parking lot and turned the keys over to the attendant, who parked the car for her. There was a sign posted in the attendant's building that read "Not responsible for loss of or damage to cars in excess of $500." Blake never saw the sign. Two hours later, a tornado hit the parking lot and destroyed Blake's car, which was valued at $10,000. Blake wants to collect $10,000 from the owner of the parking lot.

1. What is the legal relationship between Blake and the parking lot owner?

2. Is Blake bound by the limitations of liability stated on the sign posted in the attendant's building? Explain your answer.

3. Must the parking lot owner pay Blake for her loss? Explain your answer.

4. If the parking lot owner is obligated to pay Blake, what amount would the owner have to pay? Why?

# PART IX

# INSURANCE

# Chapter 35

# Property and Casualty Insurance

## CHAPTER OUTLINE

The Nature of Insurance
**Purchasing Insurance**
**The Insurance Policy**
    When Protection Begins
    Insurable Interest
    Exclusions
    Amount of Coverage
    Deductible Clause
    Claims
**Property and Casualty Insurance**
    Fire
    Burglary and Theft
    Personal and Public Liability

    Marine
    All-Risk
    Multi-Peril
**Standard Clauses in Policies**
    Coverage
    Removal of Property
    Vacancy
    Pro-Rata Liability
    Increase in Risk
    Coinsurance
    Insurable Interest
    Cancellation and Termination
    Assignment

## MULTIPLE-CHOICE QUESTIONS

On the line next to each statement, write the letter of the best answer.

1. A risk or peril that specifically is not covered by an insurance policy is called an (a) excision, (b) extrusion, (c) exclusion, (d) extension.

2. The standard fire insurance policy has been adopted in (a) all states west of the Mississippi, (b) all states east of the Mississippi, (c) Alaska and Hawaii only, (d) all states.

3. Coverage against loss or damage from a windstorm is called (a) special coverage, (b) extended coverage, (c) windstorm coverage, (d) catastrophe coverage.

4. To insure property against loss or damage from any cause, you should buy a(n) (a) all-risk policy, (b) multi-peril policy, (c) marine policy, (d) liability policy.

5. To collect under an insurance policy for damage to property, the insured must have an insurable interest at the time (a) the policy is purchased, (b) the loss occurs, (c) of purchase and the time of loss, (d) proceeds are paid.

6. To protect yourself against claims that others might make against you for injuries caused by your negligence and on your property, you need (a) public liability insurance, (b) inland marine insurance, (c) risk insurance, (d) negligence insurance.

7. An addition to an insurance policy is called a(n) (a) filler, (b) amendment, (c) memorandum, (d) rider.

8. Most policies protecting residences provide that coverage stops if the residence is vacant for more than (a) 60 days, (b) 30 days, (c) 3 months, (d) 1 year.

9. The obligation to carry a minimum amount of insurance is called (a) risk sharing, (b) coinsurance, (c) multiple coverage, (d) co-obligation.

10. Insurance that protects against loss from claims made by persons injured as a result of the insured's actions is (a) fire insurance, (b) public liability insurance, (c) personal liability insurance, (d) standard insurance.

## ACTIVITY: IDENTIFYING RISKS COVERED BY INSURANCE

Place an X in the column at the right of each statement to indicate whether the risk is covered by a standard fire policy with extended coverage.

|  | COVERED | NOT COVERED |
| --- | --- | --- |
| 1. Damage to a roof caused by lightning | | |
| 2. Breakage of windows as a result of vandalism | | |
| 3. Damage to a rug due to a hot water heater's bursting | | |
| 4. Loss of a tree during a windstorm | | |
| 5. The unexplained disappearance of a camera | | |
| 6. Smoke damage caused by a kitchen accident | | |
| 7. The collapse of a roof due to the weight of ice and snow | | |
| 8. Destruction of furniture due to a flood | | |
| 9. A broken window caused by a falling tree branch | | |
| 10. Damage to a front door during a riot | | |

## CASE PROBLEMS

Read the case problems below. For each problem, answer yes or no, and then explain your answer in the space provided.

1. Gilbey was burning some leaves in his backyard one afternoon. When he got too close to the flames, his coat caught fire and was ruined. Can he collect from his insurance company under his fire insurance policy for the damage to the coat?

2. Hanley went to a baseball game and took along a valuable camera. The camera was insured under an all-risk policy. Hanley, through negligence, left the camera in the aisle, where it was stepped on and destroyed. Can Hanley collect from the insurance company for the value of the camera?

3. Jaffey bought a painting for $2,000 and insured it for that amount. Ten years later, she discovered that the painting was actually a Rembrandt worth $2,000,000. If the painting is stolen, can Jaffey collect the full appraised value?

4. Gregg applied for an insurance policy covering loss of or damage to his motorcycle. In the application, he incorrectly stated the color of his eyes. If the motorcycle is damaged in an accident, can the insurance company refuse to pay for the damage because of the misstatement in the application?

5. Cohen lent Bridges a valuable set of china dishes for use during a party that Bridges was giving at her home. Bridges took out an insurance policy insuring the value of the china. When the china was damaged during the party, Bridges insisted that the insurance company compensate her for the loss. Was she entitled to collect?

6. Davidson insured her jewelry with two insurance agencies. If the jewelry is stolen, can she collect the full policy amount from both agencies?

_____
_____
_____

7. Hughes canceled his car insurance policy before the end of the term. Did Hughes receive a refund for the full amount of the unused premium?

_____
_____
_____

## COMPLETION QUESTIONS

In the statements below, important words have been omitted. Fill in the blanks to complete each statement.

1. A means of sharing risk of loss with others is called _____.

2. A written insurance contract is called a(n) _____.

3. The greater the risk, the higher the _____.

4. Someone who is hired by and sells insurance policies only for a specific company is called an insurance _____.

5. A risk that specifically is not covered under an insurance policy is called a(n) _____.

6. A policy that states the specific amount to be paid when a loss occurs is said to have _____ coverage.

7. To reduce premiums, many insurance companies offer policies that contain a _____ clause.

8. A material _____ on an application for an insurance policy can void the policy.

9. In the event of a loss, the first step in presenting the claim is to notify the _____.

10. After a claim is settled, the insured is asked to sign a document called a(n) _____ before payment is made.

# Chapter 36

# Automobile Insurance

## CHAPTER OUTLINE

The Need for Automobile Insurance
Types of Automobile Coverage
    Bodily Injury Liability
    Property Damage Liability
    Medical Payments
    Uninsured Motorists
    Collision
    Comprehensive Physical Damage

Who Is Covered by Automobile Insurance
No-Fault Insurance
How Premiums are Determined
Cancellation of Automobile Insurance
What to Do if You're Involved in an Accident
    At the Time of the Accident
    After the Accident
    When to Consult an Attorney

## TRUE-FALSE QUESTIONS

Indicate whether each statement below is true or false by circling T or F in the column on the right.

1. Automobile insurance is compulsory in every state.  T  F
2. The amount of insurance required varies from state to state.  T  F
3. Collision insurance pays for damage to a vehicle regardless of who is at fault.  T  F
4. A deductible feature in an insurance policy usually reduces the amount of the premium.  T  F
5. Automobile insurance protects the owner only.  T  F
6. A person's liability for injury to another person is limited to the amount of insurance coverage.  T  F
7. With no-fault coverage, an injured person can recover from her or his own insurance company regardless of who was at fault.  T  F
8. All states in the United States have no-fault laws.  T  F
9. Not all automobile accidents have to be reported to the police.  T  F
10. An insured can cancel an automobile insurance policy at any time.  T  F

## MULTIPLE-CHOICE QUESTIONS

On the line next to each statement, write the letter of the best answer.

_____ 1. Laws that ensure that the owners or drivers of cars are able to pay for the damages or injuries they cause others are called (a) coinsurance laws, (b) auto liability laws, (c) financial responsibility laws, (d) no-fault laws.

_____ 2. Injuries caused by a hit-and-run driver are covered by (a) comprehensive insurance, (b) property damage liability insurance, (c) collision insurance, (d) uninsured motorist insurance.

_____ 3. The premium for collision insurance can be reduced through (a) coinsurance, (b) a deductible clause, (c) assigned risk, (d) an omnibus clause.

_____ 4. In some states, a vehicle owner must provide proof of financial responsibility before the vehicle can be (a) registered, (b) bought, (c) sold, (d) repaired.

_____ 5. A person who operates a vehicle with the owner's consent is protected by a clause in the policy called a(n) (a) guest clause, (b) autobus clause, (c) deductible, (d) omnibus clause.

_____ 6. Cook carries comprehensive insurance on his car. All of the following types of loss or damage are covered by this insurance *except* (a) theft, (b) glass breakage, (c) collision, (d) tornado damage.

_____ 7. Filing an accident report in the case of death or injury is mandatory in (a) all states, (b) those states that have no-fault laws, (c) those states that do not have no-fault laws, (d) none of these.

_____ 8. If you injure another person in an auto accident and you carry $50,000 of liability insurance, your insurance company is responsible to the extent of (a) $100,000, (b) $50,000, (c) the no-fault threshold figure, (d) whatever the court awards.

_____ 9. Guest laws relieve drivers of liability for injuries to guests unless the driver's negligence is (a) average, (b) minimal, (c) gross, (d) zero.

_____ 10. The type of automobile insurance that permits an insured to collect medical expenses resulting from an accident, regardless of fault, is (a) liability, (b) no-fault, (c) comprehensive, (d) collision.

## ACTIVITY: PROTECTING AGAINST RISK

Indicate whether the coverages listed below protect against the risks described in the left column by placing an X in the proper column.

| | Bodily Injury | Property Damage | Medical Payments | Uninsured Motorist | Collision | Comprehensive |
|---|---|---|---|---|---|---|
| 1. Your car radio is stolen. | | | | | | |
| 2. A vandal ruins the finish on your car. | | | | | | |
| 3. A falling branch smashes your windshield. | | | | | | |
| 4. You back your car into a fire hydrant. | | | | | | |

|  | Bodily Injury | Property Damage | Medical Payments | Uninsured Motorist | Collision | Comprehensive |
|---|---|---|---|---|---|---|
| 5. Your car explodes because of a leak in the gas tank. | ___ | ___ | ___ | ___ | ___ | ___ |
| 6. You have to rent a car when yours is stolen. | ___ | ___ | ___ | ___ | ___ | ___ |
| 7. A hit-and-run driver hits your car, causing damage. | ___ | ___ | ___ | ___ | ___ | ___ |
| 8. You are hospitalized after being in an auto accident. | ___ | ___ | ___ | ___ | ___ | ___ |
| 9. Your neighbor sues you after you back into her car. | ___ | ___ | ___ | ___ | ___ | ___ |
| 10. You are injured when an unknown driver hits you while you change a tire. | ___ | ___ | ___ | ___ | ___ | ___ |

## CASE PROBLEMS

Read the case problems below. For each problem, answer yes or no, and then explain your answer in the space provided.

1. Beatty had collision coverage on her car. While driving to school one day, she made a wrong turn on a one-way street and collided with another car, damaging her own car extensively. Did Beatty have a good claim for the damage?

   _____
   _____
   _____

2. Cramer bought a new car for $8,000. Two days later, it was demolished when Cramer drove it into a tree. If Cramer had $250 deductible collision coverage on his car, what is the maximum he can collect?

   _____
   _____
   _____

# Chapter 37

# Personal Insurance

## CHAPTER OUTLINE

The Need for Personal Insurance
Life Insurance
    Whole Life Insurance
    Endowment Insurance
    Term Insurance
    Insurance for Special Purposes
    Standard Policy Clauses
    How Life Insurance Proceeds are Paid

Health Insurance
    Medical, Surgical, and Hospital Insurance
    Major Medical Insurance
    Medicare and Medicaid
    Disability Income Insurance
    Dental Expense Insurance

## MULTIPLE-CHOICE QUESTIONS

On the line next to each statement, write the letter of the best answer.

_____ 1. Life insurance is often a combination of protection and investment. The type of insurance that has no investment feature is (a) straight life, (b) endowment, (c) term, (d) universal life.

_____ 2. The least costly type of life insurance is (a) endowment insurance, (b) limited payment life insurance, (c) term insurance, (d) whole life insurance.

_____ 3. The clause in a life insurance policy that states that the insurance company cannot void a policy that has been in effect for a specific period of time for any reason other than nonpayment of premiums is the (a) incontestable clause, (b) suicide clause, (c) settlement option clause, (d) grace period clause.

_____ 4. In his application for life insurance, Meany lied about his health. The insurance company cannot cancel the policy if it discovers the lie after the policy has been in effect (a) 1 year, (b) 2 years, (c) 3 years, (d) 5 years.

Copyright © Houghton Mifflin Company. All rights reserved.

5. At age 35, Grimsby took out a life insurance policy and stated her age as 29. Grimsby died 5 years later. What effect, if any, does the misrepresentation have on the payment to the beneficiary? (a) The insurer does not have to pay the beneficiary anything because the policy is void, (b) the insurer must pay the beneficiary only half the face value of the policy, (c) the insurer must pay the beneficiary an amount adjusted for the insured's correct age, (d) the insurer must pay the beneficiary the face value of the policy because the misrepresentation had no effect on the performance of the contract.

6. Forman allowed her term insurance policy to lapse when she was laid off from work and short of money. After six months she was able to make all of her back payments and was still in good health. Which clause in her policy would require the insurance company to place Forman's policy back in force? (a) Grace period clause, (b) reinstatement clause, (c) incontestable clause, (d) waiver of premium clause.

7. Weeks purchases a life insurance policy on McKay's life and names Jones as the beneficiary. Who must have an insurable interest and at what time for this policy to be valid? (a) Jones at the inception of the policy, (b) Jones at the time of McKay's death, (c) Weeks at the inception of the policy, (d) Weeks at the time of McKay's death.

8. Johnson and Bell were engaged to be married. Johnson took out a $10,000 life insurance policy on his life and named Bell as the beneficiary. The engagement was broken. Johnson subsequently married Cochran and had a son. When Johnson died, the insurance company would be required to pay (a) his estate, (b) Cochran, (c) the son, (d) Bell.

9. When Pogue retired from her job at age 65, she became eligible for government-subsidized health insurance called (a) Medicare, (b) Medicaid, (c) unemployment insurance, (d) disability income protection.

10. Insurance that covers catastrophic illness or injury is called (a) Medicare, (b) Major Medical Insurance, (c) Medicaid, (d) Social Security.

## CASE PROBLEMS

Read the case problems below. For each problem, answer yes or no, and then explain your answer in the space provided.

1. The premium on Benson's life insurance policy was due on December 1. Benson mailed the premium on December 10, but the insurance company refused to accept it, claiming the policy had lapsed. Was the insurance company correct?

2. Harden purchased a life insurance policy. Five years later, he committed suicide. Did the insurance company have to pay the proceeds of the policy to Harden's beneficiary?

3. On August 1, 1986, Williams submitted a life insurance application to the Premier Life Insurance Company. Although he was born in 1950, he mistakenly wrote 1960 as his year of birth on the application. Last month the insurance company discovered the error in Williams's date of birth. Can the policy be declared void?

_____

_____

_____

4. Rustin purchased a 5-year term insurance policy. After 5 years, can Rustin collect the cash value of the policy from the insurance company?

_____

_____

_____

5. Milton purchased a whole life insurance policy. Several years later, she found she could no longer pay the premiums. Can the insurance company cancel the policy without any further benefit to Milton?

_____

_____

_____

_____

## MATCHING QUESTIONS

Use the following terms to identify the phrases below. On the line next to each phrase, write the letter of the term that most closely relates to it.

a. Group insurance
b. Key-man insurance
c. Limited payment insurance
d. Term insurance
e. Endowment insurance
f. Modified life insurance
g. Annuity
h. Family income policy
i. Disability income insurance
j. Whole life insurance

_____ 1. A policy that provides income during the owner's lifetime

_____ 2. An insurance policy for which premiums start out low and increase

_____ 3. A policy that insures all members of a specific group

_____ 4. Insurance purchased by business partners to insure the lives of other partners or stockholders

_____ 5. A policy that combines whole life and term insurance

_____ 6. Insurance that provides protection for a limited time

_____ 7. Insurance for which premiums are paid for a limited period of time

_____ 8. Insurance that provides protection until the insured reaches a certain age

_____ 9. A policy that provides income to a person who cannot work because of illness or accident

_____ 10. A policy offering lifetime protection and for which premiums remain the same

# Review

# Part IX Insurance

## TRUE-FALSE QUESTIONS

Indicate whether each statement below is true or false by circling T or F in the column on the right.

1. An insurance broker is employed by an insurance company to sell insurance.  T  F
2. An insurance company does not issue a policy without an application.  T  F
3. Once an insured makes the first premium payment, the insurance company is obligated on the policy regardless of the presence of an insurable interest.  T  F
4. If an insured suffers a loss that equals the deductible amount, he or she does not recover anything from the insurance company.  T  F
5. An insurance company can cancel a policy because of false information on the application even if it did not rely on the information in issuing the policy.  T  F
6. Fire insurance does not cover smoke damage caused by a fire.  T  F
7. A homeowners policy covers damage to the personal property of guests while they are on the insured's property.  T  F
8. Specific coverage in a property insurance policy becomes a problem if costs rise because of inflation.  T  F
9. An insurance company can cancel an insurance policy if the insured increases the risk of loss or damage.  T  F
10. A passenger in a car who shares the expenses of a trip is not protected by an automobile guest law.  T  F

## MATCHING QUESTIONS

Use the following terms to identify the phrases below. On the line next to each phrase, write the letter of the term that most closely relates to it.

a. Coinsurance
b. Short rate
c. Subrogation
d. Binder
e. Indemnification
f. Proximate cause
g. Release
h. Guest laws
i. Floater policy
j. Deductible

_____ 1. That part of a loss paid for by the insured

_____ 2. A legal form signed when a claim is settled

_____ 3. Laws that define responsibility toward passengers in the insured's car

_____ 4. A clause that requires an insured to maintain a certain amount of insurance

_____ 5. An insurance company's right to recover from the person responsible for the loss

_____ 6. A temporary insurance policy

_____ 7. Compensation to an insured for loss of or damage to insured property

_____ 8. The premium amount refunded to the insured when a policy is canceled by the insured

_____ 9. An all-risk policy that covers loss or damage to personal property from any cause

_____ 10. The direct or natural cause of a loss or damage

## MULTIPLE-CHOICE QUESTIONS

On the line next to each statement, write the letter of the best answer.

_____ 1. Insurance can be issued by (a) department stores, (b) savings banks, (c) churches and synagogues, (d) city governments.

_____ 2. An insurance salesperson who sells insurance issued by several companies is an (a) insurance agent, (b) issuer, (c) actuary, (d) insurance broker.

_____ 3. When an insurance company does not give a binder, a policy becomes effective when (a) the application is received, (b) the application is accepted, (c) 30 days have gone by, (d) the policy is delivered to the insured.

_____ 4. If an insured does not have an insurable interest in the life or the property insured, the (a) policy is void, (b) policy is voidable at the insured's option, (c) insured can collect only half the face value of the policy, (d) insured cannot recover any premiums paid.

_____ 5. If you own a painting valued at $5,000 and want to guarantee payment of that amount in the event of theft, regardless of the actual value at the time of the loss, you should choose insurance with (a) inflation coverage, (b) open coverage, (c) valued coverage, (d) closed coverage.

_____ 6. To be fully protected from loss of or damage to personal property for any reason, you would choose a(n) (a) all-risk policy, (b) homeowners policy, (c) multi-peril policy, (d) standard policy.

_____ 7. If a person insures property with more than one company and a loss occurs, (a) the company that issued the first policy is liable for the loss, (b) neither company is liable, (c) each company pays its pro-rata share of the loss, (d) each company must pay the full amount of the loss.

_____ 8. Property and casualty policies can be canceled (a) when a loss occurs, (b) at any time by the insured or the insurer, (c) by the insured only, (d) by the insurer only.

_____ 9. An insured who has property and casualty insurance (a) can assign the policy at any time, (b) is prohibited from assigning the policy, (c) can assign the policy with the consent of the insurance company, (d) can assign the policy only before a loss occurs.

_____ 10. Collision insurance insures against (a) injury to the insured, (b) damage to another's car, (c) injury to another person, (d) damage to the insured's car.

_____ 11. The coverage under a policy in which a specific amount is payable is called (a) closed, (b) specific, (c) open, (d) valued.

_____ 12. Concealing material information on an insurance application (a) voids the policy, (b) makes the policy voidable at the insurance company's option, (c) has no effect on the policy, (d) has no effect if the initial premium has been paid.

_____ 13. To insure a camera against any type of loss, you would purchase a (a) theft policy, (b) homeowners policy, (c) comprehensive policy, (d) floater policy.

_____ 14. Insurance coverage that pays for damage if a driver loses control of her or his car and crashes into a store window is (a) comprehensive, (b) property damage, (c) collision, (d) public liability.

_____ 15. Ward, age 40, wants to insure his life. To receive the face value of the policy when he reaches age 60, he should buy a(n) (a) term policy, (b) 20-year endowment policy, (c) 20-payment life policy, (d) annuity with payments beginning at age 60.

_____ 16. When an insured dies, the life insurance company pays the (a) face value of the policy to the beneficiary, (b) cash surrender value to the beneficiary, (c) face value to the insured, (d) cash surrender value to the insured.

_____ 17. Hubbard planned to fly from Boston to Dallas. She purchased a life insurance policy that covered her solely during the trip. This kind of policy is called a(n) (a) straight life policy, (b) term policy, (c) endowment policy, (d) annuity.

_____ 18. A life insurance company can refuse to pay the face amount of a policy if the insured commits suicide (a) before age 18, (b) before age 21, (c) within the first 2 policy years, (d) within the first 3 policy years.

# PART X

# WILLS AND ESTATE PLANNING

# Chapter 38

# Wills and Intestacy

## CHAPTER OUTLINE

The Purpose of a Will
Requirements of a Valid Will
   Testamentary Capacity
   Freedom from Duress, Fraud, and Undue Influence
   Written Form
   Witnesses
Special Wills
   Holographic Wills
   Nuncupative Wills

Limitations on Disposing of Property by Will
Making a Will
Changing or Revoking a Will
Administering a Will
   Probating the Will
   Administering the Estate
   Settling the Estate
Intestacy
Living Wills and Health Care Proxies

## MULTIPLE-CHOICE QUESTIONS

On the line next to each statement, write the letter of the best answer.

_____ 1. The estate of a person who dies without a will is distributed according to (a) federal law, (b) oral instructions left by the person before death, (c) state law, (d) local ordinance.

_____ 2. Property owned by joint tenants with the right of survivorship is distributed on one tenant's death (a) according to that person's will, (b) to the survivor(s), (c) according to state law, (d) to that person's children.

_____ 3. In most states, a valid will can be executed by a person (a) of any age, (b) under 16, (c) over 25, (d) 18 or over.

_____ 4. To be valid, a written will can be (a) typed, (b) handwritten, (c) printed, (d) any of these.

_____ 5. A completely handwritten will is called a (a) nuncupative will, (b) holographic will, (c) xerographic will, (d) de minimus will.

_____ 6. In most states a will, to be valid, must be signed by the testator (a) at the beginning of the will, (b) after the witnesses' signatures, (c) on each page, (d) at the end of the will.

_____ 7. Of the following methods, the only one that does not effectively revoke a will is (a) mutilating it, (b) sending a letter of revocation to one's heirs, (c) writing a new will, (d) destroying the old will.

_____ 8. In most states, the number of witnesses required for a will to be valid is (a) one, (b) four, (c) two or three, (d) five.

_____ 9. Persons named as beneficiaries in a will (a) can witness the will, (b) cannot witness the will, (c) should witness the will, (d) can witness the will if they are over 18.

_____ 10. The person named in a will to carry out its terms is the (a) guardian, (b) spouse, (c) administrator, (d) executor.

## COMPLETION QUESTIONS

In the statements below, important words have been omitted. Fill in the blanks to complete each statement.

1. A person who makes a will is called a(n) _____.

2. A person who dies without a will is said to have died _____.

3. Establishing a will's validity is a process called _____.

4. The _____ is the person who handles the estate of a person who dies without a will.

5. In most states, a person who is entitled to share in the estate of a person who dies intestate is called a(n) _____.

6. An oral will made in the presence of witnesses is a(n) _____ will.

7. A(n) _____ is an amendment to a will.

8. A will that expresses one's health care preferences is a(n) _____ will.

9. A gift of personal property by will is called a(n) _____.

10. The right of a(n) _____ to receive a certain portion of an estate cannot be defeated by a will's provisions.

# ACTIVITY: READING A WILL

Read the will below and answer the questions that follow.

---

I, Sam Taylor, declare that this is my will:

1. I give my wife the sum of $10 as she has enough money of her own to provide for her needs.
2. I devise my half of the home I own jointly with my wife to my good friend, Robert Fisk.
3. I bequeath the sum of $100,000 to the American Cancer Society.
4. I leave the balance of my estate, consisting of $400,000 in real estate, to my children, Janet and Mark Taylor.

                                      Sam Taylor

The above will was signed by Sam Taylor in our presence and was declared by him to be his last will. He asked us to act as witnesses, and we now sign this will as witnesses to it.

*Janet Taylor* — residing at 93 Providence Rd., Reston, Virginia

*Mark Taylor* — residing at 1628 Harrison Street, Akron, Ohio

---

1. Must Sam's wife accept the $10 as the only amount she is entitled to from his estate?
2. Can Robert Fisk acquire good title to the house under Paragraph 2 of the will?
3. Is the will invalid because Sam typed his name at the end instead of signing it?
4. Is the provision in Paragraph 3 automatically valid?
5. If Sam left $100,000 to the U.S. government as a contribution, would this kind of provision be held valid?
6. If Sam's wife had died before he did, would Robert Fisk get valid title to Sam's home?
7. Will the gifts to Sam's children be held valid?
8. If Sam had left nothing to his children, would that alone have made the will invalid?
9. Is the will considered valid without a notary's acknowledgment of Sam's signature?
10. Would this will have been valid if Sam was 17 years old when he prepared it?

# Chapter 39

# Estate Planning

## CHAPTER OUTLINE

The Need for Estate Planning
Taxes and Estate Planning
    Gifts
    The Marital Deduction
    Trusts
Developing an Estate Plan

## MULTIPLE-CHOICE QUESTIONS

On the line next to each statement, write the letter of the best answer.

_____ 1. An estate tax is imposed by (a) all states, (b) the federal government, (c) banks, (d) each city.

_____ 2. The major reason for estate planning is (a) to create an estate, (b) to provide liquidity, (c) to minimize taxes, (d) all of these.

_____ 3. The federal estate tax is a tax on (a) the gross estate, (b) the marital deduction, (c) the net estate, (d) trusts.

_____ 4. A trust set up in one's will is called a(n) (a) inter vivos trust, (b) living trust, (c) Totten trust, (d) testamentary trust.

_____ 5. The marital deduction allows property to pass to a surviving spouse tax-free (a) up to $100,000, (b) up to $250,000, (c) in an unlimited amount, (d) over $250,000.

_____ 6. Each year a married couple jointly can give tax-free gifts to individuals in the amount of (a) $6,000, (b) $12,000, (c) $10,000, (d) $20,000.

_____ 7. The person who receives benefits from a trust is called the (a) settlor, (b) heir, (c) beneficiary, (d) trustor.

8. Information needed for successful estate planning includes (a) Social Security numbers, (b) family history, (c) insurance policy information, (d) all of these.

9. The main advantage of a trust is (a) reduced income taxes, (b) reduced estate taxes, (c) flexibility, (d) liquidity.

10. Property that qualifies for the marital deduction includes (a) jointly held real estate, (b) insurance proceeds payable to a spouse, (c) jointly owned stocks, (d) all of these.

## MATCHING QUESTIONS

Use the following terms to identify the phrases below. On the line next to each phrase, write the letter of the term that most closely relates to it.

a. Beneficiary
b. Estate planning
c. Living trust
d. Marital deduction
e. Settlor
f. Trust
g. Trustee
h. Net estate
i. Testamentary trust
j. Liquidity

1. A person who turns over property to be held and managed in a trust
2. A trust set up to take effect during a person's lifetime
3. Having assets that readily can be converted into cash
4. The person who holds and manages the property in a trust
5. A person who receives benefits under a trust agreement
6. A trust set up after death through a will
7. A federal estate tax deduction available when property is transferred to a spouse under certain conditions
8. The process of planning for the management and disposition of one's assets to dispose of them properly and to minimize income and estate taxes
9. A device used to transfer property for the purpose of holding and managing it for the benefit of another
10. Assets left by an individual at death, less certain deductions permitted by law

## SHORT-ANSWER QUESTIONS

Answer each of the following questions in the space provided.

1. List the person(s) who should be consulted in developing an estate plan.

2. Briefly describe the steps involved in developing an estate plan.

3. List four different types of property that generally qualify for the marital deduction.

4. Describe three different devices that can be used to minimize estate taxes.

# Review

## Part X
## Wills and Estate Planning

**MULTIPLE-CHOICE QUESTIONS**

On the line next to each statement, write the letter of the best answer.

_____ 1. A gift of real property is called a(n) (a) legacy, (b) codicil, (c) devise, (d) attestation.

_____ 2. A will can be changed by adding a(n) (a) writ, (b) codicil, (c) attesting clause, (d) mandamus.

_____ 3. For a will to be valid, most states require that it be witnessed by (a) one person, (b) two or three people, (c) four or five people, (d) five people.

_____ 4. Which of the following is *not* required by most states for a will to be valid? (a) That the will be witnessed, (b) that the witnesses know the contents of the will, (c) that the signature of the testator appear on the will, (d) that the testator be legally competent.

_____ 5. Someone who dies without leaving a valid will has died (a) in trusteeship, (b) in codicil, (c) intestate, (d) in holography.

_____ 6. A person can change or revoke a will by (a) tearing it up, (b) executing a new will, (c) executing a codicil, (d) all of these.

_____ 7. The process of establishing a will's validity is called (a) administration, (b) testacy, (c) settlement, (d) probate.

_____ 8. A clause at the end of a will stating that the witnesses actually saw the will being signed is called a(n) (a) attrition, (b) lapse, (c) testament, (d) attestation.

_____ 9. A gift of a car in a will is an example of a (a) specific devise, (b) general legacy, (c) general devise, (d) specific legacy.

_____ 10. A will written completely in the maker's own handwriting is called a(n) (a) nuncupative will, (b) oral will, (c) holographic will, (d) hologram.

_____ 11. Disposition of an intestate's property is determined by (a) state law, (b) provisions of the will, (c) federal law, (d) local custom.

_____ 12. The choice of an executor to handle an estate is made by the (a) judge, (b) person who executed the will, (c) beneficiaries, (d) spouse of the deceased.

13. The final step in administering an estate is known as (a) probate, (b) sequestration, (c) remainder, (d) settlement.

14. In an oral will, a person can dispose of (a) real property only, (b) real and personal property, (c) personal property only, (d) none of these.

15. To be valid, in most states a will must be signed by the maker (a) at the beginning, (b) on each page, (c) immediately after the witnesses' signatures, (d) at the very end of the will.

## CASE PROBLEMS

Read the case problems below. For each problem, answer yes or no, and then explain your answer in the space provided.

1. Perkins typed a will and then added his handwritten signature at the end. The will was not witnessed. In the will, Perkins left all of his property to one sister. Perkins's other sister claimed that the will was void. Was she correct?

   _____
   _____
   _____

2. Nichols executed a will valid in all respects. In the will, she left $5,000 to her nephew. Six months later, Nichols crossed out this figure and wrote in $50,000. When Nichols died, the nephew made a claim against the estate for $50,000. Was the claim valid?

   _____
   _____
   _____

3. Burdine left a will in which she bequeathed her house to her sister provided the sister agreed to live in the house and not sell it. On Burdine's death, the sister claimed that the provision was invalid. Was she correct?

   _____
   _____
   _____

4. When he made his will, Greggs had two children, and he left all of his property to his wife and the two children. A year later another child was born, but Greggs never changed his will. When Greggs died, the first two children claimed that the third child was not entitled to share in Greggs's estate. Were they correct?

   _____
   _____
   _____

## MATCHING QUESTIONS

Use the following terms to identify the phrases below. On the line next to each phrase, write the letter of the term that most closely relates to it.

a. Probate
b. Trust
c. Intestate
d. Executor
e. Codicil

_____ 1. The personal representative of a deceased named in the deceased's will

_____ 2. An addition or amendment to a will

_____ 3. The process of validating a will

_____ 4. A person who dies without a will

_____ 5. A plan by which one turns over property to someone to hold and manage for another

# PART XI

# CONSUMER AND CREDITOR PROTECTION

# Chapter 40

# Protecting the Consumer and the Taxpayer

## CHAPTER OUTLINE

The Need for Consumer Protection
Regulation of Business Practices
   The Right to Fair Advertising
   The Right to Fair Pricing
   The Right to Refuse Unordered Goods
   The Right to Cancel Certain Contracts
   The Right to Understandable Written Contracts
   Truth in Savings Accounts
Product Standards
   The Right to Safe Merchandise
   The Right to Proper Labeling and Packaging
   The Right to Purchase Quality Vehicles

Remedies for Violation of Consumer Protection Laws
Rights of the Air Traveler
   Overbooking of Flights
   Flight Delays
   Liability for Lost, Delayed, or Damaged Baggage
   Liability on International Flights
Rights of the Taxpayer

## COMPLETION QUESTIONS

In the statements below, important words have been omitted. Fill in the blanks to complete each statement.

1. The agency primarily responsible for enforcing consumer rights is the _____.

2. The failure to disclose important product information is one form of _____.

3. Price fixing violates both state _____ and federal _____ laws.

4. A person who receives unordered goods can either _____ them or throw them away.

5. The _____ can require advertisements for certain products to carry warning labels.

6. Exaggerating the quality of merchandise is called _____.

7. An item sold below cost to entice a customer into a store is called a(n) _____.

8. Consumer contracts involving less than a certain amount of money must be written in _____.

9. Liability for injuries on international flights is limited by the _____.

10. A suit by a group claiming a violation of consumer protection laws is called a(n) _____ suit.

## SHORT-ANSWER QUESTIONS

Answer each of the following questions in the space provided.

1. List four consumer rights and give an example of each.

   _____
   _____
   _____
   _____
   _____
   _____
   _____
   _____

2. List three federal consumer agencies and describe their functions.

   _____
   _____
   _____
   _____
   _____
   _____
   _____

# CHAPTER 40

## CASE PROBLEMS

Read the case problems below. For each problem, answer yes or no, and then explain your answer in the space provided.

1. Acme Supermarket and Peach Supermarket agreed to charge the same prices for their fruits and vegetables, resulting in a lower price for consumers. Have these supermarkets violated the law?

   _____
   _____

2. Turner bought a new TV from a department store, paying for it in cash. Two days later, she tried to return it, claiming she had a right to rescind the sales contract within 3 days of the purchase. Was Turner correct?

   _____
   _____
   _____

## ACTIVITY: DESCRIBING VIOLATIONS

Look at the product packaging shown below. In the spaces provided at the right, describe any violations of consumer labeling laws.

_____

_____

_____

## ACTIVITY: REWRITING LEGALESE

Read the following clause from an actual lease and rewrite it in "plain English" in the space provided.

The landlord hereinabove named does hereby let unto the tenant hereinabove named, the premises known as 422 Cole Street, Cole, Ohio, for the term of two years commencing January 1. The tenant hereby agrees to take said premises for the aforesaid term under the terms and conditions hereinafter described.

_____
_____
_____
_____
_____

# Chapter 41

# Protecting the Borrower

## CHAPTER OUTLINE

The Use of Credit
Types of Credit
    Charge Accounts
    Installment Loans
    Bank Loans
The Right to Obtain Credit

The Right to Know What Credit Costs
The Right to Fair Credit Information
The Right to Accurate Billing
The Right to Fair Debt Collection
The Right to Legal Interest Charges
The Right to Be Relieved from Debt

## MULTIPLE-CHOICE QUESTIONS

On the line next to each statement, write the letter of the best answer.

_____ 1. Discrimination in granting credit is prohibited by the (a) Federal Trade Act, (b) Commerce Act, (c) Equal Credit Opportunity Act, (d) Fair Credit Act.

_____ 2. In deciding whether to grant credit, a creditor can consider an applicant's (a) religion, (b) geographical residence, (c) income, (d) marital status.

_____ 3. In deciding whether to grant credit, a creditor can refuse to consider income from (a) alimony, (b) a pension, (c) part-time employment, (d) gambling.

_____ 4. The money paid for the use of credit is a(n) (a) annual charge, (b) finance charge, (c) borrowing fee, (d) percentage fee.

_____ 5. A person whose credit card is stolen and who notifies the card issuer of the theft is liable for charges made with the card up to (a) the total amount charged, (b) $100, (c) $250, (d) $50.

_____ 6. An incorrect bill received by a consumer must be corrected within (a) 30 days, (b) 45 days, (c) 60 days, (d) 90 days.

_____ 7. A consumer who believes a bill is incorrect must notify the (a) Federal Trade Commission, (b) Better Business Bureau, (c) creditor, (d) local chamber of commerce.

_____ 8. Assets of a debtor that *cannot* be taken to satisfy a judgment include (a) a car, (b) a bank account, (c) stocks, (d) household furniture.

_____ 9. Usury laws generally do not apply to (a) credit card charges, (b) mortgage loans, (c) education loans, (d) vacation loans.

_____ 10. A person can file for bankruptcy (a) once a year, (b) once in a lifetime, (c) every 12 years, (d) every 6 years.

## TRUE-FALSE QUESTIONS

Indicate whether each statement below is true or false by circling T or F in the column on the right.

1. Lenders can refuse credit to someone who is receiving public assistance.     T   F
2. Creditors always can consider a potential borrower's age in determining whether to grant credit.     T   F
3. A lender must disclose the finance charge but not the annual percentage rate.     T   F
4. The law does not require that service or carrying charges added to finance charged be disclosed to a borrower.     T   F
5. If you lose a credit card because of your negligence, you may be held responsible for an unlimited amount of unauthorized charges.     T   F
6. A person who is denied credit is entitled to know the reasons why.     T   F
7. A consumer who believes a bill is incorrect does not have to make any payment on the bill until the error is corrected.     T   F
8. An agreement requiring an interest rate higher than the contract rate is usurious.     T   F
9. After being discharged in bankruptcy, a bankrupt is no longer responsible for any debts.     T   F
10. When the interest rate is not stated in a loan or credit agreement, the maximum that can be charged is called the legal rate.     T   F

## CASE PROBLEMS

Read the case problems below. For each problem, answer yes or no, and then explain your answer in the space provided.

1. Garnett needed capital to expand her business. She found a friend who agreed to lend her the money at 25% interest per year. When Garnett failed to pay the debt, her friend sued. Garnett claimed that the loan was invalid because the maximum interest rate in her state is 12%. Was Garnett legally correct?

_____

_____

_____

2. Briggs finds that her debts exceed her assets by a considerable amount, and she cannot pay her bills on time. Is bankruptcy the only solution?

_____

_____

## ACTIVITY: IS THERE A VIOLATION?

In the column at the right, indicate with an X whether or not the following actions violate borrower protection laws.

|   | VIOLATION | NO VIOLATION |
|---|---|---|
| 1. A credit card company holds a cardholder liable for charges in the amount of $25 made without the cardholder's consent. | _____ | _____ |
| 2. A bank refuses to grant a loan to a woman because she is divorced. | _____ | _____ |
| 3. A loan company fails to disclose the annual percentage rate for a loan made to a borrower to purchase a dump truck. | _____ | _____ |
| 4. A store imposes a penalty on a customer who refuses to pay for merchandise because it's defective. | _____ | _____ |
| 5. An attorney trying to collect a debt for a client repeatedly phones the debtor at her place of work. | _____ | _____ |
| 6. A collection agency advises a debtor that failure to pay the amount may result in court action. | _____ | _____ |
| 7. A bank lends money to a business and charges an interest rate 4 percent above the legal rate. | _____ | _____ |
| 8. A bank charges a higher-than-permitted interest rate because of a shortage of funds in the area. | _____ | _____ |

# Chapter 42

# Protecting the Creditor

## CHAPTER OUTLINE

Protecting Creditors' Rights
The Right to Be Paid
   Unsecured Debts
   Secured Debts
Other Methods of Protecting Creditors'
   Rights
   Suretyship
   Guaranty
   Remedies for Debtor's Default

Security Interests Created by Law
   Mechanic's Lien
   Tax Lien
   Judgment Lien
   Artisan's Lien
   Hotelkeeper's Lien

## TRUE-FALSE QUESTIONS

Indicate whether each statement below is true or false by circling T or F in the column on the right.

1. To be collectible, a debt always must be in writing.    T   F
2. An unsecured creditor can repossess the item for which credit was given.    T   F
3. A creditor can refuse to give credit unless security is given.    T   F
4. A secured loan is valid even if a financing statement is not filed.    T   F
5. In some states a secured creditor can repossess the collateral without going to court.    T   F
6. A guarantor is primarily responsible for paying the debtor's obligation.    T   F
7. If the debtor and creditor increase the interest rate on a guaranteed loan, the guarantor is freed of all responsibility on the loan.    T   F

8. A taxing authority can sell someone's property if that person fails to pay taxes.  T  F

9. If a secured creditor repossesses property and decides to sell it, the sale must be public.  T  F

10. A financing statement protects both the creditor and the public.  T  F

## CASE PROBLEM

Read the case problem below and then answer the questions that follow.

Granby wanted to borrow money from Public Bank to purchase a new car. Because Granby's credit was poor, Public Bank agreed to lend the money to Granby only if Granby's brother would act as guarantor. Granby and his brother signed the contract.

1. If Granby defaults in paying the loan, what are Public Bank's remedies?

   _____
   _____
   _____

2. If Public repossesses the car, can it sell the car at a private sale?

   _____

3. If Granby defaults on the loan, must Public first try to collect from Granby before trying to collect from his brother?

   _____

4. If Granby does not pay, can Public hold his brother liable for making the payment? Explain your answer.

   _____
   _____
   _____

5. What would happen if Granby's brother were a surety rather than a guarantor?

   _____
   _____
   _____

## MATCHING QUESTIONS

Use the following terms to identify the phrases below. On the line next to each phrase, write the letter of the term that most closely relates to it.

a. Surety
b. Collateral
c. Financing statement
d. Guarantor
e. Lien
f. Termination statement
g. Repossession
h. Judgment lien
i. Creditors' bill of rights
j. Mechanic's lien

_____ 1. A notice that a security interest no longer exists

_____ 2. The act of taking back property that is subject to a security agreement

_____ 3. A person who promises to repay a debt if the debtor fails to do so after attempts are made to collect from the debtor

_____ 4. A secured interest in property granted by law

_____ 5. Property subject to a security interest

_____ 6. Public notice of a security interest

_____ 7. A person who promises to repay the obligation of a debtor even though the creditor does not attempt to collect from the debtor

_____ 8. A lien for those who supply labor, materials, or services in the construction of buildings

_____ 9. Statutes that ensure creditors are paid

_____ 10. A lien granted to a creditor who has sued a debtor

## SHORT-ANSWER QUESTIONS

Answer each of the following questions in the space provided.

1. Assume that you operate a piano store. A customer wants to buy a piano and pay for it by making a small deposit and paying the balance over 3 years.

   a. What methods could you use to make sure that you receive the balance?

   _____
   _____
   _____

   b. If the customer is not able to make any payments after 3 months, what options do you have?

   _____
   _____
   _____
   _____

2. Describe three different types of liens used to protect a creditor's interest.

_____
_____
_____
_____
_____
_____

# Review

# Part XI Consumer and Creditor Protection

## MATCHING QUESTIONS

Use the following terms to identify the phrases below. On the line next to each phrase, write the letter of the term that most closely relates to it.

a. Loss leader
b. Collateral
c. Security agreement
d. Consumer
e. Insolvency
f. Class action suit
g. Bait and switch
h. Mechanic's lien
i. Credit
j. Secured creditor

_____ 1. The right to pay for goods and services after they have been received

_____ 2. An agreement between debtor and creditor that creates a security interest

_____ 3. A lien given to those who supply materials, labor, and services in constructing buildings

_____ 4. Advertising designed to get a consumer to select a more expensive product than the one advertised

_____ 5. An item sold at or below cost to attract customers

_____ 6. Any type of asset that can be pledged as security to a bank or other creditor

_____ 7. The inability of a debtor to pay debts as they come due

_____ 8. A person who buys goods, products, and services

_____ 9. A creditor who has a secured interest in property belonging to the debtor

_____ 10. A lawsuit filed on behalf of a group of consumers

## TRUE-FALSE QUESTIONS

Indicate whether each statement below is true or false by circling T or F in the column on the right.

1. Bait-and-switch advertising is permissible as long as the recommended item is superior to the item the consumer intended to buy.     T   F
2. Price fixing is a violation of both state and federal laws.     T   F
3. Failure to use "plain English" in a contract as required by law would make the contract voidable at the purchaser's or buyer's option.     T   F
4. Consumer rights can be enforced by groups as well as by individuals.     T   F
5. A lender can refuse to grant credit to a potential borrower solely because of that person's marital status.     T   F
6. The government can ban the sale of any product that is considered dangerous.     T   F
7. In deciding whether to grant credit, a creditor can discount the importance of income from alimony, part-time work, or a pension.     T   F
8. A security agreement is effective only if it is filed.     T   F
9. A secured creditor who repossesses property and decides to sell it must dispose of it at a public sale.     T   F
10. A secured creditor usually can repossess the collateral without first having to resort to the courts.     T   F

## MULTIPLE-CHOICE QUESTIONS

On the line next to each statement, write the letter of the best answer.

_____ 1. Consumer protection laws have been enacted at (a) the state level, (b) the county level, (c) state and federal levels, (d) regional levels.

_____ 2. If a retailer runs out of an advertised item, it must give a consumer a(n) (a) credit, (b) item of equal value, (c) refund, (d) rain check.

_____ 3. Mislabeling an item with an incorrect "suggested retail price" is an example of (a) price fixing, (b) price misrepresentation, (c) bait-and-switch advertising, (d) a loss leader.

_____ 4. A buyer's right to cancel a contract made with a door-to-door salesperson is guaranteed by the (a) Federal Trade Act, (b) Truth in Lending Act, (c) Unordered Goods Act, (d) Return of Merchandise Act.

_____ 5. A seller who violates consumer protection laws can be subject to (a) civil penalties, (b) criminal penalties, (c) both civil and criminal penalties, (d) none of these.

6. The Smyth Company began to manufacture and sell a power lawn mower that had a tendency to catch on fire. The federal government was able to protect the public by (a) forcing a recall of the mowers, (b) requiring corrective action, (c) ordering a refund, (d) all of these.

7. An unsecured debt (a) must be oral, (b) must be in writing, (c) can be either oral or written, (d) must be written and filed in the county clerk's office.

8. An unsecured creditor can collect a debt by (a) seizing the item sold, (b) bringing suit to collect, (c) obtaining an injunction, (d) all of these.

9. A secured creditor can collect a debt by (a) seizing the item and selling it, (b) bringing criminal charges against the debtor, (c) having the debtor arrested, (d) all of these.

10. A security agreement is filed to protect the (a) debtor, (b) public, (c) creditor, (d) creditor and the public.

11. Collateral for a security interest (a) can be tangible or intangible personal property, (b) must be intangible personal property, (c) must be tangible personal property, (d) can be real property.

12. In a secured transaction, collateral (a) must be in the debtor's possession, (b) must be in the creditor's possession, (c) cannot be required, (d) can be in either the debtor's or the creditor's possession.

13. Whether a person is a surety or a guarantor depends on (a) the purpose of the loan, (b) the interest rate of the loan, (c) who is primarily responsible for payment, (d) the age of the borrower.

14. Anderson supplied bricks to a contractor to construct an apartment house. If the contractor does not pay for the bricks, Anderson will be protected by filing a (a) tax lien, (b) debtor's lien, (c) mechanic's lien, (d) judgment lien.

15. A secured creditor who repossesses the collateral when a debt is not paid (a) must sell it, (b) can keep it or sell it, (c) must deliver it to the police, (d) must return it to the debtor.

16. A debtor can file a bankruptcy petition (a) every 2 years, (b) once a year, (c) every 6 years, (d) every 6 months.

17. Collecting interest in excess of the legal rate is (a) price fixing, (b) legal, (c) price misrepresentation, (d) usury.

18. If you receive an incorrect bill, you (a) need not pay it, (b) must notify the creditor, (c) must notify the Better Business Bureau, (d) can sue the creditor.

19. A person who is denied credit is entitled to know (a) the name of the credit bureau supplying the credit report, (b) the address of the credit bureau, (c) the names of people asking for credit reports, (d) all of these.

20. If your credit card is stolen and you notify the issuer, your liability is limited to (a) $100, (b) $75, (c) $50, (d) $500.

## ACTIVITY: USING CREDIT

Shown below is a retail installment credit contract. Read the contract and then answer the questions on the following page.

---

**A-1 AUTOS**     121 S. Main Street, Akron, OH 44308

**RETAIL INSTALLMENT CONTRACT**

Date: _Sept. 25_ 19 _--_

Buyer's Name (print): _Marguerita Santos_

Address: _207 E. Buchtel Avenue, Akron, OH 44325_

The undersigned Seller hereby sells and the undersigned Buyer, having been quoted both the following Cash Price and the following Deferred Payment Price, hereby buys for the Deferred Payment Price, on the terms and conditions hereinafter set forth, the following described motor vehicle, with accessories and equipment thereon, receipt and acceptance of which, in satisfactory condition, are hereby acknowledged by Buyer:

| NEW OR USED | YEAR | MAKE | BODY STYLE | MODEL NO. | NO. CYL. | FACTORY OR SERIAL # |
|---|---|---|---|---|---|---|
| Used | 1982 | CHEV | 2-door | 8-046 | 4 | AL27884625 |

**Special Accessories and Equipment**
(Check or specify those applicable)

Transmission: ☐ Automatic     ☐ Power Steering     ☐ Air-Conditioning
☑ 4-Speed                     ☑ Power Brakes       ☑ Radio
                              ☐ Power Windows      ☐ Other (specify) _____

1. Cash Price
   (incl. taxes, accessories, services) $ _1,200._
2. Downpayment
   Cash Downpayment  $ _200._
   Trade-in          $ _—_

   Yr.    Model    Make    Serial #
   Total Downpayment                       $ _200._
3. Unpaid Balance of Cash Price (1-2) $ _1,000._

4. Other Charges
   Certificate of Title Fee        $ _10._
   Registration Fee                $ _25._
   Optional Insurance              $ _—_
5. Unpaid Balance
   Amount Financed (3 + 4)         $ _1,035._
6. Finance Charge                  $ _93.15_
7. Total of Payments (5 + 6)       $ _1,128.15_
8. Deferred Payment Price (1 + 4 + 6) $ _1,328.15_
9. Annual Percentage Rate          _9%_

**PAYMENT SCHEDULE**

Buyer hereby agrees to pay to Seller the Total of Payments (Item 7 from above) in _23_ monthly installments of _$47.00_ each and one final installment of _$47.00_ on the like day of each month commencing _Oct. 1_, 19 _--_ or, if different from date of transaction, finance charge begins to accrue _Oct. 1_, 19 _--_.

Signed _Marguerita Santos_     Date: _9/25/--_

Signed _____     Date: _____

1. What is the purchase price of the car?

2. What are the total interest charges?

3. What is the total cost of the car?

## SHORT-ANSWER QUESTIONS

Answer each of the following questions in the space provided.

1. Because items end up costing more when they are bought on credit, what are the advantages of buying on credit?

2. What are the disadvantages of buying on credit?

3. With passage of the Truth in Lending Law, businesses providing credit to consumers are required to provide complete information on the cost of using credit. Write a short paragraph explaining how this law has helped consumers make wiser buying decisions.

# ANSWER KEY

# Chapter 1 Foundations of Law

**TRUE-FALSE QUESTIONS**

1. true; p. 3
2. true; p. 14
3. false—precedents; pp. 7, 10
4. true; p. 12
5. false—equity; p. 13
6. true; p. 14
7. false—common (case); pp. 7, 10
8. true; p. 12
9. true; pp. 3
10. true; p. 11

**MULTIPLE-CHOICE QUESTIONS**

1. b; p. 7
2. a; pp. 8, 9
3. b; p. 9
4. c; p. 8
5. d; p. 12
6. a; p. 11
7. d; p. 5
8. a; pp. 12, 13
9. d; p. 9
10. c; p. 9
11. a; pp. 10, 11
12. d; p. 7
13. a; p. 11
14. a; p. 12
15. a; p. 13

**SHORT-ANSWER QUESTIONS**

1. 1. Constitutions—The U.S. Constitution and the 50 state constitutions are the source of laws that establish government power and authority; 2. Statutes—The legislation consisting of laws passed by federal, state, and local governments; 3. Court decisions—The courts interpret or modify existing laws or make decisions that create precedents; 4. Administrative regulations—Rules and regulations set up by state and federal agencies that have the force of law. pp. 8–11
2. *Stare decisis* is the practice of following previous decisions; its main advantage is that it enables people to act in certain ways, knowing they can rely on established law. pp. 7, 10
3. If a lawsuit arises and money damages (the only *remedy at law*) are an unsuitable remedy, a court of equity may allow the injured party to seek nonmonetary relief such as specifically ordering the other party to perform a certain act (called specific performance) or to refrain from certain conduct (called an injunction). p. 13
4. Although law is strongly affected by ethical concepts, the law and ethics are not the same. Many rules of law are completely unrelated to ethics, for example, the rule stating you must stop at a red light. Likewise, many ethical precepts are not legally enforceable, for example, the issue of watching from shore as a person drowns in a lake. p. 4
5. *Robinson* v. *California* is a part of the U.S. law called case law (law arrived at through court decisions). More importantly, this decision by the Supreme Court became a precedent. As stated on page 10 of the text, courts in the United States makes laws that create precedents (a standard to be followed by other courts), and these precedents have the same force of law as laws passed by the United States Congress or by state legislatures. p. 10

# Chapter 2  The U.S. Court System and Its Constitutional Foundation

## MATCHING QUESTIONS

1. b; p. 18
2. i; p. 22
3. f; p. 30
4. n; p. 18
5. o; pp. 30, 31
6. k; p. 24
7. a; pp. 29, 30
8. d; p. 30
9. e; p. 29
10. g; p. 25
11. l; p. 25
12. h; p. 31

## MULTIPLE-CHOICE QUESTIONS

1. c; p. 18
2. d; p. 19
3. c; pp. 25, 27
4. d; p. 27
5. b; p. 24
6. a; p. 18
7. c; p. 18
8. c; p. 24
9. d; pp. 20, 21
10. d; p. 24
11. c; p. 21
12. a; pp. 20, 22

## SHORT-ANSWER QUESTIONS

1. In a court action, opposing parties, usually represented by attorneys, produce evidence to prove that their point of view should prevail over the other party's. It is felt that this process will bring out all evidence and that the result will be the truth.  p. 30
2. This form of government allows for an executive branch, a legislative branch, and a judicial branch. The separation of government functions into three separate branches removes the judicial system from politics and from the influence of temporary fads or ideas.  p. 29
3. Judicial review allows lower court decisions to be reversed or changed if they are not in accordance with existing law and the state and federal constitutions.  pp. 29, 30
4. A court with general jurisdiction has the power to hear almost any case brought before it. A court with limited jurisdiction has the power to hear only certain cases limited by type of case, by the amount of money involved, or by the geographic area.  p. 19
5. The appealing party must show that, had an error of law not been made, he/she would have won the case. Cost is another inhibiting factor of the appeals process. One major expense is attorney's fees. Another major expense is the cost of reducing to writing the entire record of the court trial (word for word). A copy of this record of trial must be presented to each appellate court judge so that he or she can study it in great detail.  pp. 22, 24
6. The issuance of a summons in a civil case (civil lawsuit) brings the defendant party under the jurisdiction of the court. In a criminal case, an arrest made by means of an arrest warrant issued by a judge brings a person accused of a crime (the defending party) into court. pp. 19, 20
7. U.S. Bankruptcy Court
   U.S. Court of International Trade
   U.S. Tax Court
   U.S. Claims Court  p. 24
8. Civil courts handle cases involving disputes between individuals, between a person and a business, or between businesses. Disputes are usually settled by an award of money damages to the "winning party." Criminal courts hear cases between a governmental unit—such as the state or federal government (acting for society)—and a person or business accused of a crime. Criminal courts determine whether a crime has been committed and also set punishment for those who are found guilty of committing a crime.  p. 19
9. A discussion of small claims court will be found on pp. 20–22. Three distinct advantages are listed on p. 20.

Copyright © Houghton Mifflin Company. All rights reserved.

10. The case of *Roe* v. *Wade* is a recent (1973) example of a court's power to exercise the right of judicial review. The concept of judicial review gives higher courts the power to review decisions of lower courts and to modify, change, or reverse these decisions if they are not in harmony with existing laws and constitutions. The Supreme Court case of *Marbury* v. *Madison* established the basis for the concept of judicial review by declaring an act of Congress unconstitutional. pp. 29, 30
11. Refer to p. 31 in the text.

## CASE PROBLEMS

1. a. federal; p. 24
   b. U.S. District Court; p. 24
   c. U.S. Court of Appeals; p. 25
2. a. small claims court; pp. 20, 22
   b. no; pp. 20, 22
   c. judge; pp. 20, 22
3. a. civil; p. 23
   b. state; p. 23
   c. trial; p. 23
4. No. Diversity of citizenship suits in federal court must involve $50,000 or more. p. 25

## ACTIVITY: EXPRESSING YOUR LEGAL OPINION

(Answers will vary.)

Some points for allowing an appeal:

- Appellate court judges are geographically, emotionally, and politically removed from the place of trial. This places them in a neutral position to reflect on the issues brought up at the trial.
- The process of appeal serves as a check on the proceedings in a trial court to insure that a proper interpretation of the evidence presented in a case was made by a judge.

# Chapter 3  Public Wrongs/Crimes

## COMPLETION QUESTIONS

1. corrections; p. 44
2. one year; p. 35
3. larceny; p. 38
4. entrapment; p. 44
5. indictment; p. 47
6. less than; p. 35
7. juvenile delinquent; p. 50
8. larceny; p. 37
9. Miranda warnings; p. 46
10. extortion; pp. 38,39

# SHORT-ANSWER QUESTIONS

1. See Figure 3.3, p. 45, and also pp. 44–50.
2. Rights:                                    Defenses:
   right to remain silent                     insanity
   right against self-incrimination           justification
   right to know reason for arrest            entrapment
   (*Note:* Student answers may vary. See pp. 44–50 and pp. 42–44 of text.)
3. See Table 3.1 on p. 51 of text. Also see pp. 44–54.
4. a. larceny (theft) and possession of stolen property  pp. 37–39
   b. assault  p. 36
   c. burglary and larceny (theft)  pp. 37, 38
   d. robbery  pp. 36, 37
   e. embezzlement and forgery  p. 38

# MULTIPLE-CHOICE QUESTIONS

1. b; pp. 37, 38
2. b; p. 36
3. d; p. 38
4. d; p. 43
5. d; pp. 36–39, 40–42

# ACTIVITY: CASE ANALYSIS

1. a. burglary — illegal entry with intent to commit a crime  p. 37
   b. Answers will vary. The two central facts are that coins from the burglary were found and that the police searched the rest of the house without a warrant.
   c. Chimel was found guilty of burglary.
   d. The Court found that while the search of Chimel and of the immediate area was justified, the search, without a warrant, of the entire house was not.
   e. Answers will vary.

# CASE PROBLEMS

1. Yes. The intent to commit the crime still classifies the act as burglary, even though Benton did not actually follow through with his intention.  p. 37
2. No. The low price Reese paid and the circumstances of the sale should have made him suspicious that the speakers were stolen. Courts hold that a person is guilty of a crime if he/she accepts property under the reasonable belief that it has been stolen.  p. 39
3. Yes. Marx has the defense of entrapment. The act of bringing drugs into the U.S. originated in the minds of the immigration officials and it was they who induced Marx to violate the law. This act on the part of the immigration officials constitutes the defense of entrapment. Therefore, Marx is not criminally liable.  p. 44

# ACTIVITY: WHAT'S YOUR OPINION?

1. Answers will vary, but here are some possibilities: poverty; unemployment; lack of education; alcohol and drug abuse; lack of direction by parents; influence of television; light sentences or no jail sentence (probation) given by judges; little chance of being caught (e.g., inadequate police investigation); breakdown in moral values.

Copyright © Houghton Mifflin Company. All rights reserved.

2. Obtain a warrant before making an arrest.

# Chapter 4  Private Wrongs/Torts

## MATCHING QUESTIONS

1. f; p. 68
2. b; p. 72
3. h; p. 73
4. d; p. 71
5. j; pp. 67, 68

## COMPLETION QUESTIONS

1. invasion of privacy; p. 67, 68
2. intentional; p. 61
3. theft (stealing); pp. 70, 71
4. injunction; p. 71
5. defamation; p. 66
6. *New York Times* v. *Sullivan*; p. 66
7. strict liability; p. 75
8. careless; p. 72
9. malpractice; p. 73
10. proximate (direct); p. 73

## MULTIPLE-CHOICE QUESTIONS

1. d; p. 65
2. c; p. 60
3. d; pp. 61, 73
4. b; p. 74
5. d; pp. 61, 62
6. c; p. 70
7. d; p. 65
8. a; p. 66
9. d; p. 70
10. b; p. 70
11. c; p. 73
12. d; pp. 61, 62
13. d; pp. 74, 75
14. c; pp. 62, 63
15. d; p. 73
16. d; p. 65
17. a; p. 75
18. c; p. 71
19. c; p. 60
20. b; p. 66

## CASE PROBLEMS

1. No, there has been no false arrest. For a false arrest to occur, a person must be detained against his/her will. In this case, Jones, confronted by Reed for possible shoplifting, consented and freely accompanied her (Reed) to the store manager's office.  pp. 62–64
2. Yes. An invasion of privacy has taken place because Dansig, without consent, used Langley's picture in an advertising campaign.  pp. 67, 68
3. No. Since the remark about Byrd was true, Byrd has no claim for damages on the basis of slander. Byrd, however, can sue for invasion of privacy because Dr. Springer wrongfully disclosed true information about Byrd which was not of legitimate concern to the public—in this case those in attendance at the dinner party.  pp. 65–68
4. No. Davis was negligent (i.e., he acted carelessly). He (Davis) should have foreseen that his act of walking onto the waxed floors in spite of the signs that warned customers not to, created a risk that injury could have resulted. Davis failed to act like a "reasonable person" would have acted. On the other hand, if Davis were not the average individual (e.g., minor child, sight impaired, advanced age), he might have some success in suing the restaurant. He could claim that the restaurant contributed to his (Davis's) negligence by not anticipating

dangers for certain classes of people (e.g., as a sight-impaired person he could not see the small signs; or as a minor child he was attracted to the area by the shiny floor). pp. 72–74

**SHORT-ANSWER QUESTIONS**

1. False arrest involves unlawful detainment by an authorized official—for example, a police officer—without just cause. False imprisonment occurs when a person is unlawfully forced to remain in a certain area or freedom of movement is restricted.

   (Examples will vary.) A police officer mistakes you for someone else and arrests you (false arrest). A store detective holds you in a locked room on suspicion of shoplifting (false imprisonment). pp. 33, 34
2. Refer to pp. 72–74.
3. Refer to p. 74 in the text.
4. Refer to p. 66.

# Chapter 5  Litigation and Alternatives for Settling Civil Disputes

**TRUE-FALSE QUESTIONS**

1. verdict; p. 94
2. true; p. 93
3. petit; p. 93
4. judgment; p. 94
5. true; p. 83
6. true; p. 83
7. attorney; p. 83
8. true; p. 90
9. discovery; p. 92
10. true; p. 93

**MULTIPLE-CHOICE QUESTIONS**

1. c; p. 93
2. c; p. 94
3. a; p. 94
4. b; p. 89
5. d; p. 94

**CHRONOLOGY**

1. summons and complaint
2. answer
3. discovery proceedings
4. attorneys' opening statements
5. presentation of evidence for the plaintiff
6. presentation of evidence for the defendant
7. attorneys' closing statements
8. verdict
9. appeal  pp. 86–95

## SHORT-ANSWER QUESTIONS

1. Litigation is the settlement of disputes in court or by trial. Arbitration is the nonjudicial determination of disputes; an arbitrator is chosen to hear the case and make a binding decision called an award. Mediation is similar to arbitration, except that the decision reached is not binding but advisory only.  pp. 83, 95, 96
2. Discovery enables both the plaintiff and the defendant to learn in detail the nature of the other's claim or defense. The process used in the pretrial steps of discovery ensures that all potential testimony and other evidence is available to both sides. As a result of the use of discovery as a pretrial technique, the actual trial can be shortened, or the need for a trial can be eliminated.  p. 92
3. Discovery techniques include written questions answered under oath by the opposite party; depositions—sworn statements from witnesses who, for good cause, may not be able to be present at the trial; compulsory physical and mental examinations by doctors chosen by the other party in personal injury cases; and the production for inspection of documents or other things in the possession of the other party.  p. 92
4. Costs associated with an appeal are high—the entire record of trial must be reduced to writing (word for word) and given to each appellate court judge to study; attorney's fees are higher than the normal 33.33 percent of the amount collected as money damages. The opportunities for successful appeal are limited to questions of law; i.e., the appealing party must show that he or she would have won the case if the error of law had not been made during the trial.  pp. 23, 24—Chapter 2; p. 94.
5. Refer to pp. 95–97.

## ACTIVITY: DOCUMENT ANALYSIS

1. This document, called a complaint, is one of the documents (another is a summons) used to initiate a civil action in a court of law. It sets out the facts and circumstances that the plaintiff believes are the basis for a legal action against the defendant; the complaint also states the remedy being sought by the plaintiff.  p. 86
2. Negligence of the defendant (Mary Martin) in operating her automobile, causing the plaintiff (William Jordan) to suffer great bodily injury for an extended period of time.
3. a summons  p. 86
4. allegations  p. 89
5. She should, through her lawyer, file an answer which is a written response to the allegations (claims) made by the plaintiff.  pp. 88, 89

## ACTIVITY: WHAT'S YOUR OPINION?

1. Answers will vary.
2. Answers will vary.

# Review   Part I   Understanding the Law

## TRUE-FALSE QUESTIONS

1. T; p. 4
2. T; p. 12
3. F; p. 9
4. T; p. 29
5. F; p. 27
6. T; p. 35
7. T; p. 35
8. T; p. 48, 49
9. F; p. 20
10. T; p. 7
11. F; p. 75
12. T; p. 60
13. T; p. 75
14. T; pp. 44–47
15. T; p. 93

## MULTIPLE-CHOICE QUESTIONS

1. c; p. 47
2. a; p. 93
3. b; p. 72
4. d; p. 65
5. c; p. 70
6. c; p. 86
7. a; p. 94
8. c; p. 71
9. b; p. 87
10. b; p. 47
11. a; p. 37
12. b; p. 44
13. d; p. 12
14. d; p. 7
15. c; p. 7
16. d; p. 70
17. a; p. 38
18. c; p. 94
19. a; p. 14
20. d; p. 7
21. c; p. 76
22. b; p. 20
23. b; p. 72
24. b; p. 8
25. d; pp. 25, 27
26. d; p. 12
27. d; pp. 8–11
28. c; p. 37
29. c; p. 64
30. d; pp. 62, 63
31. d; p. 11
32. a; p. 18
33. a; p. 40
34. d; p. 19
35. b; p. 19

## COMPLETION QUESTIONS

1. precedent; p. 7
2. punishment; p. 12
3. money damages; p. 75
4. discovery; p. 92
5. true; p. 66
6. reasonable; p. 73
7. carelessness; p. 72
8. fraud; p. 69
9. person; p. 62
10. punitive; p. 76

## CASE PROBLEM

1. indictment; p. 47
2. felony (2nd time); p. 39
3. district attorney; pp. 47, 49
4. subpoena; p. 93
5. in some states ("dram shop act"); p. 40

## SHORT-ANSWER QUESTIONS

1. Refer to pp. 8–11.
2. Refer to pp. 61, 72, 75.
3. Refer to Figure 3.3, p. 45, of text; also pp. 44–50.
4. Refer to pp. 95–97.
5. Answers will vary. (As background refer to Chapter 1, especially: p. 3—Why Laws Are Needed, pp. 5–7—The Functions of Law, p. 14—The Changing Nature of Law

Copyright © Houghton Mifflin Company. All rights reserved.

# Chapter 6  The Basics of Contract Law

## MULTIPLE-CHOICE QUESTIONS

1. d; p. 110
2. d; pp. 107, 109
3. a; p. 112
4. b; p. 110
5. b; p. 107
6. c; p. 111
7. c; p. 112
8. d; pp. 106, 117
9. a; pp. 108–112
10. d; pp. 106, 107
11. c; p. 108
12. b; p. 109
13. c; p. 110
14. b; p. 110
15. b; p. 109

## CASE PROBLEMS

1. a. Yes. An implied contract was formed as a result of the action of the parties rather than from spoken or written words. p. 110
   b. Yes. A contract implied in law was formed between Berger and the hospital. If she does not pay, she would benefit unjustly at the expense of the hospital; therefore, the court would require her to arrange for payment. pp. 111, 112
   c. No. The agreement between Stevens and Anderson was simply a social arrangement, and therefore no legal obligations were created. pp. 105, 106
   d. Yes. The oral offer and acceptance of the credit manager position created a binding contract. However, because the agreement was oral, enforcement will be difficult. p. 110
   e. No. A valid contract requires offer and acceptance. There is no evidence of acceptance on Martell's part. p. 106
   f. No. Because the subject matter of the contract did not exist at the time of the agreement, the contract is void. A void contract has no legal effect. p. 109
2. a. Harry Owens; p. 106
   b. James Harrington; p. 106
   c. January 9; p. 106
   d. Owens cleaned the carpet; Harrington paid money ($350). p. 107
   e. Yes. p. 112
3. a. date of agreement
   b. signature of parties
   c. consideration
   d. location of house to be painted; p. 111 (Figure 6.3)

## SHORT-ANSWER QUESTIONS

1. Answers will vary. Suggested answer: If an agreement creates a legal obligation, then it is considered to be a contract and will be enforced by the courts. However, many agreements are simply social arrangements in which the parties do not intend to create a legal obligation. Such social agreements are not enforceable as contracts in a court of law. pp. 105, 106
2. Written terms cannot easily be changed. If a misunderstanding arises later, it is easy to establish the terms actually agreed upon. p. 110
3. Consideration may be property such as a watch or a car. Consideration may also consist of doing something you are not legally bound to do, refraining from doing something you have a legal right to do, or promising to do or not to do something. p. 107
4. Refer to pp. 111 and 112.
5. A unilateral contract is one in which a promise is made by one party (the offeror) in return for the performance of a specific act by the other party (the offeree). (A promise for an act.) A bilateral contract is one in which a promise is made by one party (the offeror) in return for a promise made by another party (the offeree). (A promise for a promise.) p. 108

# Chapter 7  Agreement: Offer and Acceptance

## MULTIPLE-CHOICE QUESTIONS

1. c; p. 96
2. a; pp. 116–118
3. b; pp. 118, 119
4. d; p. 117
5. a; p. 118
6. d; p. 118
7. b; p. 120
8. b; pp. 123, 124
9. d; pp. 123, 124
10. b; p. 120
11. a; pp. 119, 120
12. d; p. 119
13. b; p. 119
14. b; p. 119
15. c; p. 119

## CASE PROBLEMS

1. Yes. Acceptance occurred when Ganze mailed the acceptance letter. The fact that the telegram and the letter arrived at the same time has no bearing in this case.  pp. 123, 124
2. No. A counteroffer terminates the original offer. Beacher rejected the original offer, and Jordan rejected Beacher's counteroffer. Therefore, no contract was formed.  p. 119
3. No. The offeree's silence would not be regarded as acceptance. Wurzer had no legal obligation to notify the publishing company.  p. 125
4. Yes. The offer was made to the general public, but it is directed to the first person who acts upon it. Since Jarvis complied with the offeror's request, she is entitled to the reward.  p. 122
5. No. An offer may be withdrawn at any time, even if the offeror has promised to hold the offer open for a stated period. No option contract existed to require the offeror to hold the offer open.  p. 120

## MATCHING QUESTIONS

1. d; pp. 119, 120
2. a; pp. 118, 119
3. b; p. 119
4. c; p. 119
5. e; p. 121

## ACTIVITY: CASE ANALYSIS

1. No. The revocation was also published, thereby ending the offer, even though Shuey did not see the revocation himself.  pp. 119–121
2. No. Shuey did not apprehend Suratt; he simply supplied information leading to his arrest. The original offer provides only a $10,000 reward for providing such information.  pp. 122, 123

# Chapter 8  Consideration

## MULTIPLE-CHOICE QUESTIONS

1. d; pp. 131, 132
2. a; p. 135
3. b; pp. 133, 134
4. a; p. 131
5. c; p. 135
6. a; p. 137
7. c; p. 131
8. d; p. 132
9. a; p. 135
10. b; pp. 133, 134
11. b; p. 137

## CASE PROBLEMS

1. No. Adler is already under contract and would have to give additional consideration, such as a longer contract period, to create a new agreement. p. 134
2. Yes. The adequacy of the consideration is unimportant. The important thing is that consideration (money) was given in exchange for the item. pp. 132, 133
3. No. The agreement to not sue (which Visca would have been legally entitled to do) when supported by valid consideration (money) is enforceable. p. 132
4. No. The promise of a gift is unenforceable because of lack of consideration. p. 131
5. No. A compromise of a disputed claim is binding on both parties. The promise of each to settle for less is supported by consideration which is each other's refraining, or a promise to refrain, from contesting the amount to be paid in court. p. 135

## SHORT-ANSWER QUESTIONS

1. Fraud; Duress; Undue Influence; Unconscionability; pp. 132, 133
2. If a party (usually the offeree) promises to perform a pre-existing legal obligation (i.e., an obligation he/she is already bound to perform), then that party has really not given up any consideration to support a new promise by the offeror to do something. (See example on p. 135 of text.) p. 135
3. Courts will apply this equity doctrine to enforce a promise unsupported by consideration on the part of the promisee (offeree) if it would be grossly unfair not to enforce the promise. A promisee may do something significant in reliance upon the promise of the promisor (even though no consideration was given by the promisee) and then have the promisor back out of his/her promise. (See example on p. 139 of text.) p. 139
4. Refer to pp. 137–139 of text.

# Chapter 9   Competent Parties

## MULTIPLE-CHOICE QUESTIONS

1. b; p. 151
2. c; p. 147
3. d; pp. 145, 146
4. b; pp. 148, 149
5. b; p. 146
6. a; pp. 151, 152
7. b; p. 148
8. c; p. 144
9. d; pp. 145, 148
10. b; p. 148
11. b; pp. 150, 151
12. c; p. 144

## CASE PROBLEMS

1. No. Once a minor ratifies a contract after reaching majority, he or she can no longer disaffirm. Karlson ratified the agreement by making payments after he turned 18, the age of majority in most states. pp. 147, 148
2. No. A self-supporting minor is liable for her or his own necessaries. pp. 148, 149
3. Yes. A minor may disaffirm a contract within a reasonable time after reaching the age of majority. pp. 145, 146
4. No. A minor may avoid a contract for other than necessaries even if the minor's age was misrepresented. The minor may be required to pay for depreciation of the tuxedo's value. pp. 145–147

## ACTIVITY: ETHICAL DILEMMA

This is a difficult question. On the one hand, a retail merchant does have an ethical responsibility to avoid taking undue advantage of a person who lacks capacity. On the other hand, the merchant must be careful not to diminish that person's freedom and dignity, to embarrass him/her, or to cause the person lacking capacity to bring a lawsuit for discrimination. Thus, there is danger in assuming a protective position toward people who are in a confused state of mind; nevertheless, merchants at the management level need to address these difficult issues and incorporate their thinking into the store's business policies.

# Chapter 10   Legal Purpose

## CASE PROBLEMS

1. No. Agreements that totally discourage marriage are illegal and void.  p. 164
2. No. An agreement made with an elected or appointed official to use her or his influence to affect the passage of a law is illegal and void.  pp. 163, 164
3. No. Agreements that interfere with the proper administration of justice are illegal and void.  p. 163
4. No. When state statutes require that a person be licensed to perform services for the general public, an agreement made with an unlicensed person is illegal, and the unlicensed person cannot legally collect for services performed.  p. 159
5. Yes. A contract in reasonable restraint of trade is valid and binding.  pp. 165, 166
6. No. An agreement with an elected or appointed official to use her or his influence to affect passage of a law is illegal and void.  pp. 163, 164
7. No. Giveaways used for promotional purposes are lawful as long as it is not necessary to purchase anything to participate. Since Rissone's participation was free, the element of consideration is lacking and the promotion is legal.  pp. 159, 160

## MULTIPLE-CHOICE QUESTIONS

1. a; pp. 160, 161
2. d; p. 159
3. a; p. 159
4. a; pp. 159, 160
5. b; p. 167
6. b; p. 157
7. c; p. 160, 161
8. c; pp. 160–162, 164–167
9. a; p. 160
10. b; pp. 165–167
11. c; pp. 166, 167
12. d; pp. 165–167
13. a; p. 163
14. a; p. 164
15. a; pp. 159, 160
16. c; p. 158
17. b; p. 162
18. d; p. 166
19. b; p. 167
20. d; p. 162

## ACTIVITY: CASE ANALYSIS

1. Breach of contract—failure of the defendant to pay for merchandise purchased.
2. The defendant's attorney argued that the checkers and boards were bought for use as games of chance, and that such games were prohibited by state law. He argued that the contract was therefore illegal and void, and that his client was not obligated to pay.
3. No. The court ruled in favor of the plaintiff.
4. That the games as used by the Fun and Games Entertainment Center were games of skill, not games of chance, and that the state law prohibited only games of chance, not games of skill.

Copyright © Houghton Mifflin Company. All rights reserved.

5. None. Generally, if both parties know that an agreement is illegal, neither can sue for breach, and neither can recover for any performance rendered. The court would probably refuse to hear the case and would leave the parties where it finds them.  p. 157

# Chapter 11    Contracts That Must Be in Writing

## TRUE-FALSE QUESTIONS

1. T; pp. 174, 175
2. T; p. 173
3. T; p. 174
4. T; p. 173
5. F; pp. 174, 175
6. T; pp. 179, 180
7. F; pp. 179, 180
8. F; p. 177
9. T; p. 179
10. T; p. 180

## CASE PROBLEMS

1. No. The promise to pay another's debt must be in writing to be enforceable.  pp. 174, 175
2. No. A promise by an executor to be personally liable for the debts of the deceased must be in writing to be enforceable.  p. 175
3. No. Contracts for the sale of property must be in writing to be enforceable, even if a down payment is made.  pp. 175, 176
4. Yes. An oral contract which by its terms can be performed within a year is enforceable.  p. 177
5. No. Contracts made in consideration of marriage must be in writing to be enforceable.  p. 176

## MULTIPLE-CHOICE QUESTIONS

1. b; pp. 174, 175
2. c; pp. 175, 176
3. c; p. 177
4. c; p. 179
5. b; p. 174
6. c; pp. 175, 176
7. a; pp. 173–177
8. d; pp. 177, 178
9. b; p. 174
10. c; p. 180

## SHORT-ANSWER QUESTIONS

1. See text pp. 179, 180.
2. When the friend promises to pay Jackson's bill if Jackson does not do so, the friend is promising to pay the debt of another. In order to be enforceable, this promise must be in writing according to the statute of frauds. When Jackson's friend, however, tells Riggins to charge the purchase to him (Jackson's friend), the friend is incurring a personal debt; he is not promising to pay Jackson's debt but instead is creating his own debt. This latter type of transaction does not have to be in writing to be enforceable.  pp. 174, 175
3. When the terms of a contract cannot possibly be performed within one year from the date the contract is entered into (not on the date that performance is to begin).  p. 177
4. See text p. 173.
5. See text pp. 175 and 176.

# Chapter 12  Transfer of Contract Rights and Obligations

### MINI-CASE

1. a; pp. 185, 186
2. c; p. 185
3. d; p. 185
4. a; p. 185
5. b; p. 188

### TRUE-FALSE QUESTIONS

1. F; p. 185
2. T; pp. 187, 188
3. F; p. 188
4. F; p. 189
5. T; p. 187
6. T; p. 188
7. F; p. 188
8. T; p. 185
9. T; pp. 185, 186
10. F; p. 191

### MULTIPLE-CHOICE QUESTIONS

1. a; p. 188
2. c; p. 191
3. b; p. 186
4. c; pp. 187, 188
5. a; p. 187

### CASE PROBLEMS

1. Yes. Blacke's must pay the finance company $600. Unless and until the obligor (Blacke's) receives a notice, the assignment has no legal effect. In this case, the obligor is free to perform for the assignor.  pp. 188–190
2. No. The right to work for someone is so personal that it cannot be assigned without permission.  p. 187
3. No. Contract obligations that require a special skill or knowledge may not be delegated without permission of the party who is to receive performance of the service.  p. 187
4. Yes. Rights of a nonpersonal nature may be freely transferred without permission.  pp. 185, 186
5. Yes. Obligations of a nonpersonal nature may be delegated without permission.  p. 186
6. Yes. You are under no obligation to accept the services of the guitarist's brother. Contracts involving special skill, knowledge, or judgment cannot be delegated without both parties' consent.  p. 187
7. No. Since the third party (the assignee) failed to notify you of the assignment, he has no legal claim against you.  p. 188

### SHORT-ANSWER QUESTIONS

1. It means that the assignee has the same rights as the assignor and does not acquire any new rights. Also, the assignee is subject to the same defenses as existed prior to the assignment.  p. 191
2. Yes, and such a clause in a contract is generally honored; however, there are some exceptions. A contract, for example, cannot prevent an assignment of the right to receive money. The statutes of some states may also place restrictions on assignments.  pp. 187, 188
3. If notice is not given after the assignment has been made, the assignee runs the risk that the obligor, not knowing of the assignment, will pay the debt (or render whatever other performance is required) to the assignor. In this case, the assignee loses all rights against the obligor.  pp. 188, 190

Copyright © Houghton Mifflin Company. All rights reserved.

4. Generally no special form is required when an assignment is made. Any oral or written words that clearly indicate a person's intent to make an assignment are sufficient. It is always best, however, to put an assignment in writing. p. 188
5. Answers will vary. The following is a suggested answer. It would not be fair to let the delegator of the duty substitute a new party in his/her place without the third party's permission and then be able to escape liability.

## ACTIVITY: CASE PROBLEM

a. This was a legal assignment; therefore, the bank may collect the $30,000 from Marlan. Marlan has a legal obligation to pay the assignee once he/she has been given notice of the assignment. pp. 185, 186
b. This was not a legal assignment; therefore, the bank may not collect the $20,000 from Pool. No contract right existed that could be assigned at the time of the so-called assignment. The thought of hiring RYCOM did not as yet create rights that could be assigned. p. 185

# Chapter 13  The Termination of Contracts: Discharge

## MULTIPLE-CHOICE QUESTIONS

1. c; p. 199
2. c; p. 197
3. a; p. 200
4. d; p. 196
5. b; p. 198
6. a; p. 200
7. d; p. 199
8. d; p. 197
9. d; p. 197
10. c; p. 199
11. d; p. 201
12. a; p. 196

## ACTIVITY: CASE ANALYSIS

Zoe would not be liable if he died or became seriously ill or disabled. Impossibility releases both parties without liability for breach of contract. p. 200

## TRUE-FALSE QUESTIONS

1. alteration; p. 201
2. substantial performance; p. 197
3. true; p. 197
4. tender of performance; p. 196
5. true; p. 199
6. rescission; p. 198
7. true; p. 199
8. performance; pp. 196, 197
9. novation; pp. 198, 199
10. true; p. 197

## CASE PROBLEMS

1. No. Death discharges a contract for personal services. p. 200
2. Yes. A contract may be discharged by mutual agreement of the parties. p. 198
3. No. Payment by check does not constitute legal tender and does not discharge the debtor from liability. p. 197

4. Yes. Unforeseen hardships that make a contract more difficult to perform after a contract is made will not discharge a contract. (In this case, the standard notebooks can be obtained elsewhere by Hardies for delivery to Davidson.) p. 201
5. Yes. Impossibility of performance due to the destruction of the subject matter terminates the contract. p. 199

## ACTIVITY: LEARNING HOW CONTRACTS ARE TERMINATED

1. Yes. The contract is valid because (a) the signatures show the parties have reached agreement (offer and acceptance), (b) there is consideration ($650 rent for the leased property), (c) the parties are competent, and (d) there is legal purpose. pp. 106, 107
2. This contract may be terminated by full or substantial performance, by agreement of the parties, through impossibility, by alteration, or by breach of contract. pp. 196–201
3. Both parties must do everything they have agreed to do in the contract; that is, Janet and William Percy must pay rent of $650 each month to Harriet Cole and must keep the premises in good condition. Harriet Cole cannot lease the property to anyone else for 2 years and cannot ask the Percys to leave for 2 years. pp. 196, 197, 198
4. Answers will vary, but likely answers will center on destruction of the leased property, such as by fire, a tornado, or an earthquake. pp. 199, 200, 201
5. Cole can take action to collect double the rent ($1300) for each month they do not pay the rent.

## ACTIVITY: LEGAL DISTINCTION

Refer to pp. 199–201 in the text.

# Chapter 14    The Termination of Contracts: Breach of Contract

## MULTIPLE-CHOICE QUESTIONS

1. b; p. 207
2. c; p. 207
3. c; p. 206
4. b; p. 208
5. b; p. 208
6. a; p. 214
7. d; pp. 209, 214
8. d; p. 210
9. d; p. 214
10. c; p. 213

## TRUE-FALSE QUESTIONS

1. T; p. 210
2. T; p. 207
3. F; pp. 212, 213
4. F; p. 214
5. F; p. 210
6. T; p. 209
7. F; p. 213
8. T; p. 209
9. T; p. 211
10. T; p. 208

## ACTIVITY: ANALYZING A CONTRACT

1. The remedies are to sue for money damages, to rescind the contract, to obtain specific performance of the contract, or to obtain an injunction to forbid a person to do a certain act. pp. 206–210

Leon may sell part or all of the stored furniture and take the amount owed out of the proceeds of the sale. Refer to contract.
3. Damages would be compensatory to reimburse Leon for the cost of storing the furniture and for any costs of selling the furniture if necessary. pp. 207, 208
4. Probably not. No specific liquidated damages have been provided for in the contract. It is unlikely that a court would award punitive damages as that would enrich Leon unfairly. Student conclusion.
5. Leon will get $150 plus any expenses incurred in selling the furniture. The remaining money will be paid to Greeley because his debt to Leon would have been paid in full. Refer to contract.

## SHORT-ANSWER QUESTIONS

1. Remedies for breach of contract are discussed on pp. 206–210 of text. (*Note:* the two major types of remedies allowed by the courts are legal remedies and equitable remedies.)
2. Material breach is discussed on pp. 206 and 207 of text.
3. Refer to p. 207 of text.
4. The waiver has the effect of eliminating the breach. As a result of the waiver, the contract is canceled with no further liability on the part of either party to the contract. p. 207
5. Specific performance is discussed on p. 209 of text.

# Review   Part II   Contracts

## TRUE-FALSE QUESTIONS

1. T; p. 132
2. F; pp. 185, 186
3. T; p. 214
4. T; p. 174
5. T; p. 215
6. F; p. 119
7. F; pp. 187, 188
8. T; p. 209
9. T; p. 173
10. F; p. 149

## MULTIPLE-CHOICE QUESTIONS

1. c; p. 109
2. d; p. 124
3. c; p. 210
4. a; p. 116
5. b; p. 135
6. c; pp. 173, 174
7. b; p. 187
8. c; p. 208
9. a; p. 200
10. c; p. 165
11. c; p. 120
12. a; p. 145
13. b; pp. 158–167
14. c; p. 207
15. c; p. 199
16. b; p. 174
17. d; pp. 199–201

## ACTIVITY: IDENTIFYING A CONTRACT

1. voidable; p. 145
2. valid; p. 144
3. void; p. 159
4. valid; p. 152
5. valid; p. 147

## ACTIVITY: ANALYZING A CONTRACT

1. Yes. The signatures on the contract indicate that agreement has been reached by the parties although there is no way of determining which party made the original offer. p. 123
2. $1,000 and the furniture. pp. 131, 132
3. Yes. p. 132
4. None. The adequacy or inadequacy of consideration has no effect on a contract when the items being exchanged (in this case furniture and money) are different. p. 132
5. Sandra G. Lockwood and S. Kathryn Long. Refer to contract.
6. Yes. Generally any adult may enter into a contract with another adult. p. 144
7. Yes. It is legal to sell personal property to another person. pp. 157, 158

## MATCHING QUESTIONS

1. g; p. 207
2. f; p. 196
3. a; p. 198
4. c; p. 206
5. b; p. 201

## COMPLETION QUESTIONS

1. voidable; p. 212
2. full performance; p. 197
3. liquidated; p. 208
4. legal tender; p. 197
5. executed; p. 112
6. consideration; p. 131
7. assignee; p. 191
8. option; p. 120
9. void; p. 157
10. breach of contract; p. 206

## ACTIVITY: CASE PROBLEMS

1. Yes. Under the common law rule, serious illness in a personal service contract discharges the contract. p. 200
2. Yes. The hardship (breakdown of factory machinery) should have been guarded against by including a contingency clause in the contract. p. 201
3. No. A contract for personal services cannot be assigned without consent. p. 187

# Chapter 15   The Sales Contract: Key Concepts

## TRUE-FALSE QUESTIONS

1. T; p. 230
2. T; p. 230
3. T; p. 226
4. T; p. 227
5. F; p. 226
6. T; pp. 231, 232
7. T; p. 226
8. T; p. 230
9. F; p. 226
10. F; p. 226

## MULTIPLE-CHOICE QUESTIONS

1. c; pp. 225, 226
2. d; p. 234
3. c; p. 231
4. c; p. 231
5. a; p. 231
6. c; p. 225
7. d; pp. 225, 226, 232
8. c; pp. 231, 232
9. a; pp. 227, 228
10. c; p. 227

## SHORT-ANSWER QUESTIONS

1. This is a sale because the dealer is supplying you with goods (the motorcycle) in exchange for your money. p. 225
2. This is not a sale because the repair shop supplied you with an intangible service rather than a product. p. 226
3. No. An oral contract for goods to be specially manufactured for the buyer is enforceable even if the amount involved is more than $500. p. 232

## ACTIVITY: ANALYZING A SALES CONTRACT

1. The seller is most likely a nonmerchant. If the seller were a merchant, the name of the business would have been listed, rather than the individual's name. p. 226
2. Under the UCC, special rules relating to sales are applied to a merchant seller. Therefore, it is necessary to know whether a seller is a merchant or a nonmerchant to know whether these rules apply. p. 226
3. No. Under the UCC, a contract for the sale of goods costing $500 or more must be in writing to be enforceable. pp. 230, 231
4. Personal property. p. 225
5. Yes. It could be set aside because under the UCC, a court can set aside a contract thought to be unfair or unconscionable at the time the agreement is made. pp. 223, 224

## ACTIVITY: COMPARISON OF RULES

The common law "mirror image" rule states that an acceptance of an offer cannot legally vary the terms of an offer—that is, the acceptance cannot add, alter, omit, or change any terms in the offer. This rule tended to obstruct the formation of a contract. The Code eliminates the mirror image rule and replaces it with a rule that is more practical in today's business world. These rules are discussed on pp. 227–230.

# Chapter 16  The Sales Contract: Transfer of Title and Risk of Loss

## MULTIPLE-CHOICE QUESTIONS

1. c; p. 241
2. b; pp. 241, 242
3. a; pp. 243, 244
4. a; p. 249
5. c; p. 241
6. a; p. 246
7. b; p. 247
8. c; p. 247
9. c; pp. 243, 244
10. a; p. 242

## MATCHING QUESTIONS

1. c; p. 241
2. d; p. 246
3. a; p. 241
4. b; pp. 244, 245
5. j; pp. 241, 242

## CASE PROBLEMS

1. No. When goods are sent FOB destination, the risk of loss does not pass until these goods reach the destination. In this case, Cobb must bear any loss that occurs before the goods reach Utica.  pp. 243, 244
2. Yes. When a consumer buys goods at a merchant's place of business, risk of loss does not pass to the buyer until he or she actually receives (takes physical possession of) the goods.  p. 242
3. No. In a sale on approval, risk of loss (and title) remain with the seller until approval is given by the consumer-buyer.  p. 244
4. Yes. The legal owner of stolen goods does not lose title (ownership) to these goods. Otterman and Redstone never received title; therefore, Philips, the true owner, can recover the rug from Redstone.  p. 247
5. Yes. Under Article 6 of the UCC, creditors may declare a bulk sale void if the buyer does not notify them at least 10 days before the sale has taken place.  (Note creditor rights under Revised Article 6.)  pp. 245, 246

## ACTIVITY: CASE PROBLEM

Gould must bear the loss. Tomari was not a merchant within the meaning of the Code (Section 2-104); therefore, the risk of loss passes upon tender of delivery (Section 2-509). Since Tomari made a proper tender by notifying Gould that the van was ready for pick-up, the loss falls on Gould.  pp. 242, 243

# Chapter 17   The Sales Contract: Performance, Breach, and Remedies for Breach

## COMPLETION QUESTIONS

1. conforming; p. 254
2. notice; p. 257
3. cover; p. 257
4. inspect; p. 255
5. accept; p. 255
6. market price; p. 258
7. purchase price; p. 260
8. insolvent; p. 261
9. remedy; p. 256
10. 10; p. 261

## SHORT-ANSWER QUESTIONS

1. A buyer may: (1) sue for breach of warranty; (2) cancel the contract and cover; (3) cancel the contract and sue for damages; (4) sue to obtain the goods (specific performance or replevin).  pp. 256–259
2. The seller may: (1) cancel the contract; (2) resell the goods and sue for damages; (3) sue to recover the purchase price; (4) sue to recover damages for nonacceptance; (5) withhold delivery of the goods; (6) reclaim the goods from the buyer.  pp. 259–262

Copyright © Houghton Mifflin Company. All rights reserved.

## MULTIPLE-CHOICE QUESTIONS

1. a; p. 261
2. d; pp. 257, 258
3. d; pp. 256, 257
4. a; pp. 259, 260
5. d; pp. 256, 259–262
6. b; pp. 255, 256–259
7. a; p. 255
8. c; p. 259
9. c; p. 257
10. a; p. 255

## CASE PROBLEM

1. For goods still in possession of the Best Co., Morgan can attempt to reclaim these goods if it does so within 10 days after discovering the insolvency. If the Best Co. had assured the Morgan Co. in writing within three months before delivery that it (the Best Co.) was in good financial condition, the 10-day limit would not apply.   pp. 261, 262
2. The Morgan Co. could stop the goods in transit if the carrier is properly notified in time to allow a stoppage before the goods are delivered to the Best Co.   p. 261
3. The Morgan Co. can completely withhold delivery of the December shipment (cancel the shipment). The Morgan Co. could resell any goods that it was able to reclaim and the goods still in its possession (December shipment) and sue for damages. For goods it could not reclaim or resell, Morgan Co. could sue Best Co. for the purchase price of the goods. Since the Best Co. is insolvent, chances of recovering damages or the purchase price are at risk.   pp. 260, 261

# Chapter 18   Product Liability: Negligence, Warranties, and Strict Liability

## TRUE-FALSE QUESTIONS

1. T; p. 267
2. F; p. 276
3. F; pp. 267, 268
4. F; p. 270
5. T; p. 271
6. F; p. 270
7. T; p. 271
8. T; pp. 271, 272
9. T; p. 270
10. T; p. 269

## MULTIPLE-CHOICE QUESTIONS

1. c; p. 269
2. a; p. 270
3. a; p. 267
4. c; p. 271
5. a; p. 270

## CASE PROBLEMS

1. Yes. The guests could sue "Chicken Delight" for breach of the implied warranty of merchantability. The guests ate the chicken in the buyer's home, so in most states they have the right to sue the immediate seller.   pp. 271, 274–276
2. Yes. Under the UCC, if the seller gives a warranty after the sale, the warranty becomes part of the original sales contract, even without consideration.   p. 270
3. Yes. When the buyer tells the seller the particular purpose for which the goods are needed and relies on the seller to select these goods, there is an implied warranty that the goods supplied will fit the needed purpose.   pp. 271, 272

4. No. In a sale, there is an implied warranty that the seller has good title to the goods. p. 272
5. Yes. The press, as manufactured, was unreasonably dangerous. The two points made by Marvin at the trial would be especially convincing to the jury. The guard should have come as standard equipment.

## ACTIVITY: UNDERSTANDING PRODUCT WARRANTIES

1. This is an express warranty because Fulton Electric Company has specifically stated in writing what it will do for the person who buys the product. p. 269
2. Yes. It states the type of warranty (full); the terms and conditions are understandable; the company agrees to repair or replace the product under the full warranty; it states the length of the warranty; it states what parts are covered (the entire product). pp. 276, 277
3. No. Under the Magnuson-Moss Warranty Act, if the manufacturer or seller elects to give a written warranty, then the implied warranties cannot be eliminated. p. 276
4. None. The warranty period stated is 12 months. p. 275, 276
5. No. The damage is the result of the owner's misuse, not of a manufacturing defect. See wording in warranty.
6. The buyer must pay for delivering the product to a repair facility. Fulton must pay for returning the product to the buyer. See wording in warranty.
7. No. Fulton's warranty specifically states that it will pay for repair work only if the work is done at one of its repair facilities. See wording in warranty.
8. No. The warranty guarantees the product to be free of manufacturing defects. The scratches are cosmetic defects. (Usually the buyer can return such a product to the store where it was purchased and ask for a new one.) See wording in warranty.
9. No. The warranty states that the company will "elect to repair or replace" the product. If the company decides to repair the product, the buyer cannot insist on a new one. See wording in warranty.
10. The warranty period would start on July 13, since the owner received it as a gift on that date. See wording in warranty.

# Review    Part III  Purchase and Sale of Goods Under the UCC

## TRUE-FALSE QUESTIONS

1. T; p. 230
2. T; p. 242
3. T; p. 243
4. T; pp. 247, 248
5. F; pp. 244, 245
6. T; p. 270
7. F; p. 272
8. F; p. 273
9. T; pp. 233, 234
10. T; p. 247

## MULTIPLE-CHOICE QUESTIONS

1. a; pp. 245, 246
2. c; pp. 269, 270
3. b; p. 272
4. b; p. 261
5. b; pp. 250, 261
6. b; p. 271
7. c; pp. 243, 244
8. d; p. 232
9. c; p. 241
10. d; p. 254
11. d; pp. 225, 226
12. d; pp. 227, 228
13. b; p. 226
14. a; p. 230
15. b; p. 228

Copyright © Houghton Mifflin Company. All rights reserved.

## ACTIVITY: UNDERSTANDING WARRANTIES

1. a; p. 269
2. c; p. 271
3. c; p. 270
4. a; p. 270
5. b; p. 242

## CASE PROBLEMS

1. Yes. Under the statute of frauds, only the party who is liable for performance of the contract must sign it in order for it to be enforceable. p. 230
2. Yes. In catalog sales, there is an express warranty that the goods will conform to the catalog description. Friske may sue for breach of the express warranty of description. p. 270
3. Yes. Since the goods were sent FOB shipping point, Friske is liable for any damage that occurs while the goods are en route to the destination, Boston. p. 243
4. No. Because this was a sale on approval, risk of loss did not pass to Jayson. The theft occurred within the 30-day approval period, so the store must bear the loss. p. 244

## SHORT-ANSWER QUESTIONS

1. Answers will vary. Sample answer: A buyer may sue on the basis of (1) negligence—the injured party must establish the manufacturer's or seller's negligence in designing, inspecting, or marketing the product; (2) breach of warranty—that is, breach of the seller's guarantee that a product is not defective and that it is suitable for its intended use; proof of negligence is not required; (3) strict liability—the issue is whether the product was unreasonably dangerous; the injured party does not have to prove fault and need not show the existence of a warranty. pp. 268–276, 277, 278
2. Answers will vary. Sample answer: In order to completely avoid making an express warranty, a merchant would have to avoid (1) using samples or models, (2) making statements or promises about the goods, (3) describing the goods. Also, under the UCC any disclaimer of express warranties will be disregarded if it is inconsistent with the words or conduct that created an express warranty. pp. 269, 270, 272, 273

# Chapter 19  Nature and Types of Commercial Paper

## MULTIPLE-CHOICE QUESTIONS

1. d; p. 288
2. a; p. 291
3. b; p. 291
4. c; p. 288
5. d; pp. 293, 294
6. c; p. 290
7. c; p. 293
8. a; pp. 292, 293
9. d; p. 292
10. c; p. 288
11. d; pp. 293, 294
12. b; p. 288
13. b; p. 293
14. b; p. 292
15. c; p. 294

## ACTIVITY: DETERMINING NEGOTIABILITY

1. NN; p. 291
2. N; p. 291
3. N; p. 293
4. N; p. 293
5. N; p. 276
6. NN; pp. 290, 291
7. NN; p. 294
8. NN; pp. 293, 294
9. N; p. 293
10. NN; p. 294

## TRUE-FALSE QUESTIONS

1. T; p. 290
2. T; p. 288
3. T; p. 288
4. F; p. 292
5. F; p. 288
6. F; p. 288
7. F; pp. 290, 291
8. F; p. 288
9. T; p. 293
10. F; p. 293

## SHORT-ANSWER QUESTIONS

1. When it is payable in a currency that is the legal currency of a particular country at the time the instrument is issued. p. 292
2. Any writing will suffice whether it is printed, typewritten, or handwritten. pp. 290, 291
3. Words. pp. 292, 293
4. Bearer. p. 293
5. The instrument is not negotiable because it is not payable at a definite time. Negotiability must be determined from the face of the instrument. p. 293

# Chapter 20    Issue, Transfer, and Discharge of Commercial Paper

## TRUE-FALSE QUESTIONS

1. T; p. 300
2. F; pp. 302–304
3. T; pp. 302–304
4. F; p. 302
5. T; p. 300
6. T; p. 304
7. T; p. 302
8. T; p. 302
9. F; p. 304
10. T; pp. 305, 306
11. F; p. 303
12. T; p. 302
13. T; p. 302
14. T; p. 302
15. F; pp. 302, 303

## MULTIPLE-CHOICE QUESTIONS

1. b; pp. 303, 304
2. a; pp. 302–304
3. d; pp. 302–304
4. d; pp. 300–302
5. c; p. 300

## CASE PROBLEMS

1. No. A bearer instrument may be negotiated by voluntary delivery. The thief did not acquire it in this manner. p. 302
2. Yes. Although the thief stole the check, he transferred it to the third party by voluntary delivery, which is proper negotiation. p. 302

## SHORT-ANSWER QUESTIONS

1. 
   a. James Tuttle
   b. Friendly Trust Bank
   c. Rachel Fellows
   d. Rachel Fellows
   e. Timothy Blanchard

2. 
   a. special; pp. 302, 303
   b. qualified; p. 304
   c. restrictive; pp. 303, 304

Copyright © Houghton Mifflin Company. All rights reserved.

## Chapter 21  Rights and Duties of Parties to a Negotiable Instrument; Holder in Due Course Status

**TRUE-FALSE QUESTIONS**

1. T; p. 311
2. F; p. 310
3. F; p. 318
4. F; p. 311
5. F; p. 318
6. T; p. 313

**CASE PROBLEMS**

1. No. Lack of consideration is not a defense against a holder in due course.  p. 316
2. No. In 1976, the FTC ruled that if a consumer gives a seller a negotiable instrument and the seller negotiates the instrument to a bank, the bank cannot become a holder in due course. pp. 319, 320
3. No. Since the maturity date (July 8) is on Sunday, Hackman cannot demand payment on that date. He should make presentment on the first regular business day following the maturity date—Monday, July 9, in this case.  p. 311

**MATCHING QUESTIONS**

1. d; p. 312
2. i; p. 313
3. f; p. 312
4. j; pp. 320, 321
5. g; p. 317
6. b; p. 317
7. e; p. 311
8. c; p. 310
9. a; pp. 310, 311
10. h; p. 313

**ACTIVITY: ANALYZING COMMERCIAL PAPER**

1. Maria Schmidt is primarily responsible.  pp. 310, 311
2. She is a holder in due course.  p. 313
3. She is a holder.  p. 313
4. A holder in due course must take the instrument for value, in good faith, and without knowledge that the instrument is overdue or dishonored or that someone has a defense against it. pp. 313–315

## Chapter 22  Checks, Electronic Fund Transfers, and the Banking System

**TRUE-FALSE QUESTIONS**

1. T; p. 328
2. T; p. 329
3. T; p. 328
4. F; pp. 332, 333
5. T; p. 334
6. F; p. 334
7. T; p. 326
8. T; p. 327
9. F; pp. 326, 327
10. F; p. 330
11. T; p. 327
12. T; p. 328
13. T; pp. 330, 331
14. F; p. 332
15. T; p. 334

## MULTIPLE-CHOICE QUESTIONS

1. c; p. 328
2. a; pp. 330, 331
3. c; p. 329
4. b; p. 326
5. d; p. 330
6. c; p. 333
7. b; pp. 332, 333
8. a; pp. 336, 337
9. b; p. 328
10. d; pp. 334, 335
11. d; p. 328
12. c; p. 327
13. a; p. 330
14. c; pp. 329, 330
15. b; p. 334
16. b; p. 328
17. d; p. 326
18. c; pp. 326, 327
19. a; p. 326
20. c; p. 337

## SHORT-ANSWER QUESTIONS

1. The bank is responsible for paying the amount of the check if there are sufficient funds and for requiring identification before cashing a check. pp. 326, 327
2. The bank is liable for any damages caused as a result of its refusal to pay, such as injury to the depositor's credit rating. p. 326
3. The depositor has to keep sufficient funds in the account to cover checks and must examine the monthly statement and advise the bank of any errors. pp. 328, 329
4. It diminishes the use of checks. The EFTS allows money to be transferred electronically from a person's bank account to that of a creditor or into the account of a store where a purchase was made. pp. 337, 338
5. The bank is liable to the depositor and must credit the depositor's account for the amount of the check. p. 328

## MATCHING QUESTIONS

1. d; pp. 331, 332
2. f; pp. 332, 333
3. e; p. 329
4. b; p. 327
5. i; p. 326
6. a; pp. 325, 326
7. k; p. 337
8. l; p. 328
9. j; pp. 330, 331
10. h; p. 333

## ACTIVITY: ANALYZING CHECKS

1. The day is incorrect (there is no April 31).
2. The name of the pharmacy is crossed out.
3. Words of negotiability (order of) are missing.
4. The amount in figures does not agree with the amount in words.
5. The signature is different from the printed name.

## ACTIVITY: CASE PROBLEM

In this case, probably not. If a bank pays in good faith without consulting the customer, it has the right to charge the customer's account for the amount of the check. This seems to be the case here. Hanson Manufacturing Co. was one of Frontier's major customers, so what the bank did seemed proper. As a practical matter, most banks usually do not pay stale checks until they have first contacted the depositor to be sure that the depositor still wishes it to be paid. pp. 326, 327

Copyright © Houghton Mifflin Company. All rights reserved.

# Review  Part IV  Commercial Paper

## MULTIPLE-CHOICE QUESTIONS

1. b; p. 302
2. a; p. 314
3. d; p. 288
4. a; p. 318
5. d; p. 315
6. c; p. 304
7. b; pp. 292, 293
8. c; p. 288
9. d; pp. 330, 331
10. b; p. 326
11. a; pp. 315, 318
12. c; pp. 292, 293
13. b; p. 292
14. a; p. 310
15. d; p. 312
16. b; p. 326

## TRUE-FALSE QUESTIONS

1. F; p. 291
2. T; p. 290
3. T; p. 293
4. T; p. 302
5. T; p. 305
6. T; pp. 305, 306
7. F; p. 316
8. T; p. 315
9. T; p. 317
10. F; pp. 326, 327
11. T; p. 327
12. F; pp. 330, 331
13. T; pp. 334, 335
14. T; p. 311
15. F; p. 292

## MATCHING QUESTIONS

1. b; p. 288
2. j; pp. 315–317
3. c; p. 304
4. i; p. 313
5. h; p. 315
6. d; p. 310
7. g; pp. 303, 304
8. f; p. 287
9. e; p. 312
10. a; p. 288

## SHORT-ANSWER QUESTION

Paying by check eliminates the need to keep large amounts of cash on hand and is safer than using cash for payments by mail. Also, once returned by the bank, checks serve as receipts and may be used as proof of payment.  p. 325

## CASE PROBLEM

No. Manhattan Bank, the payor bank, has no liability. The UCC (Section 4-403[2]) provides that an oral stop payment order is binding upon the bank for only 14 days unless confirmed in writing within that period. In this case, Antes had not confirmed this oral stop payment order in writing. p. 328

ANSWER KEY | 269

# Chapter 23 Employer-Employee Relationship

## TRUE-FALSE QUESTIONS

1. T; p. 346
2. F; p. 352
3. T; p. 346
4. T; p. 360
5. T; p. 357
6. F; p. 346
7. T; p. 349
8. T; p. 349
9. F; p. 349
10. F; p. 358
11. F; p. 357
12. F; p. 353

## CASE PROBLEMS

1. No. If her qualifications are equal to any male applicant's qualification, she cannot be refused the job because she is female. p. 34
2. No. Alliance has good cause to dismiss Steeper and will not be liable for breach of contract. p. 349
3. Yes. Workers' compensation provides benefits for loss of wages due to an injury or illness caused by the conditions prevailing at the place of employment. p. 358
4. Yes. An employee who continues to violate reasonable rules set down by an employer may be discharged. p. 349
5. No. The Age Discrimination in Employment Act applies only to persons between the ages of 40 and 65. p. 353
6. No. A nonimmigrant alien is not permitted to work in the United States. p. 360
7. No. Access to reference letters would violate the right to privacy of the writers of the letters. p. 348

## MULTIPLE-CHOICE QUESTIONS

1. b; p. 345
2. a; p. 352
3. b; p. 349
4. d; p. 358
5. c; p. 346
6. f; p. 353

# Chapter 24 Principal-Agent Relationship

## MULTIPLE-CHOICE QUESTIONS

1. c; p. 376
2. c; p. 369
3. b; p. 373
4. d; p. 367
5. d; p. 369
6. b; p. 369
7. c; p. 367
8. d; p. 372
9. c; p. 367
10. b; p. 370
11. d; p. 378
12. d; p. 375
13. b; p. 370
14. d; p. 378
15. c; p. 376

## MATCHING QUESTIONS

1. b; p. 379
2. d; p. 372
3. a; p. 369
4. c; p. 371
5. a; p. 369

Copyright © Houghton Mifflin Company. All rights reserved.

## CASE PROBLEMS

1. No. The principal must reimburse the agent for all necessary expenses incurred by the agent in carrying out the principal's business. p. 375
2. Yes. Personally benefiting from a business deal is a breach of loyalty between the agent and the principal. p. 373
3. No. A minor may act as an agent and bind the principal in contracts made with third parties. p. 368
4. Yes. When an agent's authority is revoked, third parties who have had business dealings with the agent are entitled to notice of the revocation; otherwise, the principal is responsible for unauthorized acts of the former agent. p. 379
5. No. The principal alone may not terminate an agency coupled with an interest. The agent must agree to the termination. p. 377

## ACTIVITY: IDENTIFYING VIOLATIONS

1. accurate accounting; p. 374
2. reimbursement; p. 375
3. indemnity; p. 375
4. loyalty; p. 373
5. obedience; p. 373

## ACTIVITY: FINDING THE FACTS

1. no; p. 370
2. special agent; p. 367
3. yes; p. 370
4. no; p. 370
5. yes; p. 373

# Chapter 25  Principal-Agent, Employer-Employee, and Third-Party Relationships

## COMPLETION QUESTIONS

1. express; p. 385
2. undisclosed; p. 388
3. tort; p. 387
4. ratifying; p. 386
5. express; p. 385
6. apparent; p. 386
7. party; p. 388
8. third person; p. 388
9. implied; pp. 385, 386
10. crime; p. 390

## MULTIPLE-CHOICE QUESTIONS

1. a; pp. 385, 386
2. c; p. 390
3. c; p. 388
4. d; p. 386
5. a; p. 386
6. b; p. 385
7. d; p. 388
8. b; p. 389
9. a; p. 389
10. b; p. 389

## CASE PROBLEMS

1. Yes. A principal is liable to third parties if the agent acts within the scope of authority. In this case, Maxim had implied authority to hire men to move the merchandise in this emergency. p. 385
2. Yes. A principal is liable for the torts of an agent if the torts are committed while the agent is acting within the scope of the agency. p. 387
3. No. The agent is personally liable when acting beyond the scope of authority. In this case, a salesperson has no authority (including apparent authority in this case) to contract with the TV station for a series of announcements. p. 388
4. No. An employer is not liable for the crimes committed by an employee unless the criminal activity was authorized. p. 390
5. Yes. The trip was conducted by the company and would be considered within the scope of employment. p. 387

# Review    Part V  Agency, Employment, and Labor Law

## TRUE-FALSE QUESTIONS

1. F; p. 376
2. T; pp. 385, 386
3. F; p. 386
4. T; p. 378
5. T; p. 369
6. F; p. 369
7. T; p. 357
8. T; p. 358
9. F; p. 373
10. T; p. 373

## MULTIPLE-CHOICE QUESTIONS

1. d; p. 375
2. a; p. 368
3. d; p. 386
4. b; p. 367
5. c; pp. 386, 387

## CASE PROBLEMS

1. Yes. All contracts between principals and agents that are for more than one year must be in writing. p. 370
2. Yes. Franklin had authority to perform only one specific act; this made Franklin a special agent. p. 367
3. No. Death of a principal terminates the principal-agent relationship. p. 378
4. No. The principal is liable to third parties if the agent acts within the scope of apparent authority. p. 387
5. Yes. A minor may act as an agent, and the principal is bound by all contracts made within the scope of apparent authority. p. 368

## Chapter 26  Sole Proprietorships and Partnerships

**TRUE-FALSE QUESTIONS**

1. T; p. 398
2. F; p. 397
3. T; p. 397
4. T; p. 399
5. F; p. 400
6. F; p. 400
7. T; p. 400
8. T; p. 402
9. T; p. 402
10. F; p. 402

**SHORT-ANSWER QUESTIONS**

1. A trading partnership is an association for commercial purposes, such as manufacturing; and a nontrading partnership is an association for professional purposes, such as a law firm. p. 399
2. A limited partner contributes cash or property to the business but may not take part in operations. A general partner is a fully active partner. A silent partner is inactive in a general partnership but is known to the public. A secret partner is active in the partnership but is unknown to the public. A dormant partner is neither active in the partnership nor known to the public. p. 399
3. In a general partnership, all partners share liability for debts and torts. In a limited partnership, the limited partner is not bound by the obligations of the partnership and is not liable beyond the limited investment. pp. 399, 400
4. In a limited partnership, only the limited partners have limited liability but they cannot participate in management. In an LLC, all members have limited liability and may participate in management. p. 408

**MULTIPLE-CHOICE QUESTIONS**

1. c; p. 397
2. b; p. 399
3. d; p. 405
4. a; p. 402
5. d; p. 405
6. b; p. 400
7. d; p. 398
8. d; p. 400
9. a; p. 400
10. d; p. 405

**CASE PROBLEMS**

1. No. If a specific agreement is not drawn up, all partners equally share the profits and losses. p. 402
2. Yes. The product was bought for the business so the partnership is liable for the cost. p. 404
3. No. Bankruptcy of the partnership or an individual partner dissolves the partnership. p. 405

**ACTIVITY: ANALYZING A PARTNERSHIP AGREEMENT**

1. No. Since the term of the agreement (15 years) is more than 1 year, the statute of frauds requires that the agreement be in writing. p. 400
2. Paragraph 4 states that each partner cannot engage in any other business enterprise without written permission from the other partner. p. 403

3. Paragraph 5 states that Wolfburg's share of the profits and losses will be 60 percent; Swenson's, 40 percent. p. 402
4. According to Paragraph 5, Swenson must get written permission from Wolfburg to withdraw cash or other assets from the business. pp. 403, 404
5. No. Swenson is entitled to a share of the profit because the transaction concerned partnership business. p. 403
6. The partnership will be terminated by completion of the term of the agreement (15 years), by written permission of each partner, or by death or incapacitation of one or both partners. pp. 405, 406

# Chapter 27  Corporations and Franchising

## CASE PROBLEMS

1. No. Upon dissolution of a corporation, the corporation's creditors have first claim against the assets, followed by the preferred stockholders. Common stockholders have a claim against the remainder. p. 418
2. No. A corporation has the implied power to borrow money for any proper corporate purpose. The vote to go into the plumbing business could be invalidated, however, since it goes beyond both the express and implied powers of the corporation. pp. 420, 421
3. They would need less capital and experience than normally required, would get a well-known name or logo, and would get valuable training and experience. p. 426

## MATCHING QUESTIONS

1. d; p. 418
2. f; p. 419
3. i; p. 422
4. b; p. 419
5. e; p. 421
6. j; p. 416
7. h; p. 417
8. a; p. 420
9. g; p. 417
10. c; p. 419
11. k; p. 423

## MULTIPLE-CHOICE QUESTIONS

1. b; p. 416
2. d; p. 415
3. a; p. 416
4. c; p. 416
5. d; p. 419
6. c; p. 420
7. a; p. 420
8. c; p. 422
9. d; p. 422
10. d; p. 421
11. b; p. 422
12. a; p. 414
13. c; pp. 420, 421
14. b; p. 415
15. a; p. 420
16. d; p. 418
17. a; p. 415
18. a; pp. 417, 418
19. b; p. 414
20. c; pp. 417, 418

## SHORT-ANSWER QUESTIONS

1. No. In most states a business applying for incorporation cannot choose a name that is similar to the name of an existing corporation. p. 416
2. The advantages of organizing this company as a corporation are perpetual existence, limited liability, ease of transfer of ownership, and centralized management. pp. 423, 424

Copyright © Houghton Mifflin Company. All rights reserved.

3. No. The death of a stockholder does not result in the termination of a corporation unless it's a one-stockholder corporation. p. 423
4. In double taxation, the company is taxed on a corporate income. Then the dividends paid to stockholders are taxed as well. p. 425
5. Cortillo will receive $1,875 in dividends. p. 418
6. This corporation can be dissolved in the following ways: when the term of the corporate charter ends, when the stockholders agree, when the charter is revoked, or when there is a merger or consolidation. p. 421

## Chapter 28   Government Regulation of Business

### MULTIPLE-CHOICE QUESTIONS

1. d; p. 432
2. b; p. 432
3. c; p. 432
4. b; p. 433
5. a; p. 433
6. d; p. 434
7. a; p. 434
8. c; p. 433
9. c; p. 436
10. d; p. 437
11. a; p. 433
12. b; p. 434

### SHORT-ANSWER QUESTIONS

1. Monopolies, competition, taxation, public utilities, and preservation of the general welfare and environment. p. 433
2. Legislative power sets the rules, rates, and standards. Executive power enforces the rules. Judicial power determines violations and penalties. p. 438

### CASE PROBLEMS

1. Federal Trade Commission; pp. 434, 435
2. Occupational Safety & Health Administration; p. 439
3. Securities and Exchange Commission; p. 436
4. Federal Reserve Board; p. 439
5. Federal Communications Commission; p. 439
6. Local zoning board; p. 439
7. State licensing board; p. 440
8. State Public Utilities Commission; p. 439
9. Federal Communications Commission; p. 439
10. Federal Reserve Board; p. 439
11. Environmental Protection Agency; p. 438

## Review   Part VI  Business Organization and Regulation

### MINI-CASE

1. d; p. 405
2. b; p. 406
3. d; p. 405
4. c; p. 400
5. b; p. 399

## MULTIPLE-CHOICE QUESTIONS

1. d; p. 397
2. c; p. 397
3. b; p. 399
4. a; pp. 399, 400
5. d; p. 414
6. d; p. 441
7. d; p. 420
8. b; p. 412
9. c; p. 433
10. c; p. 439

## MATCHING QUESTIONS

1. c; p. 416
2. a; p. 405
3. e; p. 432
4. b; p. 408
5. d; p. 439

## CASE PROBLEMS

1. Yes. The death of a partner dissolves a partnership. p. 405
2. No. Income earned as part of a partnership business would have to be shared with the partners. p. 403
3. No. Officers are usually liable only to the corporation unless they are guilty of fraud or deceit. p. 421
4. No. Corporations do not terminate when there is a change of ownership. p. 421
5. If Polcin is correct, her accountant may be liable for damages for negligence and/or breach of contract. If the accountant's work does not meet professional standards, the accountant may be fined or suspended from practice. p. 440

# Chapter 29  Basic Legal Concepts of Property

## COMPLETION QUESTIONS

1. personal; p. 447
2. fixture; pp. 447, 448
3. easement; p. 448
4. deed; p. 449
5. delivery; p. 449
6. adverse possession; p. 451
7. survivorship; p. 455
8. escheat; p. 450
9. the entirety; p. 455
10. zoning; p. 458

## MULTIPLE-CHOICE QUESTIONS

1. d; p. 453
2. b; p. 453
3. d; p. 454
4. a; p. 455
5. d; p. 458
6. d; p. 450
7. b; pp. 447, 448
8. d; p. 448
9. d; p. 456
10. d; p. 457

Copyright © Houghton Mifflin Company. All rights reserved.

## MATCHING QUESTIONS

1. b; p. 448
2. c; p. 450
3. g; p. 453
4. e; p. 448
5. a; p. 456
6. f; p. 457
7. d; p. 451
8. j; p. 453
9. h; p. 447
10. i; p. 449

## SHORT-ANSWER QUESTIONS

1. A joint tenancy has the right of survivorship; upon the tenant's death, the interest in the property passes to surviving tenants. In a tenancy in common, upon the death of the tenant, the interest passes to that tenant's heirs or to the person or persons named in the deceased tenant's will. p. 454, 455
2. A patent is an exclusive right to an invention and is good for 17 years. A trademark protects words or symbols used to identify a business or product and is good for 10 years. A copyright is an exclusive right to artistic and intellectual works and is good for life plus 50 years. p. 453
3. Real property may be acquired by purchase, gift, inheritance, adverse possession, accretion, or condemnation. pp. 449–452

# Chapter 30   Renting Real Property

## MULTIPLE-CHOICE QUESTIONS

1. c; p. 464
2. b; p. 464
3. a; p. 465
4. d; p. 471
5. c; p. 470
6. b; p. 468
7. b; p. 470
8. d; pp. 468, 469
9. c; p. 472
10. c; p. 470
11. a; p. 470
12. c; p. 467

## SHORT-ANSWER QUESTIONS

1. A lease is a rental agreement between the landlord and tenant. A sublease is the transfer of a portion of a lease term by the tenant to a subtenant. p. 471
2. (1) Names and addresses of the landlord and tenant
   (2) A description of the property being leased
   (3) The term of the lease
   (4) The amount of rent
   (5) The time and place to pay the rent
   (6) The signatures of the parties
   (7) The rights and duties of the landlord; pp. 467–471
3. (1) Passage of time
   (2) Agreement between parties
   (3) Agreement in the lease
   (4) Condemnation
   (5) Destruction of the leased property
   (6) Operation of law; p. 471

## ACTIVITY: ANALYZING A LEASE

1. Mark and Anna Essex. p. 464
2. Brent J. and LeeAnn McDowell. p. 464
3. One year. p. 464
4. A tenancy for years. p. 464
5. The premises are to be used as a residence, and cannot be subleased or assigned without written consent of the landlord. Also, waste is not allowed to accumulate on the premises. pp. 437, 438
6. The lease will terminate immediately without notice, and double the rent ($500) will be required as damages. pp. 468, 469
7. The landlord is responsible for paying the taxes because the lease is silent about this. p. 467
8. Tenants may sublease the property only with written consent of the landlord. p. 471
9. The tenant must give up possession of the property in good condition and repair, excepting normal wear. p. 468
10. The landlord. Fire is considered accidental and is specifically excepted as the tenant's responsibility in the lease. p. 470
11. If the tenants are sued for failure to pay the rent or to vacate the property at the end of the term of the lease, the tenants must pay the attorneys' fees. pp. 468, 469

# Chapter 31   Buying and Selling Real Property

## TRUE-FALSE QUESTIONS

1. F; p. 478
2. T; p. 478
3. T; p. 479
4. F; p. 479
5. F; pp. 481, 482
6. T; p. 481
7. F; p. 482
8. F; p. 478
9. T; p. 483
10. F; p. 486

## MATCHING QUESTIONS

1. g; p. 481
2. d; p. 486
3. a; p. 483
4. i; p. 482
5. b; p. 479
6. j; p. 489
7. c; p. 489
8. h; p. 487
9. f; p. 481
10. e; p. 486

## MULTIPLE-CHOICE QUESTIONS

1. b; p. 478
2. c; pp. 487–489
3. d; p. 479
4. c; p. 481
5. a; p. 483
6. a; p. 486
7. b; p. 489
8. c; p. 483
9. c; p. 483
10. d; p. 489
11. a; p. 479
12. b; p. 481
13. d; p. 483
14. b; p. 483
15. a; p. 459

## ACTIVITY: TYPES OF DEEDS

1. quit-claim deed; p. 487
2. bargain and sale deed; p. 488
3. warranty deed; p. 489

# Review   Part VII   Real and Personal Property

## MULTIPLE-CHOICE QUESTIONS

1. b; p. 447
2. a; p. 447
3. d; p. 448
4. b; p. 449
5. b; p. 449
6. d; p. 457
7. a; p. 449
8. d; p. 464
9. d; p. 467
10. a; p. 468
11. c; p. 465
12. a; p. 452
13. d; p. 471
14. b; p. 471
15. d; p. 486
16. c; p. 485

## TRUE-FALSE QUESTIONS

1. F; p. 453
2. F; p. 453
3. T; p. 449
4. T; p. 448
5. F; p. 451
6. F; p. 458
7. F; p. 456
8. T; p. 458
9. T; p. 450
10. F; p. 455
11. F; p. 467
12. T; p. 470
13. F; p. 470
14. F; p. 488
15. F; p. 471
16. T; p. 472
17. F; p. 482
18. T; p. 455
19. T; p. 484
20. F; pp. 488, 489

## MATCHING QUESTIONS

1. d; p. 450
2. i; p. 449
3. j; p. 454
4. f; p. 465
5. b; p. 471
6. h; p. 472
7. a; p. 481
8. e; p. 489
9. g; p. 482
10. c; p. 489

# Chapter 32   Nature and Creation of Bailments

## YES-NO QUESTIONS

1. N; p. 497
2. Y; p. 497
3. N; p. 497
4. N; p. 497
5. Y; p. 497
6. N; p. 500
7. N; p. 500
8. Y; p. 500
9. N; p. 498
10. N; p. 497
11. N; p. 501
12. Y; p. 499
13. Y; p. 499
14. Y; p. 500
15. Y; p. 497

## SHORT-ANSWER QUESTIONS

1. (1) Possession—the bailor must be in possession of the property.
   (2) Personal property—only personal property is subject to a bailment.
   (3) Delivery and acceptance—the property must change hands and be accepted by the bailee.
   (4) Return—the bailed property must be returned with little or no change. pp. 498, 499
2. Answers will vary.
3. A bailment involves transfer of possession only. A sale involves a transfer of title and possession. p. 498
4. A depositor does not expect to get back the same money deposited and therefore no bailment is created. The deposit establishes a debt from the bank to the depositor. p. 501
5. (1) upon completion
   (2) by mutual agreement
   (3) by acts of the bailor and bailee
   (4) by destruction of the bailed property
   (5) by operation of law pp. 500, 501

## MULTIPLE-CHOICE QUESTIONS

1. c; p. 498
2. d; p. 499
3. d; p. 499
4. b; p. 501
5. c; p. 498

## COMPLETION QUESTIONS

1. bailor; p. 497
2. personal; p. 498
3. bailment; p. 497
4. real; p. 498
5. express; p. 499

# Chapter 33   Bailments: Types, Rights, and Responsibilities

## TRUE-FALSE QUESTIONS

1. true; p. 505
2. gratuitous bailment; p. 510
3. reasonable; p. 505
4. true; pp. 506, 507
5. true; p. 507
6. slight; p. 511
7. gratuitous bailment; p. 510
8. consignment; p. 508
9. true; p. 505
10. true; p. 512

## SHORT-ANSWER QUESTIONS

1. Examples will vary. Sample answer:
   (1) renting
   (2) work and services
   (3) pledging
   (4) consigning
   (5) storage   p. 505
2. Answers will vary. p. 505

## MATCHING QUESTIONS

1. h; p. 507
2. e; p. 512
3. j; p. 507
4. g; p. 508
5. b; p. 507
6. d; p. 509
7. i; p. 508
8. f; p. 511
9. a; p. 508
10. c; p. 512

## CASE PROBLEMS

1. No. Brown is responsible only for slight care of the guitar. The humidity was a problem beyond his control. p. 511
2. No. Monteiro did not turn the camera over to someone else; therefore, he retained possession and no bailment was created. p. 510
3. Yes. A bailment by necessity was created when Andrews received the book; this bailment makes her responsible for exercising reasonable care. pp. 512, 513

# Chapter 34   Special Bailments

## MULTIPLE-CHOICE QUESTIONS

1. b; p. 518
2. d; p. 518
3. a; p. 518
4. c; pp. 518, 519
5. a; p. 519
6. d; p. 521
7. a; p. 522
8. c; p. 524
9. a; p. 518
10. d; p. 526

## SHORT-ANSWER QUESTION

Student examples will vary.

1. Acts of God; p. 519
2. Acts of a public enemy; p. 519
3. Acts of public authorities; p. 519
4. Fault of the bailor or guest; p. 520

## CASE PROBLEMS

1. Yes. The motel is a special bailee and is liable for the safety of its guests' property. p. 522
2. Yes. Ajax is a special bailee, and hijacking is not an exception to absolute liability. p. 519
3. No. Thurston is a resident, not a transient, so the hotelkeeper is only responsible for reasonable care. p. 521
4. No. Liability was limited by implied agreement between the parties. p. 518
5. Yes. Even though the apples were ruined by a storm, there would have been no damage but for Storage's fault. p. 519
6. No. The shipper was aware of the overripe condition and must bear the loss—no negligence by the carrier. p. 520
7. No. Cruise is a business guest and the hotel is not liable because it took reasonable care of the coat. p. 521

8. No. A hotel ceases to be liable for a guest's baggage after the guest checks out of the hotel. p. 521
9. No. A hotelkeeper may not discriminate based solely on race, color, religion, or national origin. p. 521
10. Yes. A common carrier may limit its liability for loss of goods shipped, by contract with the consignor. p. 525

# Review    Part VIII   Bailments

## TRUE-FALSE QUESTIONS

1. F; p. 500
2. F; p. 498
3. T; p. 498
4. T; p. 498
5. F; p. 505
6. T; p. 501
7. T; p. 506
8. T; p. 518
9. T; p. 521
10. F; p. 524

## MULTIPLE-CHOICE QUESTIONS

1. b; p. 501
2. d; p. 498
3. a; p. 498
4. b; p. 505
5. c; p. 501
6. b; p. 512
7. c; p. 507
8. c; p. 511
9. a; p. 506
10. b; p. 507
11. c; p. 524
12. c; p. 526
13. d; p. 520
14. a; p. 526

## CASE PROBLEMS

1. The legal relationship is bailor/bailee. p. 510
2. No. The sign was not posted in a visible area, so Blake was not made aware of the limitation. p. 506
3. No. This loss was due to an act of God, not negligence on the part of the bailee. p. 519
4. The parking lot owner would have to pay $10,000 because that is the value of the car. The limitation would not apply, because it was not visible. p. 506

# Chapter 35    Property and Casualty Insurance

## MULTIPLE-CHOICE QUESTIONS

1. c; p. 536
2. d; p. 540
3. b; p. 539
4. a; p. 539
5. c; p. 544
6. a; p. 539
7. d; p. 539
8. a; p. 542
9. b; p. 543
10. c; p. 539

## ACTIVITY: IDENTIFYING RISKS COVERED BY INSURANCE

1. covered; p. 539
2. not covered; p. 539
3. not covered; p. 539
4. covered; p. 539
5. not covered; p. 539
6. covered; p. 539
7. not covered; p. 539
8. not covered; p. 539
9. not covered; p. 539
10. covered; p. 539

## CASE PROBLEMS

1. No. The damage was caused by Gilbey's carelessness, not by hostile fire. p. 538
2. Yes. An all-risk policy covers all losses, regardless of the cause. p. 539
3. No. Jaffey can collect only up to the face value of the policy. p. 536
4. No. The misstatement was not material to the insurance company in deciding to issue the policy to Gregg. p. 534
5. Yes. Bridges had an insurable interest because she was liable to Cohen for the value of the china. p. 543
6. No. If the same property is issued with more than one company, each company is liable only for its proportionate share of the loss (pro-rata liability). p. 543
7. No. If the insured cancels the policy, he or she receives a short rate refund, which is less than the full amount of the unused premium. p. 544

## COMPLETION QUESTIONS

1. insurance; p. 533
2. policy; p. 533
3. premium; p. 533
4. agent; p. 534
5. exclusion; p. 536
6. valued; p. 536
7. deductible; p. 537
8. misrepresentation; p. 534
9. insurance company; p. 537
10. release; p. 538

# Chapter 36  Automobile Insurance

## TRUE-FALSE QUESTIONS

1. F; p. 550
2. T; p. 550
3. T; p. 554
4. T; p. 554
5. F; p. 554
6. F; p. 552
7. T; p. 555
8. F; p. 555
9. T; p. 558
10. T; p. 557

## MULTIPLE-CHOICE QUESTIONS

1. c; p. 550
2. d; p. 553
3. b; p. 554
4. a; p. 550
5. d; p. 555
6. c; p. 554
7. a; p. 558
8. b; p. 552
9. c; p. 555
10. b; p. 555

## ACTIVITY: PROTECTING AGAINST RISK

| | Bodily Injury | Property Damage | Medical Payments | Uninsured Motorist | Collision | Comprehensive | |
|---|---|---|---|---|---|---|---|
| 1. | | | | | | X | p. 554 |
| 2. | | | | | | X | p. 554 |
| 3. | | | | | | X | p. 554 |
| 4. | | | | | X | | p. 554 |
| 5. | | | | | | X | p. 554 |
| 6. | | | | | | X | p. 554 |
| 7. | | | | X | | | p. 553 |
| 8. | | | X | | | | p. 553 |
| 9. | | X | | | | | p. 553 |
| 10. | | | | X | | | p. 553 |

## CASE PROBLEMS

1. Yes. Collision insurance covers the damage regardless of who was at fault. p. 554
2. Collision coverage pays for the fair market value of the car minus the deductible. p. 554

# Chapter 37   Personal Insurance

## MULTIPLE-CHOICE QUESTIONS

1. c; p. 565
2. c; p. 565
3. a; p. 568
4. b; p. 568
5. c; p. 567
6. c; p. 569
7. c; p. 564
8. d; p. 564
9. a; p. 573
10. c; p. 572

## CASE PROBLEMS

1. No. Most policies provide a 30-day grace period. p. 568
2. Yes. The suicide occurred after a reasonable time. p. 569
3. No. A misstatement about age does not void an insurance policy. p. 567
4. No. Term insurance does not build up cash value. p. 565
5. No. Whole life insurance policies have nonforfeiture rights, ways of using the accumulated cash value to prevent a policy from lapsing. p. 570

## MATCHING QUESTIONS

1. g; p. 566
2. f; p. 564
3. a; p. 563
4. b; p. 566
5. h; p. 566
6. d; p. 565
7. c; p. 564
8. e; p. 565
9. i; p. 573
10. j; p. 564

# Review    Part IX    Insurance

## TRUE-FALSE QUESTIONS

1. F; p. 534
2. T; p. 534
3. F; p. 536
4. T; p. 537
5. F; p. 534
6. F; p. 538
7. T; p. 540
8. T; p. 541
9. T; p. 543
10. T; p. 555

## MATCHING QUESTIONS

1. j; p. 537
2. g; p. 538
3. h; p. 555
4. a; p. 543
5. c; p. 537
6. d; p. 535
7. e; p. 533
8. b; p. 544
9. i; p. 539
10. f; p. 538

## MULTIPLE-CHOICE QUESTIONS

1. b; p. 533
2. d; p. 534
3. d; p. 535
4. a; p. 536
5. c; p. 536
6. a; p. 539
7. c; p. 543
8. b; p. 544
9. c; p. 545
10. d; p. 554
11. d; p. 536
12. b; p. 534
13. d; p. 539
14. b; p. 553
15. b; p. 565
16. a; p. 563
17. b; p. 565
18. c; p. 569

# Chapter 38    Wills and Intestacy

## MULTIPLE-CHOICE QUESTIONS

1. c; p. 581
2. b; p. 586
3. d; p. 583
4. d; p. 584
5. b; p. 585
6. d; p. 584
7. b; p. 588
8. c; p. 584
9. b; p. 585
10. d; p. 587

## COMPLETION QUESTIONS

1. testator; p. 581
2. intestate; p. 581
3. probate; p. 588
4. administrator; p. 590
5. heir; p. 590
6. nuncupative; p. 585
7. codicil; p. 587
8. living; p. 590
9. legacy or bequest; p. 582
10. spouse; p. 586

## ACTIVITY: READING A WILL

1. No; p. 586
2. No; p. 586
3. Yes; p. 584
4. No; p. 586
5. Yes; p. 586
6. Yes; p. 586
7. No; p. 586
8. No; p. 586
9. Yes; p. 584
10. No; p. 583

# Chapter 39    Estate Planning

## MULTIPLE-CHOICE QUESTIONS

1. b; p. 599
2. c; p. 599
3. c; p. 599
4. d; p. 602
5. c; p. 601
6. d; p. 600
7. c; p. 602
8. d; p. 603
9. c; p. 602
10. d; p. 601

## MATCHING QUESTIONS

1. e; p. 602
2. c; p. 602
3. j; p. 599
4. g; p. 602
5. a; p. 602
6. i; p. 602
7. d; p. 601
8. b; p. 598
9. f; p. 602
10. h; p. 599

## SHORT-ANSWER QUESTIONS

1. Lawyer
   Accountant
   Insurance agent
   Bank trust officer;  p. 603
2. Seek professional help
   Decide on a plan
   Execute the plan;  p. 603
3. Property transferred by will
   Property held jointly
   Insurance proceeds payable to a spouse
   Interests created by a trust;  p. 601
4. Gifts
   Marital deduction
   Trusts;  p. 600

# Review  Part X  Wills and Estate Planning

## MULTIPLE-CHOICE QUESTIONS

1. c; p. 581
2. b; p. 587
3. b; p. 584
4. b; pp. 583–585
5. c; p. 581
6. d; pp. 587, 588
7. d; p. 588
8. d; p. 584
9. d; p. 582
10. c; p. 585
11. a; p. 581
12. b; p. 587
13. d; p. 589
14. c; p. 585
15. d; p. 584

## CASE PROBLEMS

1. Yes. A will must be witnessed unless it is a holographic will.  p. 585
2. No. Mutilating a will revokes it.  p. 588
3. Yes. Such a provision is void because it restricts the sale of property and is against public policy.  p. 586
4. No. Children born after a will is executed are included in a bequest in a will "to Children."  p. 588

## MATCHING QUESTIONS

1. d; p. 587
2. e; p. 587
3. a; p. 588
4. c; p. 581
5. b; p. 602

# Chapter 40  Protecting the Consumer and the Taxpayer

## COMPLETION QUESTIONS

1. Federal Trade Commission; p. 610
2. false advertising; p. 610
3. regulations, anti-trust laws; p. 612
4. keep; p. 613
5. Consumer Product Safety Commission; p. 616
6. puffing; p. 612
7. loss leader; p. 612
8. plain English; p. 615
9. Warsaw Convention; p. 621
10. class-action; p. 619

## SHORT-ANSWER QUESTIONS

1. (1) The right to fair advertising
   (2) The right to fair pricing
   (3) The right to refuse unordered goods
   (4) The right to cancel a contract
   Student examples will vary.  pp. 610–616

2. (1) Federal Trade Commission—prohibits false and misleading advertising.
   (2) Consumer Product Safety Commission—is responsible for product safety.
   (3) Food and Drug Administration—requires manufacturers to give consumers correct information about their products.  pp. 610–616

## CASE PROBLEMS

1. Yes. This action is price fixing, which violates state regulations and federal antitrust laws. p. 612
2. No. The right to cancel a sales contract within three days, granted under the federal Truth in Lending Law, applies only to credit purchases.  p. 614

## ACTIVITY: DESCRIBING VIOLATIONS

1. No price  p. 617
2. No quantity  p. 617
3. No ingredients  p. 617
4. No address of manufacturer  p. 617

## ACTIVITY: REWRITING LEGALESE

The landlord named above agrees to rent the property at 422 Cole Street, Cole, Ohio, to the tenant named above for a period of two years beginning January 1. The tenant agrees to the term and the following conditions.  p. 615

# Chapter 41   Protecting the Borrower

## MULTIPLE-CHOICE QUESTIONS

1. c; p. 633
2. c; p. 633
3. d; p. 633
4. b; p. 634
5. d; p. 631
6. d; p. 637
7. c; p. 637
8. d; p. 638
9. a; p. 639
10. d; p. 640

## TRUE-FALSE QUESTIONS

1. F; p. 633
2. F; p. 633
3. F; p. 634
4. F; p. 634
5. F; p. 631
6. T; p. 633
7. F; p. 637
8. T; p. 638
9. F; p. 640
10. T; p. 638

## CASE PROBLEMS

1. No. Usury laws generally do not apply to business loans; if they did, the friend would still be entitled to repayment of the loan but would forfeit the interest.  p. 639
2. No. She could ask the bankruptcy court to help her reach an agreement with her creditors to pay them, she could go to a debt-counseling service, or she could have an attorney work out a payment arrangement with her creditors.  p. 641, 642

## ACTIVITY: IS THERE A VIOLATION?

|   | VIOLATION | NO VIOLATION |        |
|---|-----------|--------------|--------|
| 1.|           | X            | p. 631 |
| 2.| X         |              | p. 633 |
| 3.|           | X            | p. 634 |
| 4.| X         |              | p. 637 |
| 5.|           | X            | p. 637 |
| 6.|           | X            | p. 638 |
| 7.|           | X            | p. 639 |
| 8.| X         |              | p. 639 |

# Chapter 42    Protecting the Creditor

## TRUE-FALSE QUESTIONS

1. F; p. 647
2. F; p. 647
3. T; p. 648
4. T; p. 649
5. T; p. 651
6. F; p. 650
7. T; p. 650
8. T; p. 652
9. F; p. 651
10. T; p. 649

## CASE PROBLEMS

1. Public Bank may repossess the car, or sue Granby's brother if it is unable to collect from Granby first.  pp. 650, 651
2. Yes; p. 651
3. Yes; p. 650
4. Yes. The guarantor is liable for payment if all attempts to collect from Granby are unsuccessful.  p. 650
5. The bank could try to collect from Granby's brother without first suing Granby for payment.  p. 649

## MATCHING QUESTIONS

1. f; p. 649
2. g; p. 651
3. d; p. 650
4. e; p. 651
5. b; p. 648
6. c; p. 649
7. a; p. 649
8. j; p. 651
9. i; p. 647
10. h; p. 652

## SHORT-ANSWER QUESTIONS

1. a. You could obtain a security agreement, a surety, or a guaranty and use the piano as collateral.  pp. 648–650
   b. You can repossess the piano and sell it, or you can sue the customer and try to obtain a judgment.  pp. 650, 651
2. (1) A mechanic's lien is given to those who supply construction labor, materials, or services.
   (2) A tax lien is given to government agencies to ensure payment of property taxes.
   (3) A judgment lien is granted to a creditor who has sued a debtor and obtained a judgment.
   pp. 651, 652

# Review  Part XI  Consumer and Creditor Protection

## MATCHING QUESTIONS

1. i; p. 630
2. c; p. 648
3. h; pp. 651, 652
4. g; p. 611
5. a; p. 612
6. b; p. 648
7. e; p. 639
8. d; p. 609
9. j; p. 648
10. f; p. 619

## TRUE-FALSE QUESTIONS

1. F; p. 622
2. T; p. 612
3. F; p. 615
4. T; p. 619
5. F; p. 633
6. T; p. 617
7. F; p. 633
8. F; p. 649
9. F; p. 651
10. T; p. 651

## MULTIPLE-CHOICE QUESTIONS

1. c; p. 609
2. d; p. 612
3. b; p. 613
4. b; p. 614
5. c; p. 619
6. d; pp. 616, 617
7. c; p. 647
8. b; p. 647
9. a; pp. 650, 651
10. d; p. 649
11. a; p. 648
12. d; p. 649
13. c; pp. 649, 650
14. c; p. 651
15. b; p. 651
16. c; p. 640
17. d; p. 638
18. b; p. 637
19. d; p. 636
20. c; p. 631

## ACTIVITY: USING CREDIT

1. $1,200.00
2. $93.15
3. $1,328.15

## SHORT-ANSWER QUESTIONS

1. One advantage is a purchaser's ability to buy more items than might be possible with cash. Another advantage is that the purchases can be paid for over a long period of time, which enables the purchaser to have more cash to spend for other things. A third advantage is that most items purchased using credit cards can be returned if the merchandise is defective or is stolen within a certain period of time after the purchase is made.
2. One disadvantage is that it costs more to buy an item on credit than it does to buy it with cash. A second disadvantage is that the availability of credit is so tempting that some people purchase more items than they are able to afford.
3. One way in which the law has helped consumers make wiser buying decisions is by requiring that the consumer be informed of the amount that the item being purchased is actually going to cost, taking into account the cost of the use of credit. This may protect a potential consumer from getting too heavily into debt. The law has also helped by enabling a consumer to compare the cost of credit from various financial sources, resulting in more intelligent financing decisions.